# THE INFLUENCE OF ANIMISM ON ISLAM

## AN ACCOUNT OF POPULAR SUPERSTITIONS

BY

SAMUEL M. ZWEMER, F.R.G.S.

New York

THE MACMILLAN COMPANY

1920

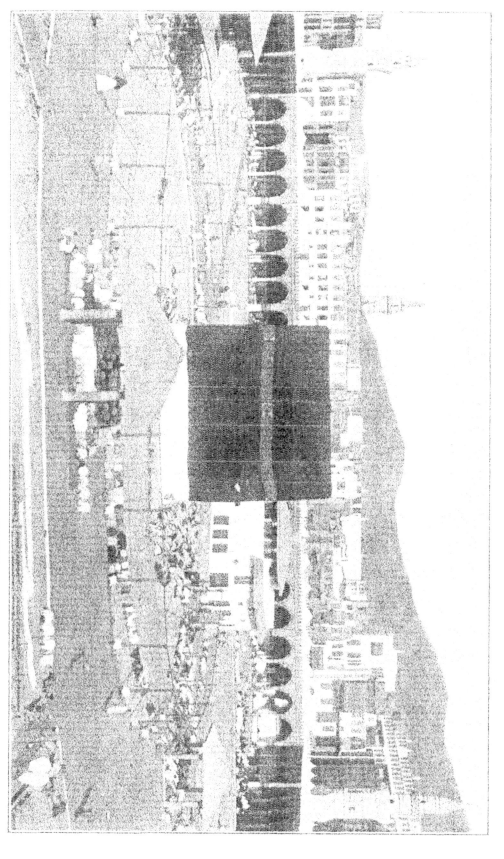

THE CENTRE OF THE MOSLEM FAITH

Pilgrims worshipping around the Kaaba. In the forefront of the picture may be seen white shrouds which are brought to Mecca, washed in Zam-zem water and then dried to be taken back for the burial of the dead.

THIS VOLUME CONTAINS
## THE A. C. THOMPSON LECTURES FOR 1918-1919
DELIVERED ON THE
## HARTFORD SEMINARY FOUNDATION
AND AT
## PRINCETON THEOLOGICAL SEMINARY
IN A COURSE OF LECTURES ON MISSIONS:

IT IS DEDICATED TO
## THE STUDENTS AND FACULTIES OF THESE INSTITUTIONS
IN APPRECIATION OF
THE INVITATION TO DELIVER THE LECTURES
AND IN PLEASANT RECOLLECTION OF
THEIR MANY COURTESIES

# PREFACE

From the standpoint both of religion and culture Animism has been described as "the tap-root which sinks deepest in racial human experience and continues its cellular and fibrous structure in the tree-trunk of modern conviction." All the great world religions show traces of animism in their sub-soil and none but Christianity (even that not completely) has uprooted the weed-growth of superstition. In this book it is our purpose to show how Islam sprang up in Pagan soil and retained many old Arabian beliefs in spite of its vigorous monotheism. Wherever Mohammedanism went it introduced old or adopted new superstitions. The result has been that as background of the whole ritual and even in the creed of popular Islam, Animism has conquered. The religion of the common people from Tangier to Teheran is mixed with hundreds of superstitions many of which have lost their original significance but still bind mind and heart with constant fear of demons, with witchcraft and sorcery and the call to creature-worship. Just as popular Hinduism differs *in toto* from the religion of the Vedas, popular Islam is altogether different from the religion as recorded in its sacred Book. Our purpose in the chapters which follow is to show how this miry clay of animism mingles with the iron of Semitic theism in the feet of the great image with head of gold that rest on Asia and Africa. The rapid spread of Islam in Africa and Malayia is, we believe, largely due to its animistic character. The primitive religions had points of contact with Islam that were mutually attractive. It stooped to conquer them but fell in stooping. The reformation of

Islam, if such be possible, must begin here. The student of Islam will never understand the common people unless he knows their curious beliefs and half-heathen practices. The missionary should not only know but sympathize. Avoiding contempt or denunciation he will even find points of contact in Animistic Islam that may lead discussion straight to the Cross and the Atonement. In popular Islam we have to deal with men and women groping after light and struggling in the mire for a firm foothold on the Rock. This book may help us to find their hand in the dark. As we read its pages we must not forget that even in Egypt and India over ninety-four per cent of the Moslem population is illiterate and therefore has no other religion than popular Islam.

S. M. ZWEMER.

# CONTENTS

# LIST OF ILLUSTRATIONS

# THE INFLUENCE
# OF ANIMISM ON ISLAM

## CHAPTER I

### ISLAM AND ANIMISM

THAT Islam in its origin and popular character is a composite faith, with Pagan, Jewish and Christian elements, is known to all students of comparative religion. Rabbi Geiger in his celebrated essay [1] has shown how much of the warp and woof of the Koran was taken from Talmudic Judaism and how the entire ritual is simply that of the Pharisees translated into Arabic. Tisdall in his " Sources of Islam " and other writers, especially Wellhausen, Goldziher and Robertson Smith, have indicated the pagan elements that persist in the Moslem faith to this day and were taken over by Mohammed himself from the old Arabian idolatry. Christian teaching and life too had their influence on Mohammed and his doctrine, as is evident not only in the acknowledged place of honor given to Jesus Christ, the Virgin Mary, John the Baptist, and other New Testament characters, but in the spirit of universalism, of conquest and above all in the mystic beliefs and ascetic practices of later Islam.

" A three-fold cord is not easily broken." The strength of Islam is its composite character. It entrenches itself everywhere and always in animistic and pagan superstition. It fights with all the fanatic devotion of Semitic

[1] " Was hat Mohammed aus dem Judenthume aufgenommen " (Wiesbaden, 1833).

1

Judaism with its exaggerated nationalism. It claims at once to include and supersede all that which Jesus Christ was and did and taught. It is a religion of compromise, of conservatism, and of conquest.

It is our purpose to show how strong is the pagan element in Mohammedanism, how many doctrines and practices of popular Islam find their explanation only in a survival of the animism of Ancient Arabia or were incorporated from many heathen sources in the spread of the faith; doctrines and practices which Islam was never able to eliminate or destroy. At the outset of our discussion it need not surprise us that a belief in demons and the old Arabian superstitions persisted in spite of Islam. Five times daily the Moslem muezzin calls out from the Mosque: "There is no god but Allah." The people repeat this and reiterate it far more than a hundred times during the day in their quarrels, feasts, fasts, rejoicings, and common conversation. But in my daily observations — and I have lived among them for more than twenty-five years — I find they have fetishes and superstitious customs which amount to as many gods as the heathen who bow down to wood and stone.[2]

[2] In the use of the word "Animism" we refer to primitive pagan practices and not to other uses of the term. William McDougall writes in his "Body and Mind" (Methuen & Co. Ltd., 36 Essex St., W. C., p. viii of Preface): "Primitive Animism seems to have grown up by extension of this notion to the explanation of all the more striking phenomena of nature. And the Animism of civilized men, which has been and is the foundation of every religious system, except the more rigid Pantheism, is historically continuous with the primitive doctrine. But, while religion, superstition, and the hope of a life beyond the grave have kept alive amongst us a variety of animistic beliefs, ranging in degree of refinement and subtlety from primitive Animism to that taught by Plato, Liebnitz, Lotze, William James, or Henri Bergson, modern science and philosophy have turned their backs upon Animism of every kind with constantly increasing decision; and the efforts of modern philosophy have been largely directed towards the ex-cogitation of a view of man and of the world which shall hold fast to the primacy and efficiency of mind or spirit, while rejecting the ani-

Now we find that Islam in Arabia itself and in the older Moslem lands was not able to shake itself free from similar beliefs and practices. To understand these aright in their origin and character it is necessary first of all to know something of what we mean by Animism. Animism is the belief that a great part if not all of the inanimate kingdom of nature as well as all animated beings, are endowed with reason, intelligence and volition identical with man. Kennedy defines it as " both a religion, a system of philosophy and a system of medicine. As a religious system it denotes the worship of spirits as distinguished from that of the gods "; [3] and Warneck says: " It would seem as if Animism were the primitive form of heathenism, maintaining itself, as in China and India to this hour, amid all the refinements of civilization. The study of Greek and old German religions exhibits the same animistic features. The essence of heathenism seems to be not the denial of God, but complete estrangement from Him. The existence of God is everywhere known, and a certain veneration given Him. But He is far away, and is therefore all but ruled out of the religious life. His place is taken by demons, who are feared and worshiped." [4]

mistic conception of human personality. My prolonged puzzling over the psycho-physical problem has inclined me to believe that these attempts cannot be successfully carried through, and that we must accept without reserve Professor Tylor's dictum that Animism ' embodies the very essence of spiritualistic, as opposed to materialistic, philosophy, and that the deepest of all schisms is that which divides Animism from Materialism."

In our treatment of Islam we do not deal with the psychology or philosophy of Animism in this sense at all. Islam as well as Christianity believes thoroughly in the existence of the soul as well as the body, and Moslem philosophy never became materialistic. The belief in life after death and in the mortality of the soul is not disputed. This book deals with the pagan interpretations of this doctrine and with superstitions connected with a belief in demons, etc., more commonly known as Animism.

[3] "Animism," by Rev. K. W. S. Kennedy, Westminster, 1914.

[4] Warneck — " Living Christ and Dying Heathenism," p. 7.

Even in Arabia the stern monotheism of the Wahabi Reformers was unable to eradicate the pagan superstitions of Islam because they are imbedded in the Koran and were not altogether rejected by Mohammed himself,—much less by his companions.

With regard to the pagan practices prevalent in early Islam, Abu'l Fida calls attention to a number of religious observances which were thus perpetuated under the new system. " The Arabs of the times of ignorance," he says, " used to do things which the religious law of Islam has adopted; for they used not to wed their mothers or their daughters, and among them it was deemed a most detestable thing to marry two sisters, and they used to revile the man who married his father's wife, and to call him *Daizan*. They used, moreover, to make the pilgrimage (*Hajj*) to the House " (the Ka'aba), " and visit the consecrated places, and wear the Ihram " (the single garment worn to the present day by a pilgrim when running round the Ka'bah), " and perform the *Tawwaf,* and run " (between the hills As Safa and Al Marwa) " and make their stand at all the Stations and cast the stones " (at the devil in the valley of Mina) ; " and they were wont to intercalate a month every third year." He goes on to mention many other similar examples in which the religion of Islam has enjoined as religious observances ancient Arabian customs, for instance ceremonial washings after certain kinds of defilement, parting the hair, the ritual observed in cleansing the teeth, paring the nails, and other such matters.[5]

Mohammed also borrowed certain fables current among the heathen Arabs, such as the tales of Ad and Thamud and some others (Surah VII 63–77). Regarding such stories, Al Kindi well says to his opponent: " And if thou mentionest the tale of Ad and Thamud and the Camel and the Comrades of the Elephant " (Surahs CV and XIV : 9) " and the like of

---

[5] Cf. Tisdall, " The Sources of the Qur'an," pp. 44–45.

these tales, we say to thee, ' These are senseless stories and the nonsensical fables of old women of the Arabs, who kept reciting them night and day.' "

When we read the account of pre-Islamic worship at Mecca we realize how many of the ancient customs persist in Islam. The principal idols of Arabia were the following:

*Hôbal* was in the form of a man and came from Syria; he was the god of rain and had a high place of honor.

*Wadd* was the god of the firmament. Special prayers for rain and against eclipse were taught by Mohammed.

*Suwah,* in the form of a woman, was said to be from antediluvian times.

*Yaghuth* had the shape of a lion.

*Ya'ook* was in the form of a horse, and was worshiped in Yemen. (Bronze images of this idol are found in ancient tombs and are still used as amulets.)

*Nasr* was the eagle god.

*El Uzza,* identified by some scholars with Venus, was worshiped at times under the form of an acacia tree (cf. Tree-worship by Moslems).

*Allat* was the chief idol of the tribe of Thakif at Taif who tried to compromise with Mohammed to accept Islam if he would not destroy their god for three years. The name appears to be the feminine of Allah.

*Manat* was a huge stone worshiped as an altar by several tribes.

*Duwar* was the virgin's idol and young women used to go around it in procession; hence its name.

*Isaf* and *Naila* were idols that stood near Mecca on the hills of Safa and Mirwa; the visitation of these popular shrines is now a part of the Moslem pilgrimage, *i. e.,* they perpetuate ancient idolatrous rites.

*Habhab* was a large stone on which camels were slaughtered. In every Moslem land sacred-stones, sacred-trees, etc., abound; in most cases these were formerly shrines of pagan (in some cases, of Christian) sanctity.

"Even in the higher religions," says Warneck, "and in the heathenism that exists in Christendom, we find numerous usages of animistic origin. Buddhism, Confucianism and Mohammedanism have nowhere conquered this most tenacious of all forms of religion; they have not even entered into conflict with it; it is only overcome by faith in Jesus Christ." Therefore these many superstitions can now no longer be styled anti-Mohammedan, although they conflict in many respects with the original doctrines of Islam. A religion is not born full-grown any more than a man, and if on attaining a ripe maturity it has cast off the form of its early youth past recognition, we cannot deny it its right to this transformation, as it is part and parcel of the scheme of nature.

"A custom or idea does not necessarily stand condemned according to the Moslem standard," writes Hurgronje, "even though in our minds there can be no shadow of doubt of its pagan origin. If, for example, Mohammedan teaching is able to regard some popular custom as a permissible enchantment against the devil or against jinns hostile to mankind, or as an invocation of the mediation of a prophet or saint with God, then it matters not that the existence of these malignant spirits is actually only known from pagan sources, nor does any one pause to inquire whether the saint in question is but a heathen god in a new dress, or an imaginary being whose name but serves to legitimate the existing worship of some object of popular reverence." [6]  Some writers go so far as to say that Animism lies at the root of all Moslem thinking and all Moslem theology. "The Moslem," says Gottfried Simon, "is naturally inclined to Animism; his Animism does not run counter to the ideal of his religion. Islam is the classic example of the way in which the non-Christian religions do not

[6] "The Achenese," pp. 287–8.

succeed in conquering Animism. This weakness in face of the supreme enemy of all religious and moral progress bears a bitter penalty. Among the animistic peoples Islam is more and more entangled in the meshes of Animism. The conqueror is, in reality, the conquered. Islam sees the most precious article of its creed, the belief in God, and the most important of its religious acts, the profession of belief, dragged in the mire of animistic thought; only in animistic guise do they gain currency among the common people. Instead of Islam raising the people, it is itself degraded. Islam, far from delivering heathendom from the toils of Animism, is itself deeply involved in them. Animism emerges from its struggle for the soul of a people, modernized it is true, but more powerful than ever, elegantly tricked out and buttressed by theology. Often it is scarcely recognizable in its refined Arabian dress, but it continues as before to sway the people; it has received divine sanction."

Other writers express a still stronger opinion. "Moslem ritual, instead of bringing a man to God," writes Dr. Adriani, "serves as a drag net for Animism," and evidence confirms this from Celebes where the Mohammedan is more superstitious even than the heathen. "Islam has exercised quite a different influence upon the heathen from what we should expect. It has not left him as he was, nor has it tempered his Animism. Rather it has relaid the old animistic foundations of the heathen's religion and run up a light, artistic superstructure upon it of Moslem customs." [7]

While Moslems profess to believe in one God and repeat His glorious incommunicable attributes in their daily worship, they everywhere permit this glorious doctrine to be buried under a mass of pagan superstitions borrowed either originally from the demon-worship of the Arabs, the Hindu

[7] "The Progress and Arrest of Islam in Sumatra," Gottfried Simon, pp. 157–9.

gods, or the animistic practices of Malaysia and Central Africa. Regarding the thirty million Moslems of the Dutch East Indies Wilkinson well says: "The average Malay may be said to look upon God as upon a great king or governor, mighty, of course, and just, but too remote a power to trouble himself about a villager's petty affairs; whereas the spirits of the district are comparable to the local police, who may be corrupt and prone to error, but who take a most absorbing personal interest in their radius of influence, and whose ill-will has to be avoided at all costs."

At first consideration one would imagine that the stern monotheism of Islam — the very intolerance of Semitic belief in Allah — would prevent compromise with polytheism. The facts are, however, to the contrary. "Belief in spirits of all sorts is neither peculiar to Acheh nor in conflict with the teaching of Islam," says Dr. Snouck Hurgronje. "Actual worship of these beings in the form of prayer might seriously imperil monotheism, but such worship is a rare exception in Acheh. The spirits most believed in are hostile to mankind and are combated by exorcism; the manner in which this is done in Acheh, as in Arabia and other Mohammedan countries is at variance in many respects with the orthodox teaching. Where, however, the Achenese calls in the help of these spirits or of other methods of enchantment in order to cause ill-fortune to his fellow-man, he does so with the full knowledge that he is committing a sin." The missionary, Gottfried Simon, goes even further when he says: "The pioneer preaching of the Mohammedan idea of God finds a hearing all the more easily because it does not essentially rise above the level of Animistic ideas; for the Mohammedan does not bring the heathen something absolutely new with his doctrine of God; his idea of God correlates itself to existing conceptions. Animism is really the cult of spirits and the souls of the departed. Yet spirit worship has not

been able to entirely obliterate the idea of God." [8]   He goes
on to show that among all the tribes of Sumatra, the images
which are incorrectly called idols are either pictures to scare
away evil spirits by their ugliness, or soul-carriers, that is to
say, pictures into which soul-stuff has been introduced by
some kind of manipulation; they therefore either introduce
soul-stuff into the house (soul-stuff = life power, life-fluid,
hence a material conception) and with it a blessing, or by an
increase of soul-stuff they ensure protection against diseases
and spirits.   The first group might perhaps best be called
*amulets,* or when they are worshiped and given food, *fetishes;* and the second group *talismans.*

In Skeat's " Malay Magic " [9] it is shown that just as in
the language of the Malays one can pick out Arabic words
from the main body of native vocabulary, so in their popular
religious customs Mohammedan ideas overlie a mass of original pagan notions.   " The Malays of the Peninsula are
Sunni Muhammadans of the school of Shafi'i, and nothing,
theoretically speaking, could be more correct and orthodox
(from the point of view of Islam) than the belief which they
profess.   " But the beliefs which they actually hold are another matter altogether, and it must be admitted that the
Mohammedan veneer which covers their ancient superstitions
is very often of the thinnest description.   The inconsistency
in which this involves them is not, however, as a rule realized
by themselves.   Beginning their invocations with the orthodox preface: *' In the name of God, the merciful, the compassionate,'* and ending them with an appeal to the Creed:
*' There is no god but God, and Muhammad is the Apostle of
God,'* they are conscious of no impropriety in addressing the
intervening matter to a string of Hindu Divinities, Demons,

[8] " The Progress and Arrest of Islam in Sumatra," Gottfried Simon,
London, pp. 48-51.
[9] Skeat's " Malay Magic," p. xiii.

Ghosts and Nature Spirits, with a few Angels and Prophets thrown in, as the occasion may seem to require."

The very wide extent of Animism is often not realized. This belief is the living, working creed of over half the human race. All South, Central and West African tribes are Animists, except where Animism has been dispossessed by Christianity. The Mohammedanism of Africa is largely mingled with it. It is the faith of Madagascar. North and South American Indians knew no other creed when Columbus landed, and the uncivilized remnant still profess it. The islanders of the Pacific and the aborigines of Australia are Animists. In Borneo and the Malay Archipelago it is strong, although a good deal affected by Hinduism. Even in China and Japan its adherents are numbered by millions. In Burma it has been stated that the nominal Buddhism of the country is in reality only a thin veneer over the real religion, which is Animism. In India, while the Census Reports record only eight and a half million as Animists, yet there are probably more than ten times that number whose Hinduism displays little else, and even the Mohammedans in many places are affected by it.

There is no agreement among scholars regarding the origin of Animism. According to a writer in the Encyclopædia Britannica, " Animism may have arisen out of or simultaneously with animatism as a primitive explanation of many different phenomena; if animatism was originally applied to non-human or inanimate objects, animism may from the outset have been in vogue as a theory of the nature of men. Lists of phenomena from the contemplation of which the savage was led to believe in Animism have been given by Dr. Tylor, Herbert Spencer, Mr. Andrew Lang and others; an animated controversy arose between these writers as to the priority of their respective lists. Among these phenomena are: trance and unconsciousness, sickness, death, clairvoyance, dreams, apparitions of the dead, wraiths, hallucinations, echoes, shadows and reflections." According to this theory evolution accounts for the growth of religious ideas. But all are not in accord with this theory; it is opposed to the Scriptures. " A dispassionate study of heathen religions," says Warneck, " confirms the view of Paul that heathenism is a fall from a better knowledge of God. In earlier days humanity had a greater treasure of spiritual goods. But the knowledge of God's eternal power and divinity was neglected. The Almighty was no longer feared or worshiped; dependence upon Him was renounced; and this downward course was continued till nothing but a dim presentiment of Him was left. The creature stepped into the place of the Creator, and the vital power, the soul-stuff and the spirits of the dead came to be worshiped." [10] This view is not exploded by science, for the Encyclopædia Britannica concludes its discussion on the subject by saying: " Even, therefore, if we can say that at the present day the gods are entirely spiritual, it is clearly possible to maintain that they have been spiritualized *pari passu* with the increasing importance of the animistic view of nature and of the greater prominence of eschatological beliefs. *The animistic origin of religion is therefore not proven.*"

Aside from the question of origin we return to its content. It is in its teaching regarding man's *soul* and the supreme importance of the immaterial that Animism affords a point of contact with such words of Christ as " What shall it profit a man if he gain the whole world and lose his own soul." It is the loss of the soul, the spirit, the invisible life-principle that the Animist fears: but this fear brings him into a life-long bondage to superstitions.

Among the Basutos in Africa it is held that a man walk-

[10] " The Living Christ and Dying Heathenism," p. 103. Compare also Ellinwood's " Oriental Religions and Christianity," p. 225.

ing by the brink of a river may lose his life if his shadow falls on the water, for a crocodile may seize it and draw him in; in Tasmania, North and South America is found the conception that the soul is somehow identical with the shadow of a man. For some of the Red Indians the Roman custom of receiving the breath of a dying man was no mere pious duty but a means of ensuring that his soul was transferred to a new body. Other familiar conceptions identify the soul with the liver or the heart, with the reflected figure seen in the pupil of the eye and with the blood. Although the soul is often distinguished from the vital principle, there are many cases in which a state of unconsciousness is explained as due to the absence of the soul; in South Australia *wilyamarraba* (without soul) is the word used for insensible. So too the autohypnotic trance of the magician or *shaman* is regarded as due to his visit to distant regions or the nether world, of which he brings back an account.

*" In many parts of the world it is held that the human body is the seat of more than one soul;* in the island of Nias four are distinguished, the shadow and the intelligence, which die with the body, a tutelary spirit, termed *begoe,* and a second which is carried on the head." " Just as among western nations the ghost of a dead person is held to haunt the churchyard or the place of death, although more orthodox ideas may be held by the same person as to the nature of a future life, so the savage, more consistently, assigns different abodes to the multiple souls with which he credits man. Of the four souls of a Dakota Indian one is held to stay with the corpse, another in the village, a third goes into the air, while the fourth goes to the land of souls, where its lot may depend on its rank in this life, its sex, mode of death or sepulture, on the due observance of funeral ritual, or many other points. From the belief in the survival of the dead arose the practice of offering food, lighting fires, etc., at the grave, at first,

maybe, as an act of friendship or filial piety, later as an act of worship. The simple offering of food or shedding of blood at the grave develops into an elaborate system of sacrifice; even where ancestor-worship is not found, the desire to provide the dead with comforts in the future life may lead to the sacrifice of wives, slaves, animals, etc., to the breaking or burning of objects at the grave or to the provision of the ferryman's toll, a coin put in the mouth of the corpse to pay the traveling expenses of the soul. But all is not finished with the passage of the soul to the land of the dead; the soul may return to avenge its death by helping to discover the murderer, or to wreak vengeance for itself; there is a widespread belief that those who die a violent death become malignant spirits and endanger the lives of those who come near the haunted spot; the woman who dies in child-birth becomes a *pontianak,* and threatens the life of human beings; and man resorts to magical or religious means of repelling his spiritual dangers." [11]

It is clear from the beliefs of the non-Mohammedans of Malaysia that all things, organic and inorganic were once credited with the possession of souls. This primitive Animism survives most distinctly in the well-known Moslem Malay ceremonies connected with the rice-soul at seed-time or harvest, but it is also traceable in a large number of other practices. We are told that whenever a peasant injures anything he must propitiate its personality, its living essence, its soul, its tutelary spirit — call it what we will. If the hunter slays a deer he must excuse himself; it is not the man but the gun or the knife or the leaden bullet that must answer for the deed. Should a man wish to mine or to set up a house, he must begin by propitiating the spirits of the turned-up soil; should he desire to fish, he will address the spirits of the sea and even the fish themselves; should he contemplate planting,

[11] " Encyclopædia Britannica," art. Animism.

he begins by acknowledging that rice has a living essence of its own which he is bound to treat with respect.   In short, he considers that all nature is teeming with life and that his own soul is walking in the midst of invisible foes.

All of these evil spirits find worshipers among Moslems in the Malay States to-day.   The *pawang* or witch-doctor and not the Moslem priest is called in to exorcise them.   This he does with old-fashioned magic with admixture of the names of Allah and Mohammed.   " The *pawang* or witch-doctor is in great demand by orthodox Mohammedan Malays, especially in times of sickness, although he often appeals openly to Siva or uses such language as the following:

" I am the equal of the Archangels,
    I sit upon God's Judgment-seat,
    And lean on the pillar of God's Throne of Glory." [12]

In reading a standard work on Animism by Kruijt, I noted the following particulars in which Animism and Islam agree.   The correspondence is the more remarkable because my experiences have been limited to East Arabia and Egypt. That is to say Islam in its cradle already had these features of paganism or primitive Animism:

The putting of blood upon the door-posts and the foundations when a house is being built (p. 23).   The special importance of the placenta as the double of the child (p. 26). Hair as the seat of the soul (pp. 26–37).   Among the pagans there are ceremonies connected with the shaving of the hair in infancy.   The Toradjas nail bits of the human scalp or shreds of hair to the palm trees to make them more fruitful. The same is done with the hair of infants.   When a mother leaves her child for a journey she ties some of her own hair to that of the child so that " the child believes the mother is still present."   Hair offerings take place as in Islam.   The

[12] Chas. E. G. Tisdall in " The Missionary Review of the World," 1916.

finger nails are connected with the soul and have spiritual value (p. 38). Also the teeth (p. 39). Spittle, perspiration, tears and the other excretions of the body all contain soul-stuff (pp. 40–47) and one may see in all the superstitions of the animist the same practices that are related of Mohammed the Prophet and his companions in Moslem Tradition. (See references given later.) The use of urine as medicine is not more common among pagans of Celebes than in Moslem lands where the practice of Mohammed the Prophet and his teaching is still supreme. One needs only to consult books like Ed Damiri, or Tub-en-Nabawi. The use of blood of animals, of saliva, of blowing, spitting and stroking in order to bring benefit to the patient is universal among animists; it was also common in early Islam and is to-day. It is recorded in early tradition that Mohammed practiced cures in this manner. In Java and Sumatra spitting is a common method for curing the sick (pp. 62–63). Among Animists amulets and anklets are worn to keep the soul in the body; at the time of death the nose, the ears, the mouth, etc., are carefully plugged up to prevent the soul escaping. These customs at the time of burial are universal also in Islam (p. 76).

Among Animists sneezing is considered unfortunate, for then the soul tries to escape from the body; yawning is on the other hand a good sign, for the breath comes inward. Perhaps for this reason the Moslems everywhere ask forgiveness of God when they sneeze, but praise Him when they yawn (pp. 92–93).

The belief that souls of men may inhabit animals such as dogs, cats, gazelles, snakes, etc., is Animistic. The same is taught in Moslem books, for example in " The Arabian Nights," which gives us a faithful picture of popular Islam. The bones of animals contain soul matter and are therefore dreaded by the animist or used for special purposes of good or ill (pp. 128). We may connect with this the belief of the Moslems that bones are the food of jinn and must not be touched. Mr. Kruijt shows in Chapter VI of his book (p. 157) that soul-stuff exists in certain metals, iron, gold, silver, lead. These are therefore powerful protectors against evil spirits. Iron objects are used to defend infants in the cradle (p. 161). The same practice is carried on in Arabia, Egypt, Persia and Morocco.

The soul after death takes its flight into the animal kingdom (pp. 171–180); especially changing to dwell in butterflies, birds, mice, lizards, snakes. May we not connect with this the teaching of Islam that the souls of Moslem martyrs go into the crops of green birds until the resurrection day? Or closer yet is the common belief in metempsychosis based upon Koran legends, developed in the commentaries. Does not the Koran teach that Jews were changed into apes and Tradition tell us that Jews and Christians were changed into hogs?

When we read the pages of Kruijt on the Fetish (pp. 197–232) we are struck in almost every paragraph with parallel beliefs current in Islam. Stones are sacred because they contain spirits. Trees are sacred for the same reason: "If a man has been successful in fighting, it has not been his natural strength of arm, quickness of eye, or readiness of resource that has won success; he has certainly got the *mana* of a spirit or of some deceased warrior to empower him, conveyed in an amulet of a stone round his neck, or a tuft of leaves in his belt, in a tooth hung upon a finger of his bow hand, or in the form of words with which he brings supernatural assistance to his side" (p. 201). Word for word this might be said of Moslems to-day.

With regard to stone-worship Kruijt tells us of sacred stones in the Indian Archipelago (pp. 204–210) which receive worship because they fell from heaven (cf. " The Black

Stone at Mecca ") or because of their special shape. Among the Dajaks of Serawak, Chalmers tells of the interior of a Lundu house at one end of which were collected the relics of the tribe. " These consisted of several round-looking stones, two deers' heads, and other inferior trumpery. The stones turn black if the tribe is to be beaten in war, and red if to be victorious; any one touching them would be sure to die; if lost, the tribe would be ruined." (p. 209.) The Black Stone at Mecca is also believed to have changed color.

Tree-worship, by hanging amulets on the tree to produce fertility or bring blessing, is common in Celebes and New Guinea (p. 215) not only, but in Arabia, Egypt and Morocco. The effect of all this, even on the conception of God in Islam, is of importance. Here also there are points of contact as well as points of contrast. " What has Animism made of God," asks Warneck, " the holy and gracious Creator and Governor of the world? It has divested Him of His omnipotence, His love, His holiness and righteousness and has put Him out of all relation with man. The idea of God has become a mere decoration; His worship a caricature. Spirits inferior to men, whose very well-being is dependent on men's moods, are feared instead of the Almighty; the rule of an inexorable fate is substituted for the wise and good government of God. Absurd lies are believed concerning the life after death, and efforts are made to master the malevolent spirits by a childish magic." Is this not true of Arabia also?

Regarding the impotence of Mohammedanism to reject animistic influences which have dragged down to its lowest levels the ideas of God, Warneck goes on to say, " Mohammedanism even with its higher idea of God, cannot introduce into the heathenism which it influences any development for the better. The heathen, who have passed over to Islam, quietly retain their demon-worship. Instead of the purer idea of God raising them, they drag it down to their own level, a proof of the tremendous down-drag which animistic religions possess " (p. 100).

" Mohammedanism," he says in another place, " has been unable to remove the fear of evil spirits.  On the contrary, it assists in the expulsion of the spirits by its *malims*.  It allows the people to go on worshiping ancestors, and adds new spirits of Arabic origin to those already worshiped. Islam nowhere appears among Animists as a deliverer " (pp. 114–115.)

The missionary is not so much concerned after all with the fact of Animism *in* Islam as he is with the utter failure of Islam to meet Animistic practices and overcome them. Gottfried Simon has shown conclusively that Islam cannot uproot pagan practices or remove the terror of spirits and demon-worship in Sumatra and Java.[13]  This is true everywhere.  In its conflict with Animism Islam has not been the victor but the vanquished.  Christianity on the contrary, as Harnack has shown, did win in its conflict with demon-worship and is winning to-day.[14]

Animism in Islam offers points of contact and contrast that may well be used by the missionary.  Christianity's message and power must be applied to the superstitions of Islam and especially to these pagan practices.  The fear of spirits can be met by the love of the Holy Spirit; the terror of death by the repose and confidence of the Christian; true exorcism is not found in the *zar* but in prayer; so-called demonic possession can often be cured by medical skill; and superstition rooted out by education.  Jesus Christ is the Lord of the Unseen World, especially the world of demons and angels. Christ points out the true ladder of Jacob and the angels of

[13] " The Progress and Arrest of Islam in Sumatra," London, 1912.

[14] Harnack: " The Mission and Expansion of Christianity," Vol. I, Book II, Chapter III.

God ascending and descending upon the Son of Man — He is the sole channel of communication with the other world. With Him as our living, loving Saviour and Friend we have no fear of " the arrow that flieth by day nor of the pestilence that walketh in darkness."

In order to guide the student for further study in regard to Animism and Islam we give the keys that will unlock the subject; for if Moslems know that we have *some* idea of their superstition they will tell us more. The subject needs thorough investigation, especially in Egypt. The best book on Animism is by A. C. Kruijt, a Dutch missionary in the East Indies, and his division of the subject is very suggestive. I here translate the table of contents of his book. Every subject leads out into a wide field of thought and investigation.

I. ANIMISM.
    (1) The Personal soul-stuff of Man found especially in the Head, the Intestines, the Blood, Placenta, Hair, Teeth, Saliva, Sweat, Tears, Urine, etc.
    (2) Means by which this soul-stuff is appropriated, e. g., Spitting, Blowing, Blood-wiping, and Touch.
    (3) The Personal Soul in Man: The Shadow, the Dream, The Escape of the Soul through Sneezing, Yawning, etc. The Were Wolf and the Witch.
    (4) The Soul-stuff of Animals.
    (5) Soul-stuff of Plants, Sacred Plants.
    (6) Soul-stuff of Inanimate Objects — Metals, Iron, Gold, etc.
    (7) The Transmigration of the Soul, especially in Animals — The Firefly, the Butterfly, the Bird, the Mouse, the Snake, the Lizard.
    (8) Special honor paid to Animals, Fetishes, Stones and Amulets.
II. SPIRITISM, OR THE DOCTRINE OF THE SOUL.
    (1) The Living Man — in regard to his Soul, its Nature.
    (2) The Life of the Soul after Death — It remains in the Grave or in the House — Its Journey to Soul Land.
    (3) The Worship of Souls — Either through a medium or without a medium — In Special Places or in Special Objects. The Priesthood that gives communication with the souls of the Departed.
III. DEMONOLOGY.
    (1) Introduction on the Creator and Creation.
    (2) The Spiritual Part of Creation.
    (3) Animals as Messengers of the Gods.

(4) Predestination.
(5) Honor of man — Saint-worship.
(6) Demi-gods.
(7) The Home of the Gods.
(8) Agricultural Gods and Sea Gods.
(9) Tree Spirits and other Demons.
(10) How demons show themselves and how one drives them away.

# CHAPTER II

ONE has only to read popular expositions of the Koran texts that refer to angels, jinn, *iblis* (the devil), *kismet* (fate), and the many traditions regarding the creation of the soul and its transmigration to realize that the world of Moslem thought and that of Animism are not distinct. Not only in popular Islam, its magic (high and low), its amulets, charms, talismans, magic squares, sacred trees, etc., but in the sacred literature of Islam we find pagan beliefs and practices perpetuated. The shortest of all monotheistic creeds, the *Kalima,* has itself become a species of magic and at least in three of the six articles of the expanded statement of orthodox belief we find animistic teaching and interpretation. " I believe in Allah and His angels, and His books, and His prophets, and the Resurrection and the Predestination of good and evil." The doctrine of God includes the magical use of His names and attributes. The doctrine of angels includes not only demonology but *jinn* fear and worship as real as in Paganism. The belief in revelation has in popular Islam almost degenerated into bibliomancy and bibliolatry. Do the *fellahin* of Egypt not take their oath on *Al Bokhari?* The prophets, especially Solomon and Mohammed, had intercourse with demons and jinn. According to the Koran and Tradition man is created with a double-ego or two souls (the Qarina) just as in the pagan mythologies. The beliefs regarding the relation of the soul to the body after death, and the doctrine of metempsychosis resemble the beliefs of Animism. Their belief in how the spirit leaves the body; the benefit of speedy burial; the questioning

21

by the two angels of the tomb; the visiting of the graves and the presentation of offerings of food and drink on the graves: all this is mixed up with pagan practices which find their parallel in Animism. Finally, the whole eschatology of Islam is a strange mixture of Judaism, Christianity and Paganism.

Some of these practices based on the creed we will recur to later; here we limit our discussion to the use of the Koran, the creed formula and the rosary in ways that are condemned by the creed itself. "There is no god but Allah" — yet His Book, His names, His very attributes are used as amulets against demon and jinn or as fetish receive the reverence due to Himself alone. Every missionary knows that the Koran itself has the power of a fetish in popular Islam. Not only is the book eternal in its origin and use for mystic purposes, but only those who are ritually pure may touch it. Certain chapters are of special value against evil spirits. It is related in Tradition, e.g. that "whosoever reads the 105th chapter and the 94th chapter of the Koran at morning prayers will never suffer pain in his teeth"! This is one reason why these two chapters, i.e. of the "Elephant" and the one entitled "Have we not expanded," are almost universally used for the early prayers. At funerals they always read the chapter "Y.S."; and then, in fear of jinn and spirits, the chapter of the Jinn. One has only to read this last chapter with the commentaries on it to see how large a place the doctrine occupies in popular Islam. The cure for headache is said to be the 13th verse of the chapter called "Al-Ana'am" or the "Cattle," which reads: "His is whatsoever dwells in the night or in the day: He both hears and knows." Against robbers at night a verse of the chapter called "Repentance" is read, etc., etc.[1] No religion has ever made so much

---

[1] Cf. Even Al Ghazali who is quoted in book of "Wird," *Mujarabat* of Ahmed Dirbi, p. 80.

of its sacred book in a magic way as Islam. Not only do we find bibliolatry, i.e. the worship of the Book, but also bibliomancy, i.e. the use of the Koran for magical or superstitious purposes. This is perhaps based on Judaism. We find that Jews used the Torah for protection purposes and in a magical way as do the Mohammedans. When a person was dangerously ill the Pentateuch was opened, and the name which first met the eye was added to the patient's name, in order to avert the evil destiny.[2]

Just as Moslems to-day use special names of God and special chapters as " cure-alls " so did the Jews of the Dispersion. The following verses in the original Hebrew were used on amulets:

| | | |
|---|---|---|
| *Genesis* | I: 1 | To make oneself invisible (S. Z. 32a). |
| | I: 1–5 | (The last letters only.) To confuse a person's mind (M. V. 25); as preservation against pollution (S. Z. 11b); and for other purposes (" Cat. Anglo-Jew. Hist. Exh." No. 1874; Schwab). |
| | XXI: 1 | To lighten child-birth (M. V. 59). |
| | XXIV: 2 | On using a divining rod (M. V. 80). |
| | XXV: 14 | Against the crying of children (M. V. 64). |
| | XXXII: 31 | Against danger on a journey (M. V. 34). |
| | XLIX: 18 | To shorten one's way on a journey (M. V. 23); in the lying-in room (M. V. 80). |
| *Exodus* | XI: 7 | For protection against a fierce dog. (For greater security, the traveler |

2 " The Jewish Encyclopedia," Vol. III, pp. 202–203.

is advised to carry a stout stick as well, which gave rise to the saying, "He has both a verse ('posuk') and a stick ('stecken') with him" applied to one well fortified on every side.)

| | | |
|---|---|---|
| | XI: 8 | To lighten child-birth (M. V. 59). |
| | XV: 2 | To shorten one's way (M. V. 24). |
| | XV: 16 | To shorten the way (M. V. 23); to insure safety in a court of law (M. V. 32); against fear (M. V. 65). |
| | XVII: 16 | Against bleeding (M. V. 45). |
| | XXII: 17 | In the lying-in room (M. V. 91). |
| | XXXIII: 23 | Against witchcraft (M. V. 41). |
| | XXXIV: 6 | To shorten the way (M. V. 23). |
| *Lev.* | I: 1 | The same (M. V. 23). |
| *Num.* | XI: 2 | Against fire (M. V. 10, 11; S. Z. 27). |
| | XI: 12 | Against the evil eye (M. V. 41). |
| | XXIII: 23 | In lying-in rooms (M. V. 91). |
| *Deut.* | VI: 4–9 | Against fever (M. V. 50). |
| | XXIII: 4 | On taking children to school (S. Z. 30b). |

A still larger number of verses were taken from the Psalms for similar purposes and used as amulets. Most common, however, was the use of the names of God and of angels.

The Koran is not only the most excellent of all books, but the essential Word of God contained therein is eternal and uncreated. It was originally written by God himself on the Preserved Tablet, then brought down in sheets (*suhuf*) to the lowest heaven on the night of Al Qadr where they

8 "Jewish Encyclopedia," p. 203.

were preserved in a place called the House of Majesty (*Beit-ul-'Izza*).   From here they were brought to Mohammed as required by circumstances in revelations.   What Professor Hurgronje says of the Moslems of Sumatra is true of all the illiterate masses in Islam and even of many of the so-called literates even in Arabia and Egypt:

" This book, once a world-reforming power, now serves but to be chanted by teachers and laymen according to definite rules.   The rules are not difficult, but not a thought is ever given to the meaning of the words; the Quran is chanted simply because its recital is believed to be a meritorious work. This disregard of the sense of the words rises to such a pitch that even pandits who have studied the commentaries — not to speak of laymen — fail to notice when the verses they recite condemn as sinful things which both they and the listeners do every day, nay even during the very common ceremony itself.

" The inspired code of the universal conquerors of thirteen centuries ago has grown to be no more than a mere text-book of sacred music, in the practice of which a valuable portion of the youth of well-educated Muslims is wasted and which is recited on a number of ceremonial occasions in the life of every Mohammedan." [4]

In all Moslems lands on the occasions of birth, death or marriage the Koran is used as a charm.   It is put near the head of the dying, and on the head of a new-born infant for good-luck.   The belief is universal in the Mohammedan world that Safar is pregnant with evil, and that one may feel very thankful when he reaches the last Wednesday of this month without mishap.   This day nowhere passes wholly without notice.   " In Acheh," says Hurgronje, " it is called *Rabn Abeh,* ' the final Wednesday.'   Many take a bath on this day, the dwellers on the coast in the sea, others in the

[4] " The Achenese," pp. 343–4.

river or at the well. It is considered desirable to use for this bath water consecrated by contact with certain verses of the Koran. To this end a *teungku* in the *gampong* gives to all who ask slips of paper on which he has written the seven verses of the Koran in which Allah addresses certain men with the word *salam* (blessing or peace)." [5]

It is the common belief in East Arabia that the Koran if wrapped in a fresh sheep-skin will withstand the hottest fire and never a page be singed or burned. I was repeatedly challenged to this ordeal with the Gospel vs. the Koran during my early missionary days at Bahrein. That the sacred character of the work is not limited to the text, but extends to paper and ink is clear from the process of insulation in taking oath. In India a hog's bristle put on the ball of the thumb which then rests on the Koran allows the swearer to perjure himself without danger. So holy a book is used therefore to drive away demons. No evil spirit visits the room where it rests on the highest shelf — the place of honor.

This belief that the Koran can drive away devils is exactly paralleled by practices in China. De Groot writes (" The Religion of the Chinese," p. 51): " I have said that classical works are among the best weapons in the war against specters. Even the simple presence of a copy, or a fragment, or a leaf of a classic is a mighty preservative, and an excellent medicine for spectral disease. As early as the Han dynasty, instances are mentioned of men having protected themselves against danger and misfortune by reciting classical phrases. But also writings and sayings of any kind, provided they be of an orthodox stamp, destroy specters and their influences. Literary men, when alone in the dark, insure their safety by reciting their classics; should babies be restless because of the presence of specters, classical passages do excellent service as lullabies."

[5] " The Achenese," p. 206.

LARGE INCENSE BOWLS IN MOSQUE AT HANKOW, CHINA

These bowls are found everywhere in China, in the courtyard or in the Mosque itself. Similar ones are used in their homes and each has an Arabic inscription from the Koran. One in my possession dates from the fourteenth century. The idea is that incense drives away demons.

Again he speaks of the magical power of the almanac (De Groot, p. 53): "No house in China may be without a copy of the almanac, or without at least its title-page in miniature, printed on purpose with one or two leaves affixed, as a charm, in accordance with the *pars pro toto* principle, and sold in shops for one coin or cash. These charms are deposited in beds, in corners and cupboards, and such like places, and worn on the body; and no bride passing from her paternal home into that of her bridegroom may omit the title-page among the exorcising objects with which her pocket is for that occasion filled."

Portions of the Koran are lithographed in colors and sold for the same purposes in Cairo, Bombay, Singapore and Madras. The fantastic combinations of Arabic script and the intaglio of the design make the charm all the more potent. Men cannot decipher it, but demons can.

In the use of the Rosary (*Subha*) and its gradual spread throughout the world of Islam we also find evidence of Animistic superstition. According to Dr. Goldziher: "It is generally admitted that the use of the rosary, which was imported into Islam, was not adopted by the disciples of Mohammed until the third century of the Hegira (622 A. D.). The following story can, at any rate, be cited in this connection. When the Abbaside Khalif, Al-Hadi (169–170 of the Hegira) forbade his mother Chejzuran, who tried to exercise her influence in political affairs, to take part in the affairs of state, he used the following words: "It is not a woman's business to meddle with the affairs of state; you should occupy your time with your prayers *and your subha*." From this it seems certain that in that century the use of the *subha* as an instrument of devotion was common only among the inferior classes and had no place among the learned. When a rosary was found in the possession of a certain pious saint, Abu-l-Kasim al-Junaid, who died in 297 of the Hegira, they attacked him for using it, although he belonged to the best society. "I cannot give up," said he, "a thing that serves to bring me nearer to God." This tradition furnishes us with rare facts since it shows us on the one hand that in the social sphere the use of the rosary was common even among the higher classes; and on the other hand that the strict disciples of Mohammed looked on this foreign innovation which was patronized by saints and pious men, with displeasure. To them it was *bia'a* that is, an innovation without foundation in the old Islamic *sunna,* and was consequently bound to stir a distrust among the orthodox.

Even later on, when the use of the rosary had for long ceased to provoke discontent in the orthodox Moslems, the controversialists, whose principle was to attack all "innovations," still distrusted any exaggerations in the usage of this practice. But like a great many things that were not tolerated at the beginning under religious forms, the rosary introduced itself from private religious life to the very heart of the mosques.

Abu Abdullah Mohammed al-'Abdari, who died 737 A.H., wrote a work of three volumes called " Al-Madkhal," which contains a lot of interesting matter on the intimate life of Islamic society, their superstitions and their popular customs, and should be studied by all who are interested in the history and civilization of the Mohammedan Orient. " Among the innovations," writes al-'Abdari, " the rosary is to be noted. A special box is made where it is kept; a salary is fixed for some one to guard and keep it, and for those who use it for Zikr. . . . A special Sheikh is appointed for it, with the title of *Sheikh al-Subha,* and with him a servant with the title of *Khadim al-Subha.* These innovations are quite modern. It is the duty of the imam of the mosque to suppress such customs as it is in his power to do so."

" The appearance of the rosary," says Goldziher, to quote

again from his paper, " and the way in which it had been adopted by the faithful of the Sunna, did not pass unperceived by the Hadith. I believe that the following story which we read in the book called ' Sunan,' written in the third century, has to do with the entrance of the rosary:

" ' 'Al-Hakam b. al-Mubarak relates on the authority of 'Amr b. Jahja, who had heard it from his father, and who in his turn had heard from *his* father: we were sitting before the door of 'Abdallah b. Masud, before the morning prayer, for we were in the habit of going to the mosque in his company. One day we encountered Abu Musa al-Ash'ari . . . and very soon Abu 'Abd al-Rahman came in his turn. Then Abu Musa said: " In former times, O Abu Rahman, I saw in the mosque things that I did not approve of; but now, thank God, I see nothing but good." " What do you mean by that ? " said the other. " If you live long enough," answered Abu Musa, " you will know. I have seen in the mosque, people who sat round in circles (*kauman hilakan*) awaiting the moment of *Salat*. Each group was presided over by a man and they held in their hands small stones. The president said to them: ' Repeat 100 *Takbir!* ' [6] and for one hundred times they recited the formula of the *Takbir*. Then he used to tell them: ' Repeat 100 *Tahlil!* ' [7] And they recited the formula of *Tahlil* for one hundred times. Then he told them also: ' Repeat 100 times the Tasbih! ' [8] And the persons who were in the group equally went through this exhortation also." Then Abu 'Abd al-Rahman asked: " What did'st thou say when thou sawest these things? " " Nothing," answered Abu Musa, " because I first wanted to find out your view and your orders." " Did you not tell them that it would have been more profitable for them to

---

[6] Takbir — to repeat *Allahu Akbar*, God is great.
[7] Tahlil — to repeat *La ilaha illa Allah* — (The Creed).
[8] Tasbih — to repeat *Subhan Allah*, God be praised.

have kept account of their sins and did you not tell them
that their good actions would not have been in vain?"   So
we together repaired to the mosque and we soon came across
one of these groups.   He stopped before them and said:
"What do you here?"   "We have here," they answered,
"small stones which help us to count the Takbir, the Tahlil
and the Tasbih, which we recite."   But he answered them in
these terms:   "Sooner count your sins and nothing will be
lost of your good works.   Woe to thee, O community of
Mohammed! with what haste you are going toward damnation?   Here are also in great numbers, companions of your
Prophet? look at these garments which are not covered with
dust, these vessels that are not yet broken; verily by him
who holds my soul in his hands, your religion can lead you
better than the contemporaries of Mohammed; will you not
at least open the door of wrong?"   "By Allah, O Abu 'Abd
al-Rahman," they cried, "we mean but to do right!"   And
he answered them:   "There are many who pretend to do
right, but who cannot get at it, it is to them that the word of
the Prophet applies:   There are of those who read the
Koran, but deny its teaching, and I swear it by God, I doubt
whether the majority of these people are not among yourselves." ' "

Other traditions show us the prophet protesting regarding
some faithful women against their using these small stones
when reciting the litanies just mentioned and recommending
the use of the fingers when counting their prayers.   "Let
them count their prayers on their fingers (ja'kidna bil ana-
mil); for an account will be taken of them."

All these insinuations found in traditions invented for the
purpose, denote a disapprobation of the use of the rosary, at
the moment of its appearance.   The use of small stones in
the litanies was, it seems, an original form of the subha, very
much like the later use of the rosary.   It is said of Abu

Huraira that he recited the *Tasbih* in his house by the aid of small stones which he kept in a purse (*jusabbih biha*). Let us also mention the severe words of Abdallah, son of the Khalif Omar, which he addressed to a person who rattled his stones in his hands during prayer (juharrik al-Hasa Bijedihi), "Do not do that, for that is prompted by the devil."

Were not the litanies ever counted in this way before the rosary was introduced? One cannot be sure. Anyway, it seems very probable that the traditions against this custom date from the time when the rosary was introduced into Islam. The Tibetan Buddhists, long before the Christian Era, used strings of beads, generally 108 in number and made of jewels, sandal-wood, mussel-shells, and the like, according to the status of their owners. Whether Islam adopted the rosary from India during the Moslem conquest is uncertain, but not improbable.

Regarding the Christian use of the rosary we read: " The custom of repeatedly reciting the Our Father arose in the monastic life of Egypt at an early time, being recorded by Palladius and Sozomen. The Hail Mary or Ave Maria, on the other hand, first became a regular prayer in the second half of the eleventh century, though it was not until about the thirteenth century that it was generally adopted. The addition of the words of Elizabeth, ' blessed is the fruit of thy womb, Jesus' (Luke 1:42), and the Angelical Salutation, ' Hail Mary, full of grace; the Lord is with thee; blessed art thou among women' (Luke 1:28), is first mentioned about 1130; but Bishop Odo of Paris (1196–1208) requires the recitation of Hail Mary together with the Our Father and the Creed as a regular Christian custom. The closing petition, ' Holy Mary, Mother of God, pray for us sinners, now and at the hour of our death,' developed gradually in the sixteenth century, and was regarded even by the council of

Besançon (1571) as a superfluous but pious custom. These facts show that the traditions which ascribe the invention of the rosary to Benedict of Nursia, Bede, or Peter the Hermit, are untrustworthy, and the same statement holds of the Dominican tradition which makes Dominic receive a vision of the Virgin commanding him to introduce the use of the rosary. At the same time, the rosary was originally an essential Dominican mode of devotion; though first arising long after the death of the founder of the order; *but while some influence may have been exercised by the acquaintance of oriental Christians with the Mohammedan Tasbih,* all the characteristics of the recitation of Our Father, like the meditations connected with it, can only be explained by the operation of specifically Christian ideas." [9]

The Rosary in Islam is at present used for three distinct purposes. It is used in prayer and *Zikr* for counting pious ejaculations or petitions. It is used for divining the will of God; and it is used in a magical way for healing. The second practice is called *Istikhara.* It is related of one of the wives of Mohammed that she said: "The Prophet taught us *Istikhara,* i.e. to know what is best, just as he taught us verses from the Book, and if any of you wants anything let him perform ablution and pray two rakk'as and read the verse: 'There is no other God, etc.' To use the rosary in this way the following things must be observed. The rosary must be grasped within the palms of both hands, which are then rubbed together; then the *Fatiha* is solemnly repeated, after which the user breathes upon the rosary with his breath in order to put the magic-power of the chapter into the beads. Then he seizes a particular bead and counts toward the "pointer" bead using the words, God, Mohammed, Abu Jahal; when the count terminates with the name of God it means that his request is favorably received, if it terminates

[9] "Schaff Herzog Encyclopedia," Vol. X.

with Abu Jahal it is bad, and if with Mohammed the reply is doubtful. Others consider it more correct to use these three words: Adam, Eve, the devil. When these words are used the Adam bead signifies approval, the devil bead disapproval, and the Eve bead uncertainty, because woman's judgment is fickle. This use of the rosary is almost universal among the common people of North Africa and Egypt.

When we remember the high idealism with which Edwin Arnold has clothed the ninety-nine names of Allah in his book on the Moslem rosary entitled " Pearls of the Faith " we enter a word of protest against the use of such glorious names for magic and sorcery. In this connection we mention a ceremony practiced among the Mohammedans of India on special occasions, called in the Arabic *Subha* and usually performed on the night succeeding a burial. The soul is then supposed to remain in the body, after which it departs to Hades, there to await its final doom. The ceremony is thus described: " At night, derwishes, sometimes as many as fifty, assemble, and one brings a rosary of 1000 beads, each as large as a pigeon's egg. Then beginning with the 67th chapter of the Koran, they say three times, ' God is one; ' then recite the last chapter but one and the first, and then say three times, ' O God, favor the most excellent and most happy of thy creatures, our lord Mohammed, and his family and companions, and preserve them.' To this they add: ' All who commemorate Thee are the mindful, and those who omit commemorating Thee are the negligent.' They next repeat three thousand times, ' There is no god but God,' one holding the rosary and counting each repetition. After each thousand they sometimes rest and take coffee; then 100 times ' (I extol) the perfection of God with his praise.' Then the same number of times: ' I beg forgiveness of God the Great'; after which fifty times: ' The perfection of the Lord the Eternal'; then ' The perfection of the Lord of

Might'; etc. (Koran XXXVII last three verses). Then two or three recite two or three more verses. This done one asks his companions, 'Have ye transferred (the merit of) what ye have recited to the soul of the deceased?' They reply, 'We have' and add, 'Peace be on the apostles.' This concludes the ceremony, which in the house of the rich, is repeated the second and third nights."

In Algeria the rosary is used by the *Taleb* in divining whether the sick will die or not. The beads are counted off in threes, if this leaves one off number the beads must be recounted in twos, if ending evenly the patient will live, if an odd one remains it means death. The rosary which is considered a holy thing is never used in vulgar magic.

In Tunisia the fortune-teller marks a place on the rosary with a thread and counts off the beads while chanting certain words, sometimes the names of the father or mother of the sick person. The required information is found by the number of beads remaining over after the recitation; if three remain to the thread, it is sickness; if two it is health.

Mr. G. B. A. Gardener, of Cape Town, says: "The rosary is sometimes worn round the neck as a cure for sickness. Those most in use are made of sandal-wood, said to come from Mecca. For magical purposes the rosary is used by counting."

Miss G. Y. Holliday of Tabriz, Persia, gives the following information: "The rosary is used to decide what medicine should be taken, what physician should be called, whether his advice should be followed or not, etc. It is also used about all the affairs of life; it is called taking the *istikhara*. In using it, the rosary is grasped by the first bead the hand happens on; from which they count to the *Khalifa*, or the large bead which is the most prominent object, saying 'bad, good,' the last bead giving the decision."

In Java the rosary is used as follows for healing the sick,

or for inducing sickness. With the rosary in the hand one reads any chapter from the Koran and up to the fifteenth verse, this verse always contains a word of talismanic power, and while this verse is being read the rosary is counted and the result follows.

In Egypt the rosary is widely used for the cure of the sick. In this case it depends on the material from which the beads are manufactured. Those made of ordinary wood or of mother-of-pearl are not valuable, but a rosary made of jet (yusr) or *kuk* (a particular kind of wood from Mecca) is valuable. In Egypt both among Copts and Moslems the rosary is used for the cure of "retention of urine" in children. It is put on the infant's neck or is laid on the roof in the starlight to catch the dew, then it is washed and the water given to the child to drink.

"In India," writes Mr. K. I. Khan of Poona, "the rosary is used to protect against the evil eye and other dangers, sometimes it is washed in water and the water given as medicine to the sick to drink."

When we consider how in all these puerile superstitions the original use of the rosary with its ninety-nine beads for the remembrance of the one true God has been lost or obscured we are forcibly reminded of the words of Warneck: "Animistic heathenism is not a transition stage to a higher religion. I think I have adduced sufficient facts to establish that, and facts do not vanish away before hypothesis. Let them produce facts to prove that animistic heathenism somewhere and somehow evolved upwards toward a purer knowledge of God, real facts, not imaginary construction of such an evolution. Any form of Animism known to me has no lines leading to perfection, but only incontestable marks of degeneration." [10]

In its doctrine of the soul before birth, after death, and in the future world, Islam is not free from animistic ideas which

[10] "The Living Christ and Dying Heathenism," Warneck, p. 10.

differ little from those of Pagans in Africa.  Al Ghazali says:  "When God Almighty let His hands pass over the back of Adam and gathered men into His two hands, He placed some of them in His right hand and the others in His left; then he opened both His hands before Adam, and Adam looked at them and saw them like imperceptible atoms.  Then God said:  'These are destined for Paradise and these are destined for hell-fire.'  He then asked them:  'Am I not your Lord?' and they replied:  'Certainly, we testify that Thou art our Lord.'  God then asked Adam and the angels to be witnesses . . . after this God replaced them into the loins of Adam.  They were at that time purely spiritual beings without bodies.  He then caused them to die, but gathered them and kept them in a receptacle near His throne. When the germ of a new being is placed in the womb of the mother, it remains there till its body is sufficiently developed; the soul in the same is then dead, yet when God Almighty breathes into it the spirit, He restores to it its most precious part, of which it had been deprived while preserved in the receptacle near the throne.  This is the first death and a second life.  Then God places man in this world till he has reached the term fixed for him."

In this teaching of the greatest Moslem theologian we have the gist of the teaching as found in the Koran and Tradition.

The Koran in many places gives a minute description of the process of death while the Commentaries based on savings of Mohammed leave no doubt of the crass materialisic ideas he held and perpetuated.  (See e.g., Suras 75; 81: 1–19; 82; 83: 4–20; 84: 1–19; and of a later period 22: 1–7.)

Death takes place by means of a poisonous lance which is held by Izra'il, the angel of death, who pierces the soul and detaches it from the body.  (Cf. Surah 32 :11.)  "As long as the soul slowly ascends from the heart through the throat, it is exposed to various temptations and doubts, but when it has been pierced by the lance and thus separated from the body, these cease. Izra'il is said to be frightful in appearance and of enormous size; his head in the highest heaven, his feet in the lowest part of the earth, and his face opposite the preserved Tablet. To a believer, however, he appears in a lovely shape, and his assistants as 'Angels of Mercy,' while to the unbelievers they are tormenting angels. The soul or spirit, according to the orthodox school, is said to be a subtle body, intimately united with the body of man, like the juice is united with the green branch of a tree. The Angel of Death also takes the life of *jinn,* of angels and even of animals." [11]

The teaching that the Angel of Death takes care of the souls of animals as well as of men's souls is clearly animistic.

Immediately after burial two large black Angels visit the dead in their graves. They are called Munkar and Nakir. The spirit of the believer, according to some authorities, is taken through the seven Heavens ino the very presence of God and then returns to the grave to reënter the body and be examined. This seems to be the teaching of Ghazali (*Durrat al Fakhira*). The same authority classifies the inhabitants of the grave as follows, and says they are of four kinds: " (1) Those who sleep on their backs till their corpses become dust, when they constantly rove about between earth and the lowest heaven; (2) those on whom God causes sleep to descend and who only wake up at the first blast of the trumpet; (3) those who remain in their graves only two or three months, then are carried away into Paradise; they perch on the trees of Paradise in the shape of birds. The spirits of martyrs are in the crops of birds. (4) Prophets and saints who may choose their own habitation."

Another animistic idea in the teaching of Mohammed is that although the whole of the human body perishes in the

[11] Klein, " The Religion of Islam," p. 81.

grave, one bone, namely the os sacrum, remains uncorrupted until the resurrection morning. It is from this bone or seed that the whole body is renewed by means of a miraculous rainstorm called " the water of life." [12]

The spirit after death enters the state (or interval), whether of time or place seems uncertain — called *Al Barzakh.*

Many curious traditions are current regarding the souls of the martyrs and their residence in the crops of green birds. One commentator says the birds are transparent, i.e. ethereal. Others say that it signifies figuratively the speed with which the souls of martyrs can travel about.

An important point and which is universally believed relates to the spirits of ordinary mortals. These remain near their graves. This accounts for the universal custom in Islam of visiting the graves of their dead on Thursday night. In India we are told, " It is a general belief among the community of Mussulmans that when a Moslem gives up the ghost his soul haunts and lurks about the place where he breathed his last for full forty days from the date of his demise: that it (the soul) comes to visit the quarter it left, with the idea and conviction that its surviving relations and acquaintances may show pity to it by offering prayers and charity for its good and salvation in the migrated region of the heaven above; that in case it finds its survivors doing good for its well-being, rest, happiness, and welfare in its changed career, it devoutly and heartily prays in return for their safety, pleasure and comfort on earth; and that in the reverse case, when it perceives its people doing naught for it or entrapped in vices opposed to the dictates of Islamic faith, it curses them and invokes on them heavenly displeasure for

[12] It is impossible to give the indecent Moslem interpretations of this term. Cf. any popular Arabic work on Eschatology.

their negligence and foolish reckless pursuits devoid of all religious principles." [13]

The special sanctity of the " night of the middle of Sha'ban," called in Arabic *Lailat Nusf Sha'ban,* is believed in by all Mohammedans. It is supposed that on that particular night Allah determines the fate of mortals during the forthcoming year. The most popular idea is that there is a celestial tree of symbolic import, on which every human being has a leaf to represent him. This tree is shaken during the night preceding the 15th of Sha'ban, causing the leaves of all those who are to die during the coming year to fall.

In Arabia many watch through a part or the whole of this night and offer up a prayer, invoking Allah's mercy, and beseeching him to blot out from his eternal book the calamities and adversity destined for the suppliant.

" Throughout the whole of the Indian Archipelago," says Hurgronje, " this month, Sha'ban, is especially dedicated to the commemoration of the dead. This does not imply grief for their loss, but rather care for their souls' repose, which is not inconsistent with merrymaking. This solicitude for the welfare of the departed exhibits itself by the giving of religious feasts. According to the religious or learned conception this is done in order to bestow on the deceased the recompense earned by this good work; according to the popular notion it is to let them enjoy the actual savor of the good things of the feast."

Not only in visiting the graves of the dead, but in the very method of burial Moslems are animists in practice whatever they may be in creed. " It is fear," says Warneck, speaking of the Animists in Malaysia, " that leads them to place food on the dead man's grave; to bring him his tools

[13] " Moslem Festivities," by Mohammed Ameer Ali — Calcutta, 1892, p. 42.

and coin, that his shadow may use them in the other world and be content. The inhabitants of many islands sacrifice some one, preferably a slave, at the grave in order that they themselves may be spared. The impelling motive is always fear, not grief nor pity. To prevent the soul of the dead from returning to the living, thorns are laid upon the corpse, which is firmly bound, *its thumbs and toes tied together,* ashes put in its eyes, an egg placed in its armpits, all with the view of making it incapable of movement." [14]

According to a Moslem tradition also, it is the universal practice to tie the toes of the dead together before burial but then to loosen them when the body has been lowered into the grave. The construction of the grave itself with its characteristic *lahdi* in all Moslem lands, can only be explained by beliefs which are animistic. Coffins are never used for burial, but a niche, *lahdi,* is made on one side of the open grave.

The contents of any book on the subject of Eschatology are an index to this world of Moslem-animistic thought. The terrors of the grave are real in popular Islam, and such books have a larger sale than any other religious literature.

Here follows for example the table of contents of El Hamzawi's "*Masharik-ul-Anwar*" on this subject. In every chapter there are points of contact with animism and signs of old pagan belief and practices perpetuated:

I. WHAT HAPPENS TO THE DEAD BEFORE BURIAL.

    1. What he should do while he is still here.

    2. What he should do when death approaches.

    3. How the spirit leaves the body.

    4. The benefit of speedy burial.

II. WHAT HAPPENS IN THE GRAVE.

    1. How the questions are asked by the two angels.

[14] "The Living Christ and Dying Heathenism," p. 59.

2. How he must answer.
3. On the joy and pain that results.
4. Where the spirits go.
5. Warning to the living.

III. ON VISITING THE GRAVE.
    1. Its desirability.
    2. The right times.
    3. What to do.
    4. Are the dead conscious?
    5. Traditions of the Prophet.
    6. Who of the Prophet's family were buried in Egypt.

IV. SIGNS OF THE HOUR AND THE END OF THE AGE.
    1. Minor signs of the hour.
    2. The appearance of the Mahdi.
    3. The appearance of anti-Christ.
    4. The return of Jesus.
    5. The Beast — Gog and Magog.
    6. The first blast of the trumpet.

V. THE RESURRECTION.
    1. The number of trumpet blasts.
    2. The one who blows.
    3. How they arise from the graves.
    4. In what form do they come?
    5. Do they arise naked or dressed?
    6. The books.
    7. The intents of the heart.

VI. THE PLACE OF JUDGMENT.
    1. Where the judgment takes place.
    2. The conditions of those who appear.
    3. The day of accounts.

    4. The robes and the throne.
    5. The *sirat* and the scales.
    6. The intercession.
    7. The scales of justice.
    8. The pond.

VII. ON THE THINGS THAT CONCERN HEAVEN AND HELL AND THE VENGEANCE OF GOD.


In this survey of the present use of the creed and the clear teaching based on some of its six articles, the conclusion is irresistible that the monotheism of Islam has degenerated in popular belief to a much larger degree than is generally appreciated. It is idle to talk of pure monotheism when dealing with popular Islam.

# CHAPTER III

## ANIMISTIC ELEMENTS IN MOSLEM PRAYER

ONE of the most impressive rites of Islam is the daily prayer ritual. It has elicited the admiration of many who have observed it, and, ignorant of the real character and content of Moslem prayer interpreted it entirely from the Christian standpoint. What is understood by prayer, however, in Christendom, and what the Moslem calls by the same name are to a degree distinct conceptions. In the punctilious regard of position, prostration, ablution and the peculiar gestures and movements of the hand, the head and the body it is clear that prayer is more than a spiritual exercise. Moslems themselves are at a loss to explain the reason for many of the details which they have learned from their youth. The various sects in orthodox Islam can be distinguished by the casual observer most easily in the method of ablution and in the prostration of the prayer ritual.

Theodore Nöldeke of Germany, and the Dutch scholar Prof. A. J. Wensinck have made a special study of the origin and detail of the prayer ritual, the latter more especially of the Moslem laws of ablution.[1][2] Further study of the sources given and long experience in many Moslem lands have led to the following observations and conclusions on the subject.

In the preparation of the five daily prayers, especially in the process of ablution — the object of the Moslem seems to be to free himself from everything that has connection with

[1][2] Der Islam, Band IV, Animisme und Daemonenglaube.
Der Islam, Band V, Heft I, " Die Entstehung der muslimischen Reinheitsgesetzebung," von A. J. Wensinck.

The "*Paiza*" or Restaurant board from China. This hangs over every place where pure (Moslem) food is sold. The Arabic inscriptions contain the text of the Koran regarding purity of food, the name of the shop-keeper and date, while in the center surrounding the ablution-vessel are words which signify the absolute ritual purity of all that is sold.

It is significant that the Turkish flag appears with the Chinese flag at the top.

supernatural powers or demons as opposed to the worship of
the one true God. That is the reason for its supreme importance. Wensinck tells us that these beliefs have little or
nothing to do with bodily purity as such, but are intended to
free the worshiper from the presence or influence of evil
spirits. It is this demonic pollution which must be removed. In two traditions from Muslim we read, " Said the
Prophet: ' If any of you wakens up from sleep then let him
blow his nose three times. For the devil spends the night in
a man's nostrils.' " And again: " Said Omar ibn el-
Khitab (may God have mercy on him): ' A certain man
performed ablution but left a dry spot on his foot.' When
the Prophet of God saw it he said: ' Go back and wash
better,' then he returned and came back to prayer. Said the
Prophet of God: ' If a Moslem servant of God performs the
ablution when he washes his face every sin which his face has
committed is taken away by it with the water or with the
last drop of water. And when he washes his hands the sin
of his hands are taken away with the water or with the last
drop of water. And when he washes his feet all the sins
which his feet have committed are taken away with the water
or with the last drop of water until he becomes pure from
sin altogether.' " Goldziher has shown in one of his essays
that, according to Semitic conception, water drives away
demons.

That ablution in Islam as taught by Mohammed to his
disciples was originally not intended to remove physical un-
cleanness but was a ceremonial precaution against spiritual
evil, of demons, etc., is evident when we compare it with the
ablutions practiced by pagan races in their ritual. For
example, Skeat describes the bath ceremony as practiced at
Perak:

" Limes are used in Perak, as we use soap. When a Malay
has resolved on having a really good ' scrub ' they are cut in

two and squeezed (*ramas*) in the hand. In Penang a root called *sintok* is usually preferred to limes. When the body is deemed sufficiently cleansed, the performer, taking his stand facing the East, spits seven times, and then counts up to seven aloud. After the word *Tujoh* (seven) he throws away the remains of the limes or *sintok* to the West, saying aloud, *Pergi-lah samua sial jambalang deripada badan aku ka pusat tasek Pawjangi,* 'Misfortune and spirits of evil, begone from my body to the whirlpool of the lake Paujangi!' Then he throws (*jurus*) a few buckets of water over himself, and the operation is complete."

"The ceremony just described is evidently a form of purification by water. Similar purificatory ceremonies form an integral part of Malay customs at *birth, adolescence, marriage, sickness, death,* and in fact at every critical period of the life of a Malay."[3]

According to al-Bokhari the washings before prayer should always begin on the right side of the body and not on the left. Another tradition gives the value of the hairs of the Prophet when they fell in the washing-vessel. The Prophet used to wash his feet when he wore sandals by simply passing his hands over the outside of the sandals; the object, therefore, cannot have been to cleanse impurity but to ward off demons. Another tradition is given as follows: According to 'Abd-el-Rahman, a man came to Omar ibn el-Khattab and said, "I am in a state of impurity and cannot find water." Ammar ibn Yasir said to Omar ibn el-Khattab, "Do you remember the day that you and I traveled together. You did not make your prayers, but I rolled myself in the sand and prayed. When I told the Prophet of this, he said, 'That was enough,' and so saying he took some earth in his hands, blew on it and then rubbed his face and hands with it."[4][5] 'Abd-el-Rahman was witness when "Amar said to

---

[3] Skeat's "Malay Magic," p. 278.
[4] [5] "Les Traditions de Bokhari," by O. Houdas, p. 126.

Omar," " We were in a detachment and we were in a state of impurity, etc. . . ." and he uses the words: " he spat on his hands " instead of " he breathed."

These two traditions from Bokhari also show the value ascribed to the animistic custom of blowing and spitting.

There are a number of traditions regarding spitting in a mosque. It must in no case be done in front of any one, nor to the right hand but to the left.[6]   According to Annas Ibn Malek, to spit in a mosque is a sin: one may expiate it by wiping up the spittle. Again, in entering a mosque one must put the right foot forward first for fear of evil consequences. In the same way we are told that a man who was carrying arrows in his hand entered a mosque, and the Prophet cried: " Hold them by the point." The only reason for this command, as is shown by its connection, is that the points of the arrows or other sharp instruments might arouse *jinn* or damage the value of prayer. We also find traditions concerning such Animistic practices as crossing the fingers or the limbs at the time of prayer.

In regard to the ritual ablution, (*ghasl*), after certain natural functions, Wensinck remarks, " Das Geschlechtsleben stand in semitischen Heidentum unter den Schutze gewisser Götter und war ihnen somit geweiht. Die männlichen und weiblichen Prostituierten bei den Pälastinichen und babylonichen Heiligtumern sind ja bekaunt genug. Ich brauche darüber kein wort ze verlieren. Weil nun der betreffende Gott für den Monotheismus Dämon geworden ist, so ist auch sein Kult, das Geschlechtsleben, den Monotheismus dämonisch." There are many traditions which assert a close relationship between sleep and the presence of Jinn. It

[6] Bokhari: Chap. 33. Cf. Muslim, Vol. I, 207 — Arabic edition. " No one must enter or approach a mosque if he has eaten onion, or garlic, because the angels hate the smell as much as human beings do." Muslim: Vol. I: 210.

is during sleep that the soul, according to animistic belief, leaves the body. Therefore, one must waken those who sleep, gently, lest the soul be prevented from returning. Not only during sleep, but during illness demons are present; and in Egypt it is considered unfortunate for any one who is ceremonially unclean to approach a patient suffering from ophthalmia.

The Moslem when he prays is required, according to tradition, to cover his head, especially the back part of the skull. This according to Wensinck is also due to animistic belief; for evil spirits enter the body by this way. Goldziher has shown that the name given to this part of the body (*al qafa*) has a close relation to the kind of poetry called Qafiya, which originally meant a poem to wound the skull, or in other words, an imprecatory poem. It is therefore for the dread of evil powers which might enter the mind that the head must be covered during prayer. References are found to this practice both in Moslem tradition and in the Talmud, on which they are based. Again it is noteworthy that those places which are ritually unclean, such as closets, baths, etc., are considered the habitation of demons.

According to tradition a Moslem cannot perform his prayer without a *Sutra* or some object placed between himself and the Kibla (the direction of Mecca) in order, " that nothing may harm him by passing in between." Of this custom we speak later. The call of the Muezzin according to Al-Bokhari drives away the demons and Satan.[7] No one dares to recite the Koran, which is a holy book, without first repeating the words, " I take refuge in God against Satan the accursed." We may add to all this what Mittwoch has shown in his book " Zur Entstehungsgeschichte des islamischen Gebets und Kultus," that the Takbir itself (that is the cry *Allahu Akbar,* God is greater), one of the elements of daily prayer, is a cry

[7] Bokhari: Kitab al Adhan: Section IV.

against demons.   The raising of the hands during prayer and
the movement of the forefinger is perhaps to ward off the
spirits of the air,[8] or it may have a connection with the
*Qanut*.   Others say that the spreading out or the stretching
forth of the fingers and arms is to prevent any idol or thing of
blasphemy being hidden between the fingers or under the
armpits, a ruse used formerly by the unbelievers and discovered by the Angel Gabriel.

Among the Arabs before the time of Mohammed and among
Moslems to-day, sneezing, especially during prayer, is an
ominous sign and should be accompanied by a pious ejacula-
tion.   This also is clearly animistic; among the tribes of
Malaysia the general belief is that when one sneezes, the soul
leaves the body.   At the close of the prayer, as is well-known,
the worshiper salutes the two angels on his right and left
shoulders.   When one sneezes one should say, " I ask forgiveness of God "; when one yawns, however, the breath
(soul) passes inward and one says, " Praise be to God."

Not only the preparations for prayer and prayer itself but
the times [9] of prayer have a distinct connection with the
animistic belief.   The noon-day prayer is never held at high
noon but a short time *after* the sun reaches the meridian.
Wensinck points out that this is due to the belief that the
sun-god is really a demon and must not be worshiped by the

[8] I am told by my sheikh from Al-Azhar that according to Moslem
tradition it is bad luck (Makruh) to drink water or any liquid while
one is standing.   If, however, one is compelled to drink standing one
should move his big toe rapidly as this will ward off all harm.   We
find here the same superstitious custom of warding off evil spirits by
moving the first toe up and down as that of the finger at the end of
the ritual prayer.

[9] Prayer is forbidden at three particular periods: at high noon because the devil is then in the ascendant; when the sun is rising because it rises between the horns of the devil, when the sun is at the setting because it sets between the horns of the devil.   ."Ibn Maja ": Vol.
I, p. 195.

monotheist.   According to al-Bokhari the Prophet postponed the noon-day prayer until after high noon for " the greatest heat of the day belongs to the heat of hell." Nor is it permitted to pray shortly after sunrise for " the sun rises between the horns of the devil." According to Abu Huraira and Abdallah ibn 'Omar, the prophet of God said: " When it is excessively hot wait until it is cool to make your prayers, for intense heat comes from hell."

Abu-Dzarr said:   The Muezzin of the Prophet had called for the noon-prayer.   " Wait until it is cooler, wait until it is cooler, or wait . . ." said the Prophet.   Then he added: " Great heat is of hell: so when it is excessively hot wait until it is cool, then make your prayers." Abou-Dzarr [10] adds:   " And we waited until we saw the shadow declining."

That certain hours of the day are unlucky and must be guarded against is a pagan belief probably based on their fear of darkness.   Maxwell, quoted by Skeat (page 15), says: " Sunset is the hour when evil spirits of all kinds have most power.   In Perak, children are often called indoors at this time to save from unseen dangers.   Sometimes, with the same object, a woman belonging to the house where there are young children, will chew *kuniet terus* (an evil-smelling root), supposed to be much disliked by demons of all kinds, and spit it out at seven different points as she walks round the house.

" The yellow glow which spreads over the western sky, when it is lighted up with the last rays of the dying sun, is called *mambang kuning* (' the yellow deity '), a term indicative of the superstitious dread associated with this particular period." [11]

In this connection it is curious to note that the unlucky times among the Malay people correspond exactly with the

[10] " Al-Bokhari," translated by Houdas (Paris, 1903), p. 190.
[11] Skeat's " Malay Magic," p. 15.

INTERIOR COURT OF THE MOSQUE OF AL 'AZHAR, CAIRO

In the upper left-hand corner of this university mosque where 6,000 students receive instruction, one may see the old Moslem sun dial which indicates the hours of prayer.

)

periods appointed for Moslem prayer. Among the Malays
each of these periods has a special meaning and a special
guardian deity, one of the Hindu divinities. The table given
corresponds very closely to the Moslem prayer schedule.
" Perhaps the oldest and best known of the systems of lucky
and unlucky times is the one called *Katika Lima,* or the Five
Times. Under it the day is divided into five parts and five
days form a cycle: to each of these divisions is assigned a
name, the names being Maswara (Maheswara), Kala, S'ri,
Brahma, and Bisnu (Vishnu), which recur in the order
shown in the following table or diagram: [12]

|           | *Morning* (pagi) | *Forenoon* (tengah naik) | *Noon* (tengah hari) | *Afternoon* (tengah turun) | *Evening* (petang) |
|-----------|---------|----------|---------|------------|---------|
| 1st day | Maswara | Kala | S'ri | Brahma | Bisnu |
| 2nd day | Bisnu | Maswara | Kala | S'ri | Brahma |
| 3rd day | Brahma | Bisnu | Maswara | Kala | S'ri |
| 4th day | S'ri | Brahma | Bisnu | Maswara | Kala |
| 5th day | Kala | S'ri | Brahma | Bisnu | Maswara |

The most interesting thing of all, however, is the tradition
regarding the Sutra. The word means something that covers
or protects; from what is it a protection and why is it used?
The Commentaries do not explain what the Sutra really
means but it is very clearly a protection against demons, as
is shown by the traditions given. [13]

According to Ibn Omar, on the feast day (when the fast
was broken) the Messenger of God gave him an order when he
went out to bring him a stick and to stick it before him and
it was before this stick that he made his prayers, while the
faithful were ranged behind him. He did the same thing
when he traveled and it is from this that the emirs took the
custom. Other authorities say the Sutra of the Prophet was
the short spear or the camel-saddle, or his camel when
kneeling. [14]

[12] Skeat's " Malay Magic," p. 545.
[13] See " Muslim," Vol. I, pp. 190, 193, 194, and Zarkani: " Com. on
al-Muwatta," Vol. I, p. 283.
[14] " Ibn Maja," Vol. I, p. 156, lines 10–12.

A curious tradition is given by Abu Dawud on the authority of Ibn Abbas who said, "I think the Apostle of God said, 'If one of you prays without a sutra (a thing set up by a praying person) before him, his prayer is apt to be annulled by a dog, or an ass, or a pig, or a Jew, or a Magi, or a menstruating woman; if they pass before him they ought to be punished on that account, with the pelting of stones.' " [15]

Abu-Johaifa said: "The Prophet went out during the heat of the day and when he came to El-Batha and prayed two *rakas* for the noon-prayer and the evening prayer, he stuck a pike before him and made his ablutions. The faithful washed themselves with the rest of the water." [16]

The following tradition is most important as it shows what the Sutra originally meant. The reference to the demon is animistic: "Abu Salih es-Sam'an said: 'I saw something that separated him from the crowd. A young man of the Bni Abu Mo'ait trying to pass before him, Abu Said gave him a push full on the chest. The young man looked round for another way out and not finding any, he returned. Abu Said pushed him back still more violently. The young man cursed him and then went and told Merwan of Abu Said's conduct. The latter at this moment entered and Merwan said to him: "What is the matter with you, O Abu Said, that you thus treat one of your own religion?" "I have heard the Prophet pronounce these words," answered Abu Said, "when one of you prays, let him place something before him which will separate him from the public, and if any one tries to pass between turn him away and if he refuse to leave let him use force, *for it is a demon.*" ' " [17] Muslim adds: [18] "If any of

[15] Ad-Damiri's "Hayat Al-Hayawan," Vol. I, p. 708.
[16] "Les Traductions de Bokhari," Houdas, p. 179.
[17] "Les Traductions Bokhari," Houdas, p. 181.
[18] "Muslim," Vol. I, p. 193.

you pray do not allow any one to pass between himself and the Sutra for it protects from the demons."

The *Sutra* or guard placed before the one in prayer is usually some object such as a stone or a stick placed at a certain distance from the one praying: i.e. about one foot beyond where his head would touch the ground. It is also a sign that none must pass before him, but never used except by men of mature years and serious mind, and then only in open or public places, never in a room or house-top. If stones are used they must never be less than three, otherwise it would seem as if the stone were the object of worship.

There are cases in which passing before one at prayer is counted as sin either to the pray-er or to the one passing, i.e.:

(a) If he who prays is obliged to pray in the public way, and there is no other way of passing except before him, there is sin neither to the pray-er or to the passer-by.

(b) If he who prays chooses a public place in preference to one less exposed and one passes in front of him, who could as easily have gone behind, sin is accounted to both of them.

(c) If he who prays chooses a public place in preference to one less exposed and the one who passes has no choice but to go in front of him sin is accounted to him who prays.

(d) If he who prays chooses an unexposed place and some one deliberately passes in front when there is space behind, sin is accounted to the passer-by and not to him who prays.

"The practices among the Shiah Moslems differ in some respects from those of the Sunnis," says Miss Holliday of Tabriz, Persia. "A Shiah about to pray takes his place looking toward the Kibla at Mecca; if he be a strict Moslem he lays before him nearest the Kibla and where he can put his forehead upon it, the *Muhr* which is indispensable. It generally consists of earth from Kerbela, compressed into a small tablet and bearing Arabic inscriptions; it is various in shape. If one has not this object, he can use a common stone, a piece of wood or a clod of earth; in the baths they keep small pieces of wood for the convenience of worshipers. With regard to wood, they say all the trees in the world came from heaven, and their life is directly from God, so they are holy objects. The Kerbela talismans are called ' turbat ' as being made from holy earth from the tomb city of the Imam Hussain. On the side nearest him of the *muhr* the worshiper lays a small pocket comb, then next to himself the rosary.

" After prayer, they point the right forefinger first in the direction of the Kibla, saluting Mohammed as the *Son of Abdullah* and the Imam Hussain 'grandson of the Prophet, son of Fatima,' then to the east saluting Imam Riza as the *Gareeb,* or stranger, at Meshhed in Khorassan, then to the west, saluting the Imam Mahdi, as the *Sahib-i-zaman* or Lord of the Age. The back is to the north; this looks like sun-worship."

Among the customs which are forbidden during prayer is that of crossing or closing the fingers. They should be held widely spread apart. We have the following tradition in Ibn Maja:[19] " Said the Prophet: ' Do not put your fingers close together during prayer. It is also forbidden to cover the mouth during prayer.' " Another tradition reads that the Apostle of God saw a man who had crossed his fingers during prayer or joined them close together; he approached him and made him spread his fingers.[20]

That the yawning, to which reference was made, has connection with spirits and demons is evident from a tradition given in the same paragraph, namely: " If any of you yawn, let him put his hand upon his mouth for verily the devil is laughing at him."

The Moslem lives constantly in dread of evil spirits; this is

[19] Vol. I, p. 158.
[20] Vol. I, p. 158.

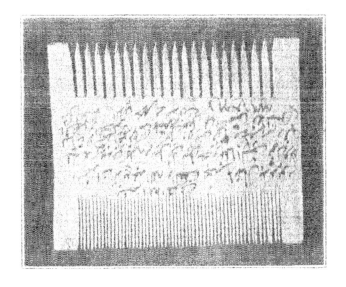

### THE TURBA AND AMULETS

In the upper left-hand corner is a TURBA or bit of pressed sacred clay from Kerbela used in daily prayer (see Chap. 31). The others are amulets made of stone and used against scorpion bite; one of them contains a magic square. The conical amulet is worn by Moslem women to facilitate child birth. It contains a portion of the 19th Psalm in Arabic with Moslem introduction.

shown by other traditions regarding the prayer ritual. For example, we read in the Sunnan of Ibn Maja [21] that Mohammed forbade prayer being made on or near watering places of camels because camels were created by devils. It is an old superstition that Satan had a hand in the creation of the camel; the explanation is given in the commentators. We are solemnly told that the fingers must be spread so as to afford no nestling place for evil demons and that therefore the method of washing the hands (*Takhlil*) consists in rubbing the outspread fingers of both hands between each other. (Ibn Maja, Vol. I, p. 158, Nasai, Vol. I, pp. 30, 173, 186–7.) The last reference is particularly important as it shows that Mohammed inculcated the practice of moving the first finger during prayer.[22] Undoubtedly the practice of combing the hair with the fingers outspread (*Takhlil esh-Sha'ar*) to which al-Bukhari refers (Vol. I, p. 51) has a similar significance. Some of the sects do not spread the fingers of the right hand during prayer but make a special effort to spread those of the left. This may be because the left hand is used for ablutions and therefore is specially apt to be infected by demonic influence.

We give further reference to all such practices as recorded in a standard work on tradition, the *Sunnan* of An-Nasai.[23]

[21] Vol. I, p. 134.

[22] Takhlil is not only used of the fingers but of the toes as well, there also demons lurk. (*See* Sha'arani's "Lawa'ih al Anwar fi Tabakat al Ahjar," p. 26.)

[23] In prayer there should be no gaps in the ranks of the worshipers lest Satan come between. Vol. I, p. 131.

One should blow the nostrils three times when awakening so as to drive away the devil. Ibid., Vol. I, p. 27.

The Prophet forbade sleep in bath-rooms because they are the abode of devils. Ibid., Vol. I, p. 15.

The Prophet forbade facing the Kibla when fulfilling a call of nature, for fear of Satan. Ibid., Vol. I, p. 15.

The separation of the fingers (p. 30): the fingers of the right hand

The niche in a mosque that shows the direction to which prayer is made called the *Mihrab,* i.e., " the place of fighting," or perhaps, the instrument by which we fight the demons? There are many traditions concerning Mohammed's struggle with *afrits* and Jinn in a mosque. The most interesing one is given in Muslim (Vol. I, p. 204). " Said the Apostle of God (on him be prayers and peace): ' A certain demon of the Jinn attacked me yesterday in order to stop my prayers, but, verily, God gave me victory over him. I was about to tie him to the side of a pillar of the pillars of the Mosque so that ye might get up in the morning and behold him, all of you, when I remembered the prayer of my brother Solomon: " O Lord, forgive me and give me a dominion such as no one ever had," and after that God set the demon free! ' " The *Mihrab* in a mosque, I am told, takes the place of the *Sutra* outside of a mosque and serves the same purpose.

The forming of ranks in Moslem prayers as they face the *Mihrab,* is most important and therefore they are extremely careful of it. There are many traditions in this respect which can only have relation to belief in *Jinn.* For example, not only must the worshipers stand in a row, but in a mosque it is considered most important to stand so close together that nothing can possibly pass between. They stand ready like soldiers in massed-formation. Here is the tradition:

Anas states that the Prophet said: " Observe your ranks, for I can see you from behind my back." " Each one of us," he adds, " put his shoulder in touch with his neighbor's and his foot with that of his neighbor." [24] We must add to

should be closed tight during prayer and of the left hand spread out, but the forefinger should remain straight. Ibid., Vol. I, p. 186.

The forefinger should be bent when giving witness. Ibid., p. 187.

The fingers should be moved. Ibid., p. 187.

Turning the head around during prayer is caused by the devil. Ibid., Vol. I, p. 177.

[24] Houdas' al Bukhari (French Trans.), p. 243; see also al Nasai, Vol. I, pp. 173 and 186-7.

this another superstition, namely, it is bad luck to pray on the left hand of the Imam.   Ibn-'Abbas said: " On a certain night I made my prayers together with the Prophet.   As I was placing myself on his left, the Messenger of God taking hold of me by the back of my head, placed me on his right. After having made our prayers, he lay down and rested until the muezzin came to look for him.   Then he got up and made his prayers *without making his ablutions.*" [25]

We have already spoken of the lifting of the hands in prayer.   This is an important matter for discussion in all works of *Fiqh.*

In the prayer called *Qunut,* which takes place during and as part of the morning prayer (*Salat*), the hands are raised in magical fashion.   Goldziher believes the original significa- tion of this was a curse or imprecation on the enemy; such was the custom of the Arabs.   The Prophet cursed his ene- mies in this way.   So did also the early Caliphs.   In Lane's Dictionary (Art. Qunut) we find the present prayer given as follows:   " O God, verily we beg of Thee aid, and we beg of Thee forgiveness.   And we believe in Thee and we rely on Thee, and we laud Thee well, and we will not be unthankful to Thee for Thy favor, and we cast off and forsake him who disobeys Thee: O God, Thee we worship and to Thee we per- form the divinely-appointed act of prayer, and prostrate our- selves; and we are quick in working for Thee and in serving Thee; we hope for Thy mercy, and we dread Thy punish- ment; *verily (or may) Thy punishment overtake the unbe- lievers.*"   It is said of the Prophet that he stood during a whole month after the prayer of daybreak cursing the tribes of Rial and Dhukwan.   We read in Al-Muwatta (Vol. I, p. 216) that at the time of the *Qunut* they used to curse their enemies, the unbelievers, in the month of Ramadhan.   Later on this custom was modified or explained away.   Al-Bukhari

[25] Houdas' al Bukhari (French Trans.), p. 244.

even wrote a book on the subject as to when the hands might be lifted in prayer.

There is no doubt regarding the origin of the *Qunut* prayer. We learn from Yusuf as Safti in his commentary on *Ibn Turki's* well-known book on *Fiqh* (p. 157): " The reason for the legislation concerning the Qunut is as follows: One day there came to the Prophet certain unbelievers who pretended that they had become Moslems and asked him that he would give them aid from among his Companions as a troop against their enemies. So he granted them seventy men from among the Companions; when they departed with them, however, they took them out to the desert and killing them threw them into the well Mayrah. This became known to the Prophet and he mistrusted them and was filled with wrath and began to curse them saying: ' O God, curse Ra'ala and Lahyan and Beni Dhakwan because they mocked God and his Apostle. O God, cause to come down upon them a famine like in the days of Joseph and help el-Walid ibn el-Walid and the weak company of Mecca.' Then Gabriel came down to him and told him to keep quiet, saying, ' God did not send you a reviler and a curser but verily he sent you as a mercy. He did not send you as a punishment. The affair does not concern you; for God will either forgive them or punish them. They are the transgressors.' Then he taught him the *Qunut* aforementioned, *i. e.,* the prayer now used."

In spite of the assertion of God's unity there are many other things connected wih Moslem prayer which show pagan magic, such as the power through certain words and gestures to influence the Almighty. These practices were prevalent before Islam. Professor Goldziher mentions the custom of incantation (Manashada) similar to that practiced by the heathen *Kahins*. Of certain leaders in the early days of Islam it was said: " If so and so would adjure anything upon God he would doubtless obtain it."

Not only in formal prayer (*Salat*) but also in the *Du'a* (petition) there are magical practices, especially in the prayer for eclipse by the raising of the hands. We are told (al-Bukhari) that on one occasion the Prophet while praying for rain raised his hands so high that one could see the white skin of his arm-pits. In the case of *Du'a* therefore, the Kibla is said to be heaven itself and not Mecca.

Another gesture used in *Du'a* is the stroking of the face, or of the body with the hands. This custom, borrowed from the Prophet, also has magical effect. At the time of his death the Prophet put his hands in water and washed his face with them, repeating the creed.

Goldziher refers especially to magical elements in the prayer for rain,[26] and against eclipses of the sun or moon. These, like excessive drought, were explained and combated by the pagan Arabs in a superstitious manner. Mohammed forbade them to recognize in such phenomena anything more than special manifestations of the omnipotence of the Creator, yet ordained in this case also certain ritual prayers, to be continued as long as the eclipse lasted.

No Mohammedan questions for a moment that the omnipotence of God reveals itself in these eclipses — indeed no doctrine is more popular than that of the omnipotence of God and predestination — yet in the ranks of the people all kinds of superstitions prevail in regard to such phenomena. In these temporary obscurations of sun and moon they discern the action of malignant spirits and do not regard the performance of a simple service of prayer as a sufficient protection. " In Acheh, as in other Mohammedan countries, these prayers are left to the representatives of religion, the *teunkus* and *leubes,* while the people of the *gampong* keep up a mighty

[26] See al Bukhari who gives certain chapters on magical formulas to be used on this occasion. Certain of the companions of the Prophet were celebrated as rain-makers.

uproar beating the great drum of the *meunasah,* and firing off guns and sometimes even cannons in order to frighten away the enemies of the sun and moon.   Various sorts of *ratebs* are also held in order to relieve the suffering heavenly body." [27]

That Moslem prayer has become paganized among the Malays is well known.   The whole ceremony of sowing rice and reaping the first crop is thoroughly animistic, and yet it is carried on with Moslem-pagan prayers and invocations. Among many examples we give the following from Skeat.[28] He describes how a woman gathers in the first fruits.

" Next she took in one hand (out of the brass tray) the stone, the egg, cockle-shell and candle-nut, and with the other planted the big iron nail in the center of the sheaf close to the foot of the sugar-cane.   Then she took in her left hand the cord of tree-bark, and after fumigating it, together with all the vessels of rice and oil, took up some of the rice and strewed it round about the sheaf, and then tossed the remainder thrice upwards, some of it falling upon the rest of the company and myself.

" This done, she took the end of the cord in both hands, and encircling the sheaf with it near the ground, drew it slowly upward to the waist of the sheaf, and tied it there, after repeating what is called the ' Ten Prayers ' (*do'a sapuloh*) *without once taking breath:*

" The first, is God,
The second, is Muhammad,
The third, Holy Water of the five Hours of Prayer by Day and
    Night,
The fourth, is Pancha Indra,
The fifth, the Open Door of Daily Bread,
The sixth, the Seven Stories of the Palace-Tower,
The seventh, the Open Door of the rice-sifting Platform,

[27] Hurgronje's " The Achenese," pp. 285–6.
[28] Skeat's " Malay Magic," p. 240.

The eighth, the Open Door of Paradise,
The ninth, is the child in its Mother's Womb,
The tenth is the Child created by God, the reason of its creation
    being our Lord,
Grant this, 'Isa!
Grant this, Moses!
Grant this, Joseph!
Grant this, David!
Grant me, from God (the opening of) all the doors of my daily
    bread, on earth, and in heaven."

In Algeria the usual posture used in prayer for rain is standing upright with the elbows bent and palms turned upwards. Prayers for rain must only be done out of doors and with old clothes on, the *burnous* being worn inside out to express distress and need.

For eclipse of the sun a long prayer is made standing with hands down at the side, fingers extended, then a long prayer while the hands are bent on the knees. These two positions are repeated with each prayer.

In Yemen, at the first of the year, if there is a drought five cows are brought to a special mosque and each one in turn is driven around the mosque three times by a huge crowd of young men, who constantly pray or recite the Koran. In case of an eclipse water is put in large trays in the open air and the people peer into this water searching for the moon's reflection, but in this prayer also is not forgotten.

In 1917 there was a total eclipse of the moon visible in Egypt. As might well be expected the eclipse greatly excited the Egyptian masses, who were very much impressed by the fact that it coincided with Ramadan and the war. Pans and drums as well as other noise-making appliances were beaten by them as long as the phenomenon was visible, and even after its disappearance, many servants refused to go to sleep on the roofs.

Among the Turkish Moslems there is a superstition regarding the value of "rain stones" called *Yada Rashi,* or in Persian *Sangi Yada.* This superstition dates from before their conversion to Islam but still persists and spread to Morocco. In Tlemcen the Moslems in time of drought gather 70,000 pebbles which are put in seventy sacks; during the night they repeat the Koran prayers over every one of these pebbles, after which the bags are emptied into the *wady* with the hope of rain.[29]

This service of prayer is also occasionally held in Java, under the name *istika;* but a more popular method of rain-making is "giving the cat a bath," which is sometimes accompanied by small processions and other ceremonies. "In Acheh, so far as I am aware," says Dr. Snouck Hurgronje, "the actual custom no longer survives, though it has left traces of its former existence in sundry popular evpressions. 'It is very dry; we must give the cat a bath and then we shall get rain,' say the padi-planters when their harvest threatens to fail through drought."

"In Tunis and Tripoli," Major Tremearne tells us, "if there is no rain, and the crops are being ruined, the Arabs go in procession outside the city with drums and flags, and pray for rain, and, according to Haj Ali, cows are made to urinate and the roofs of the houses are wetted with water by the Arabs and Hausas with them as a means of bringing down rain. But if there is no result the negroes are summoned to use their magic."

"In Northern Algeria, amongst the Magazawa of Gobir, the rain was made to fall and to cease in the following manner, according to Haj Ali. The rain-makers were nine in number and would go round with wooden clubs to a *tsamiya* (tamarind) or a *ganje* (rubber) tree near the gate of the town, and sacrifice a black bull, the blood being allowed to

---

[29] Goldziher in the " Nöldeke Festschrift," Zauber Elemente im Islamischen Gebet, p. 316.

flow into the roots. Then four pots of *giya* (beer) were brought, and were drunk by the rain-makers. After this, the eldest of the nine (Mai-Shibko) would rise, put on the hide and call out: " You Youths, You Youths, You Youths, ask the Man (Allah) to send down water for us, tell the Owner of the Heavens that men are dying here, ask him to spit upon us." The eight others would rise and stand around the old man, and call out in a loud voice what they had been told to say, and add: " If you do not send rain we will kill this old man. We are true to you, see, we have sacrificed a bull to you." Then brandishing their weapons in the air, they would continue: " If you do not send down the rain, we will throw up our clubs at you." [30]

Regarding prayers for rain offered up by the Mohammedans in China we glean the following from the *Revue du Monde Musulman* (Vol. 26, p. 89, article by G. Cordier): " A procession is formed headed by the *ahong,* or priest, carrying three objects which I will here describe:

" (1) A sack filled with 7,000 stones, very clean and which have been gathered from the bed of some river near by. These may be said to represent a sort of rosary as ten prayers are repeated over each stone.

" (2) A sword of the shape employed in the mosques but without a sheath. On the handle of this sword is inscribed the words *pao-kien, i. e.,* the ' precious sword,' and in Arabic the creed. This sword is made of wood and is covered with inscriptions in Arabic characters and carried in a case made of yellow linen.

" (3) A tablet made of brass. The Chinese call it *Chao p'ai,* that is to say the ' Tablet that is planted.' The Moslems call it *t'ong P'ai,* ' Tablet of brass,' and in Arabic *lukh nahas.* This tablet is also covered with Arabic inscriptions.

[30] " The Ban of the Bori," pp. 185, 189.

" Forty-four flags covered with quotations from the Koran are also carried in these processions, and as they march prayers are chanted.   Arriving at Hei-long-t'an, the source of the black dragon, the procession halts near the basin called *Etang du dragon*.   There a Moslem beats the water with the sword while the prayers are continued.

" This done an *ahong* holding the brass tablet gets into the water and throws it in so as to make a fish come out (others say a water snake).   When this is caught they place it in some water taken from the same source and carry it back to the mosque and is kept there until the rain comes down. When this happens it is taken back to the basin where it is again thrown in." [31]

In conclusion we may here give four of the short final chapters of the Koran that are used at the time of the five daily prayers and which contain allusions to animistic and pagan practices current in Arabia before Islam.   It is true that the beautiful opening chapter of the Koran with its lofty theism and the chapter of the Forenoon with its pathetic reference to Mohammed's childhood are frequently on Moslem lips.   So also is the chapter of the Unity (CXII).   But what thoughts a Moslem has when he repeats the following chapters, if he understands the words, we may learn from the commentaries.   After reading what they tell us there remains little doubt that paganism entered Islam by the door of the Koran!

" In the name of the merciful and compassionate God.

" Verily, we sent it down on the Night of Power!

---

[31] " A few days ago," writes Miss H. E. Levermore of Tsinchow, " the Moslems had a rain procession,— a thing rarely known with them.   It is said once before they had one, and the informer significantly adds, ' and they revolted just after.'   In this procession there was no noise, great order and devotion being observed.   The Moslems walked the streets carrying incense and reading their incantations.   Two chairs carrying Moslem sacred books were caried, whilst the priests had open Arabic Korans in their hands."

" And what shall make thee know what the Night of Power is ? — the Night of Power is better than a thousand months !

" The angels and the spirits descend therein, by the permission of their Lord with every bidding.

" Peace it is until rising of the dawn ! " [32]

. . . . . . . . . .

" In the name of the merciful and compassionate God.

" By the snorting chargers.

" And those who strike fire with their hoofs.

" And those who make incursions in the morning,

" And raise up dust therein.

" And cleave through a host therein.

" Verily, man is to his Lord ungrateful; and, verily, he is a witness of that.

" Verily, he is keen in his love of good.

" Does he not know when the tombs are exposed, and what is in the breasts is brought to light ?

" Verily, thy Lord upon that day indeed is well aware." [33]

. . . . . . . . . .

" In the name of the merciful and compassionate God.

" Say, ' I seek refuge in the Lord of the daybreak, from the evil of what He has created ; and from the evil of the night when it cometh on ; and from the evil of the blowers upon knots ; and from the evil of the envious when he envies.' " [34]

. . . . . . . . . .

" Say, ' I seek refuge in the Lord of men, the King of men, the God of men, from the evil of the whisperer, who slinks off, who whispers into the hearts of men — from jinns and men.' "

[32] [33] [34] " The Quran," Part II. Translated by E. H. Palmer. Suras 97, 100, 113, 114.

# CHAPTER IV

## HAIR, FINGER-NAILS AND THE HAND

IT must not surprise us that a great deal of animism and old Arabian superstition persist in Islam. The words of Frazer apply in this connection:[1] " As in Europe beneath a superficial layer of Christianity a faith in magic and witch-craft, in ghosts and goblins has always survived and even flourished among the weak and ignorant, so it has been and so it is in the East. Brahminism, Buddhism, Islam may come and go, but the belief in magic and demons remains un-shaken through them all, and, if we may judge of the future from the past, is likely to survive the rise and fall of other historical religions." He goes on to say, " With the common herd, who compose the great bulk of every people, the new religion is accepted only in outward show, because it is im-pressed upon them by their natural leaders whom they can-not choose but follow. They yield a dull assent to it with their lips, but in their hearts they never really abandon their old superstitions; in these they cherish a faith such as they cannot repose in the creed which they nominally profess; and to these, in the trials and emergencies of life, they have recourse as to infallible remedies when the promises of the higher faith have failed them, as indeed such promises are apt to do."[2]

---

[1] " The Scapegoat," pp. 89–90.

[2] This is true, alas, even in Christendom. But outside its pale, " Superstition has sacrificed countless lives, wasted untold treasures, embroiled nations, severed friends, parted husbands and wives, parents and children, putting swords and worse than swords between them; it has filled jails and mad-houses with innocent or deluded victims; it

What is here written has reference to the popular customs observed by Moslems in all lands and connected with hair-cutting, nail-trimming, and the use of the hand as an amulet, the latter especially in lower Egypt and North Africa.   Cus-

has broken many hearts, embittered the whole of many a life, and not content with persecuting the living it has pursued the dead into the grave and beyond it, gloating over the horrors which its foul imagination has conjured up to appall and torture the survivors.   How numerous its ramifications and products have been is merely hinted in the following list of subjects given as cross-references in a public library catalogue card: *Alchemy, apparitions, astrology, charms, delusions, demonology, devil-worship, divination, evil eye, fetishism, folk-lore, legends, magic, mythology, occult sciences, oracles, palmistry, relics, second sight, sorcery, spiritualism, supernatural, totems* and *witch-craft.*   This force has pervaded all provinces of life from the cradle to the grave, and, as Frazer says, beyond.   It establishes customs as binding as taboo, dictates forms of worship and perpetuates them, obsesses the imagination and leads it to create a world of demons and hosts of lesser spirits and ghosts and ghouls, and inspires fear and even worship of them." *

Professor F. B. Dresslar of the University of California prepared a list of those things with which superstition was connected in that State.   He secured the list through questions to grown-up people in the present century.   It was as follows:  Salt, bread and butter, tea and coffee, plants and fruit; fire, lightning, rainbow, the moon, the stars; babies, birds, owls, peacocks and their feathers, chickens, cats, dogs, cows, swine, horses, rabbits, rats, frogs and toads, fish, sheep, crickets, snakes, lizards, turtles, wolves, bees, dragon flies; chairs and tables, clocks, mirrors, spoons, knives and forks, pointed instruments, pins, hairpins, combs, umbrellas (mostly unlucky), candles, matches, tea-kettle, brooms, dishcloths, handkerchiefs, gardening tools, ladders, horseshoes, hay; days of the week and various festivals or fasts, especially Hallowe'en, birthdays; various numbers, counting, laughing, singing, crying; starting on a journey and turning back, two persons simultaneously saying the same thing, passing in at one door and out at another, walking on opposite sides of a post, stepping on cracks, sneezing, crossing hands while shaking hands, use of windows as exits, stumbling; itching of palm, eye, nose, ear, or foot; warts, moles; various articles of dress, shoes, precious stones, amulets and charms, rings, money; wish-bones; death and funerals, dreams, spiritisms, weddings, and initials.

---

* "The New Schaff Herzog Encyclopedia of Religious Knowledge," Vol. XI, p. 169.

toms which have in many cases been approved and perpetuated by the example of Mohammed himself.

According to Skeat there are certain portions of the human frame which are considered invested with a special sanctity, and require special ceremonies among the pagans. These parts of the anatomy are the head, the hair, the teeth, the ears and the nails. He says in regard to hair and its sacred character: " From the principle of the sanctity of the head flows, no doubt, the necessity of using the greatest circumspection during the process of cutting the hair. Sometimes throughout the whole life of the wearer, and frequently during special periods, the hair is left uncut. Thus I was told that in former days Malay men usually wore their hair long, and I myself have seen an instance of this at Jugra in Selangor in the person of a Malay of the old school, who was locally famous on this account. So, too, during the forty days which must elapse before the purification of a woman after the birth of her child, the father of the child is forbidden to cut his hair, and a similar abstention is said to have been formerly incumbent upon all persons either prosecuting a journey or engaging in war. Often a boy's head is entirely shaven shortly after birth with the exception of a single lock in the center of the head, and so maintained until the boy begins to grow up, but frequently the operation is postponed (generally, it is said, in consequence of a vow made by the child's parents) until the period of puberty or marriage. Great care, too, must be exercised in disposing of the clippings of hair (more especially the *first* clippings), as the Malay profoundly believes that " the sympathetic connection which exists between himself and every part of his body continues to exist even after the physical connection has been severed, and that therefore he will suffer from any harm that may befall the severed parts of his body, such as the clippings of his hair, or the parings of his nails. Accordingly he takes care that those severed portions of himself shall not be left in places where they might either be exposed to accidental injury, or fall into the hands of malicious persons who might work magic on them to his detriment or death." [3]

According to animistic beliefs the soul of man rests not only in his heart but pervades special parts of his body, such as the head, the intestines, the blood, placenta, hair, teeth, saliva, sweat, tears, etc.   The means by which this soul-stuff is protracted or conveyed to others is through spitting, blowing, blood-wiping, or touch.   In all of these particulars and under all of these subjects we have superstitions in Islam that date back to pagan days but are approved in and by Moslem tradition and in some cases by the Koran itself.

In the disposal of hair-cuttings and nail-trimmings among Moslems to-day, and their magical use, there is clear evidence of animistic belief.   People may be bewitched through the clippings of their hair and parings of their nails.   This belief is world-wide,[4] " To preserve the cut hair and nails from injury," says Frazer, " and from the dangerous uses to which they may be put by sorcerers, it is necessary to deposit them in some safe place.   In Morocco women often hang their cut hair on a tree that grows on or near the grave of a wonder-working saint; for they think thus to rid themselves of headache or to guard against it.   In Germany the clippings of hair used often to be buried under an elder-bush.   In Oldenburg cut hair and nails are wrapped in a cloth which is deposited in a hole in an elder-tree three days before the new moon; the hole is then plugged up.   In the west of Northumberland it is thought that if the first parings of a child's nails are buried under an ash-tree, the child will turn out a fine singer.   In Amboyna before a child may taste sago-pap for the first time, the father cuts off a lock of the infant's

[3] Skeat's " Malay Magic," pp. 43–45.
[4] " Taboo and the Perils of the Soul," pp. 274–275.

hair, which he buries under a sago-palm. In the Aru Islands when a child is able to run alone, a female relation shears a lock of its hair and deposits it on a banana-tree. In the Island of Rotti it is thought that the first hair which a child gets is not his own, and that if it is not cut off it will make him weak and ill. Hence, when the child is about a month old, his hair is polled with ceremony. As each of the friends who are invited to the ceremony enters the house he goes up to the child, snips off a little of its hair and drops it into a cocoanut shell full of water. Afterwards the father or another relation takes the hair and packs it into a little bag made of leaves, which he fastens to the top of a palm-tree. Then he gives the leaves of the palm a good shaking, climbs down, and goes home without speaking to any one. Indians of the Yukon territory, Alaska, do not throw away their cut hair and nails, but tie them up in little bundles and place them in the crotches of trees or wherever they are not likely to be disturbed by beasts. For they have a superstition that disease will follow the disturbance of such remains by animals. Often the clipped hair and nails are stowed away in any secret place, not necessarily in a temple or cemetery or at a tree, as in the case already mentioned."

It is remarkable that in Arabia, Egypt and North Africa everywhere this custom of stowing away clippings of hair and nails is still common among Moslems and is sanctioned by the practice of the Prophet.

Among the Malays hair offerings are made to-day in thoroughly pagan fashion, but it is interesting that the shorn locks are not buried under the threshold as they were before Islam, but are now sent to Mecca. We quote from Skeat a description of the ceremony at a wedding when the bride's locks are cut:

" The cocoanut containing the severed tresses and rings is carried to the foot of a barren fruit-tree (*e. g.,* a pomegranate tree), when the rings are extracted and the water (with the severed locks) poured out at the tree's foot, the belief being that this proceeding *will make the tree as luxuriant as the hair of the person shorn,* a very clear example of ' sympathetic magic.'   If the parents are poor, the cocoanut is generally turned upside down and left there; but if they are well-to-do, the locks are usually sent to Mecca in charge of a pilgrim, who casts them on his arrival into the well Zemzem." [5]

In North Africa a man will not have his hair shaved in the presence of any one who owes him a grudge.   After his hair has been cut, he will look around, and if there is no enemy about he will mix his cuttings with those of other men, and leave them, but if he fears some one there he will collect the cuttings, and take them secretly to some place and bury them. With a baby this is said to be unnecessary, as he has no enemies — a surprising statement.   Nails are cut with scissors and they are always buried in secret.   One can see this superstition also in the account given of a charm described by Captain Tremearne,[6] which consists of certain roots from trees mixed with a small lock of hair from the forehead and the partings of all the nails, hands and feet, *except those of the index fingers.*   The fact of this exception clearly shows that we deal again with a superstition that has come from Arabian Animism, as we shall see later.

In Bahrein, East Arabia, they observe a special order in trimming the finger-nails and bury the discarded trimmings in a piece of white cloth saying *Hatha amana min 'andina ya Iblis yashud lana al Rahman.*[7]   They bury hair-combings in the same way expecting to receive them back on the day of resurrection.   Concerning the thumb, they think it has no account with God because it can do no evil alone.

[5] Skeat's " Malay Magic," p. 355.
[6] " The Ban of the Bori," p. 57.
[7] " O Satan, this is a safe deposit from us as God is our witness."

The belief that cut hair and nails contain soul-stuff and therefore may be used for spiritual communion leads Moslems to hang their hair on the tombs of saints together with shreds of their garments, nails, teeth, etc. On the great gate of Old Cairo, called *Bab-el-Mutawali,* this also takes place and one may watch a constant procession of men, women and children having communion with the saint who dwells behind or under this gateway and seeking through personal contact with the doorway by touching, breathing, etc., to carry away the blessing.

In connection with this superstition Rev. L. E. Högberg, of Chinese Turkestan,[8] tells of the popular belief that " during the last days, Satan will appear on earth riding on a *Merr dedjell* (Satan's mule). Every hair on the mule's body is a tuned string or musical instrument. By the music furnished in this way all the people on earth are tempted to follow Satan. Great horns grow out on their heads, so that they can never return through their doors. The faithful Mohammedan has, however, a way of salvation. He has carefully collected his cut-off nails, and placed them under the threshold, where they have formed a hedge, blocking the door so as to prevent the household from running after Satan! " Again the hair and nails have special power assigned to them as a protection for the soul against evil !

In many parts of the Moslem world such as in East Arabia, human hair is used by native doctors of medicine as a powerful tonic. It is generally administered as tincture or decoction. In this respect the hair of saints has more value than ordinary hair. I have known of a case where a learned *kadi* sent to the barbers to collect hair in order to prepare such a powerful tonic. Miss Fanny Lutton writes from Muscat, Arabia: " Just in front of the Mission compound is a

[8] Correspondence in a magazine called *Central Asia* for December, 1916.

Mosque, and in the compound of the Mosque is a saint's grave. I have witnessed some queer heathenish performances there. Only a short time ago a crowd of women, men and children were assembled. A woman brought her one-year-old son to have his head shaved over the grave. A cloth was spread to receive the hair and it was afterwards tied to a small flagpole at the head of the grave, and then a new red flag was also attached which must be left there until it fades and wears out, when it must be replaced with a new one and with similar ceremonies. Refreshments were partaken of by the visitors sitting around the grave and much merriment was indulged in. *Helwa* (candy) was thrown over the grave and rose water was sprinkled all over the grave. Then the company as well as the mother and child were marched three times around the grave and led out of the grounds walking backwards, for those who perform the vow must never turn their backs on the grave as they leave. This hair is very efficacious for various ills. Yesterday I saw the keeper, who is a very wicked woman, approach the grave. Her first act was to stoop down and kiss the earth at the head of the grave. She then tore off some of the rag that was wrapped around the hair and took a portion of the hair and tied it in a bundle and delivered it to the woman that had come with her. No doubt the women had been sent to get this for some serious case that would not yield to other treatments, and so the Mullah (priest) or woman reader had been called to the case and had prescribed the hair which the patient must wear to keep off evil spirits."

Special chapters are found in the lives of Mohammed the prophet on the virtues of his *fadhalat,* spittle, urine,[9] blood,

---

[9] There are traditions in Bukhari and Muslim to show the sacred power of Mohammed's blood, spittle, etc. It is also taught that even the excreta of the prophet of Arabia were free from all defilement. Cf. "Insan al Ayun al Halebi," Vol. II, p. 222.

etc., including his hair. We read, for example, in the life of Mohammed by Seyyid Ahmed Zaini Dahlan: [10]   " When the Prophet had his head shaved and his companions surrounded him they never suffered a single hair to fall to the ground but seized them as good omens or for blessing. And since His Excellency only had his hair cut at the times of the pilgrimage this had become *sunna,* so it is related in the *Mawahib,* and he who denies it should be severely punished." And Mohammed bin Darain relates:   " I said to Obeid al Suleimani, ' I have a few hairs of the Prophet which I took from Anas,' and he replied, ' If I had a single hair it would be more to me than all the world.' "   Because of this belief, hairs of the Prophet's beard and in some cases of other saints in Islam are preserved as relics in the mosques throughout the world, *e. g.,* at Delhi, Aintab, Damascus, etc. To give a recent instance, the population of Safed in Palestine, according to a missionary correspondent, " was all excitement in the early days of July, 1911, because a veritable hair from the beard of the Prophet had been granted them as a gift by the Sultan. A Christian builder was engaged to restore a mosque of the Binat Yacob, where the famous relic now finds shelter. The mayor of the city took the journey to Acre in order to accompany the relic to its resting-place. The correspondent goes on to relate some of the marvels that were told as to the virtues connected with the hair of the Prophet. Twenty soldiers, fully armed, escorted the relic." [11]

This same relic was the object of the most energetic search among Moslems from the earliest period of Islam. According to Goldziher the hair was worn as an amulet, and men on their deathbeds directed by will that the precious pos-

[10] Margin of *Sirat al Halabi,* Cairo Edition, 1308 A.H., vol. iii, pp. 238–9.

[11] Der Christliche Orient, Sept., 1911.

session should go down with them and mingle with the earth. Jafar-ibn-Khinzabu, the vizier of an Egyptian prince, had three such hairs which at his death were put into his mouth, and his remains, according to his last testament, were carried to Medina. Impostors and charlatans were not slow to turn to advantage the credulity of the devout. Let us listen to Abdul Jani ul-Nabulusi, the famous traveler. He met on his pilgrimage to Medina a learned Mohammedan from India, Ghulam Mohammed by name. "He told me," the traveler narrates, "that in the countries of India many people possess Mohammed's hair, many have but a single hair, but others own more, up to twenty. These relics are shown to all those who would inspect them reverently. This Ghulam Mohammed tells me that one of the saintly men of the lands of India annually exhibits such relics on the ninth day of Rabi-ul-Aval, that on those occasions many people gather round him, learned and pious, perform prayers to the Prophet and go through divine service and mystic practices. He further informs me that the hairs at times move of their own accord, and that they grow in length and increase in number, so that a single hair is the propagator of a number of new ones." "All this," comments our traveler, "is no wonder, for the blessed apostle of God has a prolonged divine existence which is manifested in all his noble limbs and physical components. An historian relates that Prince Nur-ud-Din possessed a few of the Prophets's hairs in his treasury, and when he neared his dissolution he directed in his testament that the holy relics be deposited on his eyes, and there they remain in his grave to this day. He (the historian cited) goes on to inform us that every one who visits the mausoleum of the prince combines with the intention of visiting the ruler's tomb the hope that the magical relics preserved therein would produce their blissful effect. The tomb could be seen in the academy at Damascus built by the prince." [12]

The statements made in books of Moslem law leave no doubt that hair is considered sacred and may not therefore be sold or in any way dishonored. We read in the *Hedaya*,[13] a great commentary on Moslem law,—" The sale of human hair is unlawful, in the same manner as is the *use* of it, because, being a part of the human body, it is necessary to preserve it from the disgrace to which an exposure of it to sale necessarily subjects it. It is moreover recorded, in the *Hadith Sharif*, that ' God denounced a curse upon a *Wasila* and a *Mustawasila*.' (The first of these is a woman whose employment it is to unite the shorn hair of one woman to the head of another, to make her hair appear long; and the second means the woman to whose head such hair is united). Besides, as it has been allowed to women to increase their locks by means of the wool of a camel, it may thence be inferred that the use of human hair is unlawful."

" In Tunis," writes Mr. E. E. Short, " nail parings are buried; hair trimmings the same or burnt. If the latter are carried away by the wind the person will suffer from giddiness of the head. One informant gave Friday as the day for trimming the hair and nails, another Saturday. The reason for the practice seems to be that the parings might be found again and then when questioned one could answer that they had been properly buried. (Does not this point to a very materialistic conception of the resurrection body?)"

In Algeria it is believed that if nail trimmings are thrown on the ground Satan makes use of them; if trodden on, their late owner might become very ill, and it is unlucky if water is poured on them. They are used in magic and if mixed with food cause illness or death.

[12] " The Moslem World," Vol. I, p. 306.
[13] Hamilton's " Hedaya," Vol. II, p. 439.

In Cape Town the same superstitions prevail among Indian Moslems with regard to hair and nail trimmings.

In Persia the hair and nail trimmings are sometimes preserved in bottles as part of the body, which will be needed by it at the resurrection. This was the practice of an old gatekeeper on the missionary premises at Urumia; the mischievous missionary's son took pleasure in hunting for his treasure and carrying it off, then witnessing his subsequent anger and grief.[14]

"When a girl reaches what the Achenese regard as a marriageable age without having yet had a suitor for her hand, it is believed that there must be some supernatural agency at work. It is looked upon as certain that she must have in some part of her body something *malang* or unpropitious, which stands in the way of her success.

"The numerical value of the initial letter of her name is assumed as the basis of a calculation for indicating the part of her body which is to blame. When this has been ascertained, the girl is placed on a heap of husked rice (*breuch*) and the spot indicated is slightly pricked with a golden needle, so as to draw a little blood. This blood is gathered up by means of a wad of tree cotton (*gapeueh*) which is then placed in an egg, part of the contents of which have been removed to make room for it. A little of the girl's hair and some parings of her nails are enclosed in a young cocoanut leaf, and finally all these things are thrown into the running water of the nearest river or stream."[15]

In Java nails may not be cut on Fridays and never after dark. They are always wrapped up and buried and the following words repeated, "Abide here until I die and when I die follow me." Hair clippings must be put in a cool spot or the person will suffer. They must never be burned.

---

[14] Letter from Miss S. Y. Holliday of Tabriz.
[15] "The Achenese," p. 296.

Others say they must always be put into the river or flowing water. If left to fly about they will make the pathway to heaven difficult. A special order is observed in trimming the finger-nails.[16]

Among the Malays special exposure to danger is believed to occur whenever portions of a man — such as the hair or the nails — are severed from the parent body, the theory being that injury to such discarded portions may in some way be used to affect the living body itself. A Malay husband, if he found his wife treasuring up a lock of his hair, would regard her conduct with extreme suspicion.[17]

Sometimes by the use of a waxen or other image, or by the exhibition of a " sample " such as the parings of a man's nails or the clippings of his hair, the wizard conveys to the world of ghosts a knowledge of the person he wishes them to attack — and the ghosts are ever ready to profit by the hint so kindly given.[18]

That all this is really a piece of heathenism is clear to the student of comparative religion.

In Africa also the witch doctor or *oganga* makes special use of hair, teeth, nails, etc., just as in Islam. Nassau writes:[19]   " If it be desired to obtain power over some one else, the *oganga* must be given by the applicant, to be mixed in the sacred compound, either crumbs from the food, or clippings of finger-nails or hair, or (most powerful!) even a drop of blood of the person over whom influence is sought. These represent the life or body of that person. So fearful

[16] Dr. B. J. Esser, Poerbolinggo, Java, in a letter.
[17] " Malay Beliefs," p. 53.
[18] Regarding the hair of Mohammed, a legend is told among the Malays that on his journey to heaven on the monster Al-burak, they cleft the moon and when Mohammed was shaved by Gabriel the houris of heaven fought for the falling locks so that not a single hair was allowed to reach the ground. " Malay Beliefs," p. 43.
[19] " Fetishism in West Africa," p. 83. " Malay Beliefs," p. 72.

are natives of power being thus obtained over them, that they have their hair cut only by a friend; and even then they carefully burn it or cast into a river. If one accidentally cuts himself, he stamps out what blood has dropped on the ground, or cuts out from wood the part saturated with blood."

Superstitions in regard to finger-nails are common throughout the whole world and are undoubtedly animistic in their origin. Dresslar mentions a number as current in Christendom: [20]

> "Cut your nails on Monday, cut them for health;
> Cut them on Tuesday, cut them for wealth;
> Cut them on Wednesday, cut them for news;
> Cut them on Thursday, a pair of new shoes;
> Cut them on Friday, cut them for woe;
> Cut them on Saturday, a journey to go;
> Cut them on Sunday, you cut them for evil
> And all the week you'll be ruled by the devil."

We are not surprised therefore, to find in Islam so many superstitions mentioned in connection with the paring of the nails, some of which doubtless came through Judaism, others directly from Arab paganism. According to the *Haggadah*,[21] "every pious Jew must purify himself and honor the coming holy day by trimming and cleaning the nails beforehand. The Rabbis are not agreed as to when they should be pared; some prefer Thursday, for if cut on Friday they begin to grow on the Sabbath; others prefer Friday, as it will then appear that it is done in honor of the Sabbath. It has, however, become the practice to cut them on Friday and certain *poskim* even prohibit the paring of the nails on Thursday." Moslems also have special days for this purpose. The Jews believe that the parings should not be thrown away. The Rabbis declare that he who burns them

[20] "Superstition and Education," p. 72.
[21] "Jewish Encyclopedia," Art. *Nails*.

is a pious man (*Hasid*), he who buries them is a righteous one (*zaddik*), and he who throws them away is a wicked one. The reason for this is that if a pregnant woman steps on them the impurity attached to them will cause a premature birth.[22]

In the order of cutting the nails the Jews have borrowed from the Zoroastrians while the Mohammedans seem to have borrowed from the Jews. According to Mohammed the order of procedure is remembered by the word *Khawabis* which indicates the initials of the names of the five fingers of the hand. First one is to attend to the *Khansar* (little finger), then the *Wasti* (middle finger), then the *Abham* (thumb), then the *Binsar* (ring finger), and last of all to the *Sababa* (index finger). The *Sababa* means the " finger of cursing " — derived from the root *sabba* — to curse. Moslems generally follow this practice without knowing the reason of what they do. The cuttings of the finger-nails are never thrown away but are either wrapped in a paper, buried under the door-mat or carefully put into a chink of the wall. Similar superstitions exist among the animistic tribes of the South Seas. " In Morocco," says Mr. Haldane, " they begin at the small finger on the right hand, finishing with the thumb, and then commencing with the small finger on the left hand. Some, however, hold that the little and middle finger with the thumb must be done first and then the two remaining ones afterwards. Friday is the best day for this work. Nail-parings must be carefully buried. They are not so particular about hair and beard trimmings, but still they ought to be put in some out-of-the-way place where they will not be trod upon. Why these things are so no one can tell; it's the custom." In Yemen the following customs are observed. While many Arabs hold that there is no particular order of paring the nails nor any reason for keeping and burying the parings, others are very particular to begin with the little finger and to collect every scrap of the paring in a piece of cloth or cotton-wool and then to bury the lot, saying that this was their prophet's custom. Others who also bury the parings say that one ought always to begin with the fore-finger of the right hand, as it is the most honorable of all the digits. As a rule the hair is not buried; although in very exceptional cases it is.

The custom connected with hair cutting or shaving and the trimming of the nails during the pilgrimage ceremony at Mecca is well know. As soon as the pilgrim assumes the *Ihram* or pilgrim dress he must abstain from cutting his hair or nails. This command is observed most scrupulously. We read in a celebrated book of law [23] that " The expiatory fine of three *modd* of foodstuffs is only incurred in full when at least three hairs or three nails have been cut; one *modd* only being due for a single hair or a single nail, and two *modd* for two hairs or two nails. A person who is unable to observe this abstinence, should have his whole beard shaved and pay the expiatory fine." When the pilgrimage is terminated and the ceremony completed, the head is shaved, the nails are cut and the following prayer is offered: " I purpose loosening my *Ihram* according to the Practice of the Prophet, Whom may Allah bless and preserve! O Allah, make unto me every hair, a Light, a Purity, and a generous Reward! In the name of Allah, and Allah is Almighty! " After this prayer strict Moslems carefully bury their hair and nail-trimmings in sacred soil.[24]

We pass on to superstitions connected with the human hand. Mr. Eugene Lefebure writes: [25] " There never was

[23] *Minhaj et Talibin* Nawawi, p. 120.
[24] Burton's " Pilgrimage," Vol. II, p. 205.
[25] " Bulletin de la Societé de Géographie d'Alger et de l'Afrique du Nord," 1907, No. 4.

a country where the representation of the human hand has not served as an amulet. In Egypt as in Ireland, with the Hebrews as with the Etruscans, they attribute to this figure a mysterious power." Our illustrations show different forms of this superstition. The use of the hand in this connection is very ancient, perhaps it has some connection with the laying on of hands. The laying of hands on the head as a sign of dedication is found in the Bible, where one gives up one's own right to something and transfers it to God. (Ex. XXIX: 15, 19; II. Chron. XXIX: 23.) Again, the hands are placed on the head of the animal whose blood is to be used for the consecration of priests or for the atonement of the sins of the people. The same ceremony was used in transferring the sins of the people to the scapegoat and with all burnt offerings except the sin-offerings. The laying of hands on the head of a blasphemer should also be noted here. Jacob, on his death-bed, placed his right hand on the head of Ephraim. The Levites were consecrated through the laying on of hands by the heads of the tribes. The time-honored prototype of ordination through laying on of hands is the consecration of Joshua as successor to Moses. This rite is found in the New Testament and in the Talmud and was observed at the appointment of members of the Sanhedrin. It was gradually discontinued in practice, however, although it was preserved nominally. Islam makes a religious and ritual distinction between the right and left hand. Many dark and uncanny interpretations and suggestions are connected with matters referring to the left side of the body, the left hand, the left foot, etc. These go back to great antiquity and are well-nigh universal. In Islam the left hand is never used for eating; Tradition tells us that the devil eats with the left hand; the Moslem must never spit to the right or in front of him but to the left. Whether the origin of this

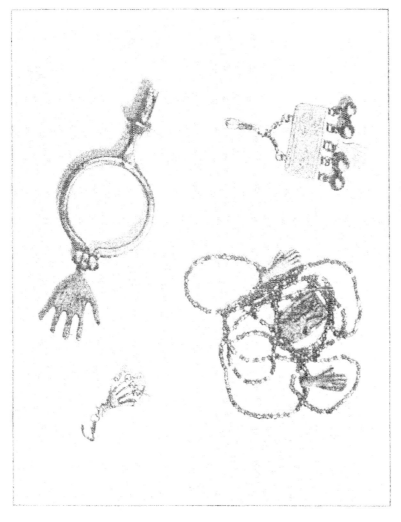

## HAND-SHAPED AMULETS

The one in the upper right-hand corner is one-fourth the real size, made of brass and put on the harness of horses, etc. The one in the lower right-hand corner is used as a brooch, generally manufactured in silver or gold. The other two are in the shape of earrings and necklace.

superstition is due to physical causes or to ritual practice, such as ablution, cannot be easily decided.[26]

In Judaism a priest's hands, represented as in benediction, on a tombstone indicate that the deceased was descended from the family of Aaron; on the title-page of a book they indicate that the printer was descended from the family of Aaron. The hand is also represented on the walls of synagogues and on mirrors. A hand is generally used as a pointer for the Torah. A hand with two ears of grain and two poppy-heads is seen on coins. Two hands joined together are often represented on "*ketubah*" blanks and on the so-called "*siflones-tefillah*" there is a hand hewing a tree or mowing down flowers. A hand either inscribed or cast in metal, was often used as an amulet.

[26] Dresslar remarks concerning similar beliefs in the United States, "Experiments upon school children show that there is more disparity between the right and left sides of the body of the brighter pupils than there is between the right and left of the duller ones. Doubtless this same augmented difference holds throughout life, or at least to the period of senescence. It is nothing more nor less than the result of specialization which increases as growing thought-life calls upon the right members of the body for finer adjustment and more varied and perfect execution. Hence, the right members become more the special organs of the will than the left, induce a greater proportion of emotional reaction, and altogether become more closely bound up with the mental life. That this specialization gives an advantage in accuracy, strength, control, and endurance of the right side there can be no doubt. But it seems equally certain that it introduces mental partialities not at all times consistent with well-balanced judgment, or the most trustworthy emotional promptings. Indeed this difference is recorded in the meaning and use of the two words, dextrous and sinister. The thought that relates itself to the stronger side is more rational than that which deals with the weaker and less easily controlled half.

"In addition to this fundamental basis for psychic differentiation with respect to the left and right, it is probable that the beating of the heart, strange and wonderful to the primitive mind, had some influence in connecting the left side with the awful and mysterious." ("Superstition and Education," pp. 206–207.)

We now turn to Moslem superstitions of this character. A missionary in Morocco writes: " Of all the talismans by which Moorish women ward off the evil eye with all its danger, none possesses so much magic power as a silver ornament worn on the breast and called *Khoumsa*. Its virtue lies in its five points, that number, in whatever form presented, being the most potent of protective agencies. In Moorish folk-beliefs it means the dispersion to the four corners of the earth, of any malign influence which has been directed against the life of the wearer." In Palestine this goes by the name of *Kef Miryam;* in Algeria the Moslems very appropriately named these talismans *La Main de Fatima,* and from this source another superstition has been developed: the mystic virtue of the number five, because of the five fingers of the hand or its sinister power.[27]

" The hand of Fatima," says Tremearne,[28] " is a great favorite in Tunis, and one sees it above the great majorities of doorways; in Tripoli there is hardly one, and this is only to be expected, since the sign is an old Carthaginian one, representing not the hand of Fatima at all, but that of Tanith. It has been thought, however, that the amulet is so curiously similar to the thunderbolt of Adad, worn in the necklet of the Assyrian kings along with emblems for the sun, the moon, and Venus, that it may be a survival of that." [28]

The hand is often painted upon the drum used in the bori (devil) dances in Tunis. It is held up, fingers outstretched and pointing towards the evil-wisher, and this, in Egypt, North Africa and Nigeria, has now become a gesture of abuse. In Egypt the outstretched hand pointed at some one is used to invoke a curse. They say *yukhammisuna,* or " He throws his five at us," i.e. he curses. Not only the hand but

[27] Mr. Lefebure in his short work, " La Main de Fatima," has gathered all that is known on the subject.
[28] " The Ban of the Bori," p. 174.

the forefinger is used for this purpose. It is therefore called, as we have seen, the *Sababa*. Goldziher gives many examples of how the fore-finger was used in magical ways long before its present use in testifying to God's unity. A controversy arose in Islam very early about the raising of the hands in prayer. It is regarding the position of the hands that the four sects have special teaching and can be distinguished. Perhaps this also indicates a magical use of the hand. In Egypt the hand is generally used as an amulet against the evil eye. It is made of silver or gold in jewelry, or made of tin in natural size, and is then suspended over the door of a house. The top of a Moslem banner is often of this shape. It is used on the harness of horses, mules, etc., and on every cart used in Alexandria we see either a brass hand or one painted in various colors. The following points are to be noted. It is unlucky to count five on the fingers. All Egyptians of the Delta when they count say: " One, two, three, four, in-the-eye-of-your-enemy." Children, when at play, show their displeasure with each other by touching the little finger of their two hands together, which signifies separation, enmity, hatred. The same sign is used by grown-up people also to close a discussion.

The origin of the stretching out of the hand with the palm exposed toward the person was explained by my sheikh in this way: Tradition says that at one time a woman who saw Mohammed became very much enamored with his handsome presence, and Mohammed fearing she would work some power over him, raised his hand (said to be the right one) and stretched it out to one side in front of him with the palm exposed toward the woman, and at the same time he repeated Sura 113. When he did this the covetous glance passed between his two fingers and struck a nail in a tree near by and broke it in pieces!

Finally we may add the curious custom also common in

Egypt, of dipping the hand in the blood of a sacrifice and leaving its mark upon doors, foundations of buildings, animals, etc., in order to consecrate them or protect them from evil influences.  In the next chapter on the *'Aqiqa* sacrifice we will refer to the prevalence of blood sacrifice in early Islam, and its significance.  The practice of dipping the hand in blood and putting marks on the door-post may go back to the story of Israel in Egypt, but the present use of the hand in this way is mixed with all manner of superstition.  Who can unravel the threads in the tangled skein of Moslem beliefs and practices?  There is much Judaism, as Rabbi Geiger has shown; more perhaps even of Christian ideas prevalent in Arabia at the time of the Prophet; but most of all Islam in its popular forms is full of animism and of practices which can only be described as pagan in origin and in tendency.

# CHAPTER V

## THE 'AQIQA SACRIFICE

AMONG the many points of contact between Christianity and Islam (and the points of departure, from which the faithful missionary can launch out into the very heart of the Gospel message), there is one which has not received the emphasis it deserves. We refer to the 'Aqiqa ceremony, observed by every Moslem household throughout most Moslem lands after the birth of a child, and concerning which the Traditions are so full. According to Moslem religious law, the expiatory sacrifice is made on the seventh day; it is commendable on that occasion to give the child its name, shave off the hair on its head, make an offering to the poor, and kill a victim. According to some authorities, if the offering of the 'Aqiqa has been neglected on the seventh day by the parents, it can be done afterwards by the child himself when he has become of age.

The root of the word 'aqiqa is 'aqqa, he clave, split, rent. It is used especially in regard to the cutting off of an amulet when the boy becomes of age. It is also used in the expression "'Aqqa bi sahmi" (He shot the arrow towards the sky), or of the sacrifice of 'Aqiqa (He sacrificed for his new-born child). It is interesting to note that the use of this word in every connection seems to have reference to expiation or redemption. According to Lane the arrow as well as the sacrifice was called 'aqiqa: " and it was the arrow of self-excuse: they used to do thus in the Time of Ignorance (on the occasion of a demand for blood-revenge); and if the arrow

¹ Lane's " Arabic-English Lexicon," Vol. V.

returned smeared with blood, they were not content save with the retaliation of slaughter; but if it returned clean, they stroked their beards, and made reconciliation on the condition of the blood-wit; the stroking of the beards being a sign of reconciliation; the arrow, however, as Ibn-ul-'Arabi says, did not return otherwise than clean. The origin was this: a man of the tribe was slain, and the slayer was prosecuted for his blood; whereupon a company of the chief men collected themselves together to the heirs of the slain, and offered the blood-wit, asking forgiveness for the blood; and if the heir was a strong man, impatient of injury, he refused to take the blood-wit; but if weak, he consulted the people of his tribe, and then said to the petitioners, ' We have, between us and our Creator, a sign denoting command and prohibition: we take an arrow, and set it on a bow, and shoot it towards the sky; and if it return to us smeared with blood, we are forbidden to take the blood-wit, and are not content save with the retaliation of slaughter; but if it return clean, as it went up, we are commanded to take the blood-wit ': so they made reconciliation."

The word 'aqiqa in Moslem literature, however, no longer refers to the ceremony of the arrow, which belongs to the Time of Ignorance. 'Aqiqa in Tradition signifies: either the hair of the young one recently born, " that comes forth upon his head in his mother's womb," some say of human beings only and others of beasts likewise; or the sheep or goat that is slaughtered as a sacrifice for the recently born infant " on the occasion of the shaving of the infant's hair on the seventh day after his birth, and of which the limbs are divided and cooked with water and salt and given as food to the poor." Al Zamakhshari " holds it to be thus called from the same word as applied to the hair; but it is said to be so-called because it is slaughtered by cutting the windpipe and gullet and the two external jugular veins."

The 'Aqiqa sacrifice is referred to in nearly all the stan-

dard collections of Traditions, generally under *Bab-al-Nikah.*
In books of *Fikh,* it is mentioned under the head of
" sacrifice " and " offerings." The most detailed account of
*Al-'Aqiqa* I have found in the celebrated book on *Fikh,* by
Ibn Rushd el Kartabi. He treats this subject under six
heads: (1) On whom it is incumbent; (2) Where; (3)
For whom it should be offered and how many offerings should
be made; (4) The time of the ceremony; (5) Its manner;
(6) What is done with the flesh.

" Now in regard on whom it is incumbent one of the sects,
namely the literalists, say that it is necessary in every case,
but most of them say it is only following the custom of the
Prophet (*sunna*), and Abu Hanifa says it is not incumbent
and not *sunna.* But most of them are agreed that he means
by this that it is optional. And the reason for their disagreement is the apparent contradiction of two traditions,
namely, that a tradition of Samra concerning the Prophet
reads, ' Every male child shall be redeemed by his *'aqiqa,*
which is to be sacrificed for him on his seventh day, and so
evil shall be removed from him.' This tradition would indicate that the sacrifice was incumbent: but there is the evident meaning of another tradition which reads as follows:
' When Mohammed was asked concerning Al 'Aqiqa he said,
" I do not love Al 'Aquq (ungrateful treatment), but to
whomsoever a child is born let him make the ceremony for
his child." ' This tradition infers that the custom is praiseworthy or allowable, and those who understand from it that
it is praiseworthy say that the *'Aqiqa* is *sunna,* and those who
understand from it that it is allowed say it is neither *sunna*
nor incumbent. But those who follow the tradition of Samra
say it is incumbent. In regard to the character of the sacrifice, all the learned are agreed that everything that is permitted in this respect for the annual sacrifice is permitted in
the case of the *'Aqiqa* from the eight classes of animals, male

and female. Malik, however, prefers the ewe as a sacrifice in his sect, and he disagrees whether the camel or the cow is sufficient. The rest of the authorities on *Fikh* say that the camel is better than the cow and that the goat is better than the sheep. And the reason for their disagreement is again due to the discrepancy of Tradition. For the Traditions of Ibn Abbas say that the Prophet of God performed the *'Aqiqa* ceremony for Hassan and Hussain by a ram for each. Another saying of his is, ' For a girl a ewe and for a boy two ewes, according to Abu Dawud.'

" In regard to the one for whom the ceremony is performed, the majority of them are agreed that the *'Aqiqa* should be performed for the male and the female in infancy only. The exception to this is Al Hassan, who says no *'Aqiqa* shall be given for the girl, and some of them allow the *'Aqiqa* to be performed for adults. And the proof with the majority of the authorities that it is limited to infants is the saying of Mohammed ' on his seventh day,' and the proof of those who disagree is the tradition related by Anas, that the Prophet performed the ceremony of 'Aqiqa for himself when he was called to be a prophet. ('Aqqa 'an nafsihi ba'adma bu'atha b'n nabuwa.) Proof that it is allowed for girls is his saying, ' for a maiden one ewe and for a boy two.' On the other hand, the proof that it should be limited to the male infants is his saying, ' Every boy child is under obligation to have his *'Aqiqa*. But as regards the number of victims the learned are also disagreed. Es Shafi, however, says, and with him agree Abu Thaur and Dawud and Ahmad, ' The *'Aqiqa* of the girl to be one ewe and of the boy two.' And the cause of their disagreement is the disagreement of Tradition. For we have a tradition of Um Karz related by Abu Dawud, that the Prophet said in the *'Aqiqa* the boy shall have two similar ewes and the girl one. And this undoubtedly means that there shall be a difference in the number of victims in the case of the boy or the girl. The other tradition, however, that Mohammed himself performed the ceremony for Hassan and Hussain with one ram each, compels a different interpretation.

" As regards the time of this ceremony, the majority are agreed that it shall be on the seventh day after birth. Malik does not count in this number the day on which the child is born, if he is born in the daytime. Abd ul Malik, however, counts it in. Ibn al Kasim says if the 'Aqiqa is performed at night-time the hair of the sacrifice shall not be cut off. The companions of Malik disagree regarding the time of the cutting of the hair. It is said to be the usual time of the sacrifice, namely forenoon. Others say immediately after dawn, basing their statement upon what is related by Malik in his Hadaya. And there is no doubt that those who permit the annual sacrifice at night permit this sacrifice also. It is also stated that the 'Aqiqa is permitted on the 14th day or the 21st.

" As regards the sunna of this ceremony and its character, it is like the sunna of the annual sacrifice, namely, that the victim must be free from blemishes as in that case, and I know no disagreement among the four schools in this respect whatever.

" As regards the flesh of the victim and its skin and the other parts, the law is the same as in regard to the flesh of the annual sacrifice, both as regards eating, alms to the poor, and prohibition of sale. All authorities are agreed that generally the head of the infant was smeared with blood in pre-Islamic times, and that this custom was abrogated in Islam, basing it upon a tradition of Baridah, viz., ' In the Days of Ignorance when a child was born to any one of us, we sacrificed a sheep for him and smeared his head with its blood. When Islam came, we were accustomed at the time of the sacrifice to shave the infant's head and to smear it with saffron.' Hassan and Katadah, however, make exception to this statement, and they say that the head of the young child shall be wiped with a piece of cotton which has been dipped in the blood, and in the Days of Ignorance it was thought commendable to break the bones of the sacrifice and to cut them from the joints. And they disagree regarding the shaving of the head of the new-born child on the seventh and the alms equal in weight to the hair in silver. Some say that it is commendable, others say it is optional. Both of these opinions are based upon Malik, and I find the custom that it is commendable better. For it is based upon a saying of Ibn Habib, according to what is contained in Al Muwatta, viz.: ' That Fatima, the daughter of the Prophet of God, shaved the hair of Hassan and Hussain and Zainab and Um Kuthum, and then she gave in alms the value of the weight in silver.' " So far the summary of the ceremony according to orthodox Tradition.

We turn from this account of the ceremony as given in Moslem books of jurisprudence to the present practice in Moslem lands. Herklots tells us that in India " the 'Aqiqa sacrifice takes place on the seventh day, called Ch'huttee, or on the fortieth day, called Chilla, in some cases on any other day that is convenient. It consists in a sacrifice to God, in the name of the child, of two he-goats, if the new-born be a boy; and of one, if a girl. The he-goat requires to be above a year old, and suheeh-col-zaz (or perfect and without a blemish); he must not be blind in one or both eyes, or lame, and is to be skinned so nicely that no flesh adhere to his skin, and his flesh so cut up that not a bone be broken. It being difficult to separate the flesh from the smaller bones, they are boiled and dressed with the flesh remaining; while in eating, the people are enjoined to masticate and swallow the softer bones, and the meat is carefully taken off the larger ones without injuring the bone. The meat is well boiled, in order that it may be more easily separated from the bones. This is served up with *manda, chupatee,* or *rotee.* While they are offering it, an Arabic sentence is repeated; the signification of which runs thus: 'O Almighty God. I offer in the stead of my own offspring, life for life, blood for blood, head for head, bone for bone, hair for hair, and skin for skin. In the name of God do I sacrifice this he-goat.' It is meritorious to distribute the food to all classes of people, save to the seven following individuals, viz.: the person on whose account the offering is made, his parents, and his paternal and maternal grandfathers and grandmothers; to whom it is unlawful to partake of it. The bones, boiled or unboiled, skin, feet and head, are buried in the earth, and no one is allowed to eat them."

The custom he describes in such detail was taken by him verbatim from the lips of Jaffur Shurruf, a native of the Deccan, who belonged to the Sunni or orthodox sect. He goes on to tell us that the shaving of the head, which is called *Moondun,* takes place on the same day, or, in the case of the rich, the ceremony is performed some days later. Those who can afford it have the child's head shaved with a silver-mounted razor and use a silver cup to contain the water, both of which after the operation are given as a present to the barber. The hair is weighed, and its weight in silver is distributed among the religious mendicants. The hair itself is tied up in a piece of cloth and either buried in the earth or thrown in the water.

Another curious custom is thus described: " Those who can afford it have the hair taken to the water-side, and there, after they have assembled, musicians and the women, and offered *fateeha* in the name of Khoaja Khizur over the hair, on which they put flour, sugar, ghee, and milk, the whole is placed on a raft or *juhaz* (a ship), illuminated by lamps, the musicians singing and playing the whole time, they launch it on the water.   Some people at the time of *moondun,* leave *choontees* (or tufts of hair unshaved) in the name of particular saints, and take great care that nothing unclean contaminates them.   A few, vowing in the name of any saint, do not perform *moondun* at all, but allow the hair to grow for one or even four or five years; and either at the expiration of the appointed season, or a little before or after, proceed to the *durgah* (or shrine) of that saint, and there have the hair shaved.   Should it happen that they are in a distant country at that time and have not the means of repairing to his shrine, they perform *fateeha* in his name, and have the hair shaved at the place where they may happen to be.   Such hair is termed *jumal chontee,* or *jumal bal.*   This ceremony is, by some men and women, performed with great faith in its efficacy."

According to Lane, the ceremony of *'Aqiqa* was not universal in Egypt in his day.   It has become less common since. Where it is observed, a goat is sacrificed at the tomb of some saint in or near their village.   The victim is called *'Aqiqa,* and is offered as a ransom for the child from hell.   The gift to the poor and the shaving of the head in all its detail as in Indian practice, however, still prevails among the villagers. The shaving of the head has been taken over by the Copts, and is practiced by them as well as by the Moslems.   In the case of wealthy Copts a sum of money, equal in value to the weight of the hair of the infant in gold, is given to the poor.   In Arabia the custom is common everywhere.

According to Doughty, there is no question in the minds of the Arabs to-day as to the significance of the rite of sacrifice: " When a man child is born, the father will slay an ewe, but the female birth is welcomed in by no sacrifice.   Something has been already said of their blood-sprinkling upon breakland, and upon the foundation of new buildings; this they use also at the opening or enlarging of new wells and waters.

Again, when their *ghrazzu* riders return with a booty (*feyd* or *chessab*), the women dance out with singing to meet them; and the (live) *chessab*,[2] which they say 'is sweet,' is the same evening smeared with the blood of a victim. Metaad, a neighbor of mine, sent me a present of the meat of a fat goat, which he had sacrificed for the health of a sick camel; and 'now,' said the Arab, 'it would certainly begin to amend.' Rubba, the poor herdsman, made a supper to his friends, dividing to them the flesh of a she-goat, the thank-offering which he had vowed in his pain and sickness. Swoysh, sacrificing the year's mind, [sic] for his grandsire, distributed the portions at his tent, but we sat not down to a dish. They are persuaded that backwardness to sacrifice should be to their hurt. All religious sacrifices they call *kurban*. I have seen townsmen of Medina burn a little *bakhur*, before the sacrifice, for a pompous odor, 'acceptable to God,' and disposing our minds to religion — Where all men are their own butchers, perhaps they are (as the Arabs) more rash-handed to shed human blood. When they sacrifice to the *jan* they sacrifice to demons. If one sacrifice for health, the death of the ewe or the goat they think to be accepted for his camel's or for his own life, life for life."

In Morocco the ceremony is also well-known. " On the morning of the name-day," says Budgett Meakin, " the father or nearest male relative slaughters the sheep, exclaiming as he cuts the throat, ' In the Name of the Mighty God: for the naming of so-and-so, son (or daughter) of so-and-so.' Referring to the mother, who is asked to give the child a name. In the evening a feast is made of the sheep, the nurse receiving as her perquisite the fleece and a fore-leg, with perhaps a present of cash besides, in return for her presence for seven days. The mother sits in state on a special chair brought by the nurse."

2 Doughty refers to animals such as sheep or horses taken as booty.

In Sumatra, we are told " The Mohammedan law recommends an offering of two sheep or goats for a male, and one for a female child, by preference on the seventh day after birth, but if this be impossible then at some later date, even when the child is quite grown up." This sacrifice is called *'aqiqa* and is not only known but is actually practiced in Acheh under the name of *hakikah*. In Acheh, no less than in other parts of the E. Indian archipelago, the people of Mekka have done their best to foster the doctrine that it is an extremely meritorious act to offer this sacrifice for the child in the holy city. The Mekka folk thus of course reap the profits on the sale of the goats and at the same time enjoy their share of the meat. Many Achenese are, however, aware that the *hakikah* is more properly offered at home. The choice of some later occasion for this sacrifice, and not the seventh day after birth is also common in Acheh.

The ceremony is performed among the Malays as follows: " A few days later the child's head is shaved, and his nails cut for the first time. For the former process a red lather is manufactured from fine rice-flour mixed with gambier, lime, and betel-leaf. Some people have the child's head shaved clean, others leave the central lock (jambul). In either case the remains of the red lather, together with the clippings of hair (and nails?) are received in a rolled-up yam-leaf (*daun k'ladi diponjut*) or cocoa-nut (?) and carried away and deposited at the foot of a shady tree, such as a banana (or a pomegranate?).

" Some times (as had been done in the case of a Malay bride at whose ' tonsure' I assisted), the parents make a vow at a child's birth that they will give a feast at the tonsure of its hair, just before its marriage, provided the child grows up in safety.

" Occasionally the ceremony of shaving the child's head takes place on the 44th day after birth, the ceremony being called *balik juru.* A small sum, such as $2.00 or $3.00, is also sometimes presented to a pilgrim to carry clippings of the child's locks to Mecca and cast them into the well Zemzem, such payment being called *'kekah* (*'aqiqa*) in the case of a boy and *kurban* in the case of a girl." [3]

The custom prevails also in China, although so much else of the Moslem ritual has there been modified or suppressed. A Koranic name, called King-ming, is given to the child within seven days of its birth, and a feast is celebrated. " The rich are expected to kill a sheep, two if the child is a male, and the poor are to be fed with the meat. In selecting the name the father has to hold the child with its face turned towards Mecca and repeat a prayer in each ear of the child. Then taking the Koran he turns over any seven pages, and from the seventh word of the seventh line of the seventh page gives the name." (Marshall Broomhall, " Islam in China.") Here as elsewhere the naming of the child and the *'Aqiqa* are closely related.

In Mecca, on the seventh day after the birth of a child, a wether is usually killed. According to Snouck Hurgronje, the people there do not connect this with the *'Aqiqa* ceremony which may take place later. For the rest the ceremonies are observed by the calling of God's name in the right ear of the infant and giving the call to prayer in its left ear. A short *Khutbah* is given at the naming of the child and a present of silver given to the poor. On the fortieth day the infant is dressed in beautiful clothes, generally of silk, and handed at sunset by the mother to one of the eunuch guardians of the *Ka'aba* who lays it down near the door of the *Ka'aba.* For ten minutes the child remains under the protection of the shadow of the *Ka'aba.* Then the mother performs the evening prayer and carries the infant home.

In the Punjab, according to Major W. Fitz G. Bourne, the

[3] Skeat's " Malay Magic," pp. 341–342.

ceremony is universal. He writes: " On the sixth day after birth, the mother is bathed, all the women of the family assemble, and a feast takes place, called 'Chhati.' On the seventh day both male and female relations are invited, and a great feast takes place. The child's head is shaved, and the hair weighed against silver, which is given to the poor. The barber places a small brass cup before the assembly, into which all present put silver.[4] A sacrifice of one or two he-goats in the case of a male child, and of a she-goat in the case of a female child, is made. This ceremony is called ' Aqiqa' and is solemnized by repeating a given prayer in Arabic."

In regard to Malaysia and especially Celebes, we have interesting information about the practice prevalent among Bare'e-speaking Toradja's, by Dr. N. Adriani and the Rev. A. D. Kruijt. They say, " The Mohammedans on the south coast believe that when a child dies before its third year it has no sins, and therefore, its soul is taken directly to Allah. After the third year, however, a sacrifice is required, for a boy two goats, for a girl one. This sacrifice is called the *Mosambale,* or *'Aqiqa.* The time differs, and is chiefly dependent on the prosperity of the family. If there is, however, a death in the family or the child is ill, no effort is spared to secure the necessary sacrifice. The father himself must slay the goat. If the father has died before the *'Aqiqa* ceremony, then a portion of the father's personal possessions must be used to purchase the *'Aqiqa* sacrifice; for example, a piece of his clothing or outfit. When the sacrifice takes place the father says ' bis millah,' etc. (I sacrifice the *'Aqiqa* of so-and-so, who is the child of so-and-so. . . .) The popular opinion is that when the child dies afterwards it rides the goat which has been sacrificed for it in order to welcome its father in the other world. On the presentation of

---

[4] This is also the custom in Egypt.

this sacrifice, they assert, that the future character of the child is dependent for good or for ill. The child whose morals are corrupt is described as one for whom no proper 'aqiqa offering has been made. Possibly this representation rests on a curious misunderstanding of the Arabic word 'aqiqa and the other Arabic word haqiqa, which means 'reality,' so that the people imagine that the two words are closely related."

In Afghanistan the practice is well-known; and in addition to that of the 'Aqiqa we learn of other vicarious sacrifices that are prevalent. Dr. Pennell says, " All Muhammadan nations must, from the origin of their religion, have many customs and observances which appear Jewish, because they were adopted by Muhammed himself from the Jews around him; but there are two, at least, met with among Afghans which are not found among neighboring Muhammadan peoples, and which strongly suggest a Jewish origin. The first, which is very common, is that of sacrificing an animal, usually a sheep or a goat, in case of illness, after which the blood of the animal is sprinkled over the doorposts of the house of the sick person, by means of which the angel of death is warded off. The other, which is much less common, and appears to be dying out, is that of taking a heifer and placing upon it the sins of the people, whereby it becomes qurban, or sacrifice, and then it is driven out into the wilderness."

All this testimony from many Moslem lands concerning the prevalence of a practice which is based upon the highest authority, namely, Sunna, is of course deeply interesting to the student of comparative religion; and for the theories on the subject, some of which are fanciful in the extreme, the reader is referred to such authorities as Frazer in his " Golden Bough " or the special treatise of Prof. G. A. Wilkens, " Ueber das Haaropfer." Perhaps the best explanation of the origin of this sacrifice from the standpoint of comparative religion is that given by W. Robertson Smith in his book, "Kinship and Marriage in Early Arabia." He says, "Shaving or polling the hair was an act of worship commonly performed when a man visited a holy place or on discharging a vow (as in the ritual of the Hebrew Nazarites). At Taif, when a man returned from a journey, his first duty was to visit the *Rabba* and poll his hair. The hair in these cases was an offering to the deity, and as such was sometimes mingled with a meal offering. So it must have been also with the hair of the babe, for Mohammed's daughter Fatima gave the example of bestowing in alms the weight of the hair in silver. The alms must in older times have been a payment to the sanctuary, as in the similar ceremony observed in Egypt on behalf of children recovered from sickness; and the sacrifice is meant, as the Prophet himself says, ' to avert evil from the child by shedding blood on his behalf.' This is more exactly brought out in the old usage—discontinued in Moslem times—of daubing the child's head with blood, which is the same thing with the sprinkling of the ' living blood ' of a victim on the tents of an army going out to battle, or the sprinkling of the blood on the doorposts at the Hebrew passover. The blood which ensures protection by the god is, as in ritual of blood-brotherhood, blood that unites protector and protected, and in this, as in all other ancient Arabian sacrifices, was doubtless applied also to the sacred stone that represented the deity. The prophet offered a sheep indifferently for the birth of a boy or a girl, but in earlier times the sacrifice seems to have been only for boys.[5] Some authorities say that the ceremony fell on the seventh day after birth, but this is hardly correct; for when there was no 'aqiqa offered the child was named and its gums rubbed with masticated dates on the morning after birth. The Arabs were accustomed to hide a new-born child under a cauldron till the morning

[5] Compare the Tradition already cited.

light; apparently it was not thought safe till it had been put under the protection of the deity. I presume that in general the sacrifice, the naming, and the symbolical application of the most important article of food to the child's mouth, all fell together and marked his reception into partnership in the *sacra* and means-of-life of his father's group. At Medina Mohammed was often called in to give the name and rub the child's gums — probably because in heathenism this was done by the priest. Such a ceremony as this would greatly facilitate the change of the child's kin; it was only necessary to dedicate it to the father's instead of the mother's god. But indeed the name *'aqiqa,* which is applied both to the hair cut off and to the victim, seems to imply a renunciation of the original mother-kinship; for the verb *'aqqa,* " to sever," is not the one that would naturally be used either of shaving hair or cutting the throat of a victim, while it is the verb that is used of dissolving the bond of kindred, either with or without the addition of *al-rahim.* If this is the meaning of the ceremony, it is noteworthy that it was not performed on girls, and of this the words of the traditions hardly admit a doubt.[6] The exclusion of women from inheritance would be easily understood if we could think that at one times daughters were not made of their father's kin. That certainly has been the case in some parts of the world."

In his later work, " The Religion of the Semites," however, Professor Smith says that a fuller consideration of the whole subject of the hair offering convinces him that the name *'aqiqa* is not connected with the idea of change of kin, but is derived from the cutting away of the first hair. " I apprehend that among the Arabs . . . the *'aqiqa* was originally a ceremony of initiation into manhood, and that the transference of the ceremony to infancy was a later innova-

[6] On the contrary, the Traditions leave the matter uncertain except as regards the practice of the Jews.

tion, for among the Arabs, as among the Syrians, young lads let their hair grow long, and the sign of immaturity was the retention of the side locks, which adult warriors did not wear. The cutting of the side locks was, therefore, a formal mark of admission into manhood, and in the time of Herodotus it must also have been a formal initiation into the worship of Orotal,[7] for otherwise the religious significance which the Greek historian attaches to the shorn forehead of the Arabs is unintelligible. At that time, therefore, we must conclude that a hair-offering, precisely equivalent to the 'aqiqa, took place upon entry into manhood, and thereafter the front hair was habitually worn short as a permanent memorial of this dedicatory sacrifice. It is by no means clear that even in later times the initiatory ceremony was invariably performed in infancy, for the name 'aqiqa which in Arabic denotes the first hair as well as the religious ceremony of cutting it off, is sometimes applied to the ruddy locks of a lad approaching manhood, and figuratively to the plumage of a swift young ostrich or the tufts of an ass's hair, neither of which has much resemblance to the scanty down on the head of a new-born babe. It would seem, therefore, that the oldest Semitic usage both in Arabia and in Syria, was to sacrifice the hair of childhood upon admission to the religious and social status of manhood."

It does not seem very clear, however, that either of these theories is altogether satisfactory. Is it not more probable that we have in this Moslem custom another Jewish element in Islam connected with the Old Testament doctrine of sacrifice, especially the redemption of the first-born? (Compare Exodus XIII: 11–22 XXXIV: 19.) If in addition to all the resemblances to the Jewish practice already noted further testimony were necessary, it would be sufficient to refer to the statement made in the commentary of Al

[7] Orotal = Allah Ta'ala, God Supreme,—Z.

Buchari as the key to this true *Sunna* of the Prophet: " For the female child one ewe — and this abrogates the saying of those who disapprove a sacrifice for a girl — *as did the Jews, who only made 'aqiqa for boys.*"    (On the authority of 'Araki in Tirmidhi — Fath-ul-Bari V. 390.)

An additional proof would be the injunction of 'Ayesha, " That not a bone of this sacrifice should be broken."    Surely the observation of the *'Aqiqa* ceremony may well lead us to use Exodus XII and John XIX with our Moslem brethren, pointing them to the " Lamb of God which taketh away the sin of the world," and who is the true Redeemer also of childhood; who Himself took little children into His arms and blessed them.    I have recently prepared a leaflet on this subject for Moslems, entitled *" Haqiqat ul 'Aqiqa "* (The True Explanation of the 'Aqiqa) calling attention to some of these traditions and pointing out the teaching of the Old Testament regarding the redemption by the sacrificial Lamb, and showing that without the shedding of blood there is no remission of sin.    That the Moslem himself once recognized the vicarious character of this sacrifice and its deeper significance of atonement is perfectly evident from the prayer used on this occasion.    In one of the books of devotion published in Hindustani and printed at Calcutta, this prayer reads as follows: " O God, this is the 'Aqiqa sacrifice of my son so-and-so; its blood for his blood, its flesh for his flesh, its bone for his bone, its skin for his skin, its hair for his hair.    O God! make it a redemption for my son from the Fire, for truly I have turned my face to Him who created the heavens and the earth, a true believer.    And I am not of those who associate partners with God.    Truly my prayer and my offering my life and my death is to God, the Lord of the worlds, who has no partner, and thus I am commanded, and I belong to the Moslems."    After using this prayer the manual of devotion states that the sacrifice shall be slain by the father of the child while he crys " *Allahu akbar.*"

We may well imagine that under the Old Testament law a similar intercessory prayer was offered by the pious Israelite when presenting his sacrifice on behalf of the first-born. According to Jewish Talmudic law, every Israelite was obliged to redeem his first-born son thirty days after the latter's birth. At the redemption the father of the child pronounces these words, " Blessed art thou in the name of Him who commandeth us concerning the redemption of the son." In the case of the first-born they also observe the custom of *Ahlakah,* that is cutting the boy's hair for the first time. This took place after his fourth birthday. According to the Jewish Encyclopædia, it was also customary in Talmudic times to weigh the child (sic) [8] and to present the weight in coin to the poor. According to Rabbi Joseph Jacobs among the Beni Israel there is a custom that if a child is born as the result of a vow its hair is not cut until the sixth or seventh year. It is usual in all these cases to weigh the hair cut off and give its weight in coin to charitable purposes.

Who can fail to see that the Moslem custom is borrowed from Judaism, however much there may be mingled in the latter of early Semitic practice, the origin of which is obscure? Is there perhaps some connection also with the *Akedah* [9] prayer and ceremony observed among the Jews? The term refers to the binding of Isaac as a sacrifice, and this Biblical incident plays an important part in the Jewish liturgy. The earliest allusion occurs in the Mishnah, and the following prayer is found in the New Year's Day ritual: " Remember in our favor, O Lord our God, the oath which Thou hast sworn to our father Abraham on Mount Moriah;

[8] This must be a misprint, even in so careful and accurate a work, for " hair of the child."

[9] 'Akedah — the binding or knotting of a rope.

consider the binding of his son Isaac upon the altar when he suppressed his love in order to do Thy will with a whole heart! Thus may Thy love suppress Thy wrath against us, and through Thy great goodness may the heat of Thine anger be turned away from Thy people, Thy city and Thy heritage. . . . Remember to-day in mercy in favor of his seed the binding of Isaac." (Jewish Encyclopædia.) Dr. Max Landsberg says: " In the course of time ever greater importance was attributed to the 'Akedah. The haggadistic literature is full of allusions to it; the claim to forgiveness on its account was inserted in the daily morning prayer; and a piece called 'Akedah was added to the liturgy of each of the penitential days among the German Jews." In any case we notice that among the Jews as among Moslems attempts are made to explain away the significance of this prayer and sacrifice as relating to the idea of the atonement. Accordingly, many American reform rituals have abolished the 'Akedah prayers.

It is the fashion of the day in liberal Theology, Moslem and Jewish as well as Christian, to explain away the idea of expiation and atonement in the Old Testament as well as in the New. The altar with its blood sacrifice is as great a stumbling-block to such thinkers as the Cross of Christ; *but the place of the altar and of the Cross are central, pivotal, and dominant in the soteriology of the Bible.* We cannot escape the clear teaching of God's Word, that " without the shedding of blood there is no remission of sin "; that " the lamb of God was slain before the foundation of the world ": that the Son of God came " to give His life a ransom for many." The missionary, therefore, as well as the reverent student of the Old Testament, is not satisfied with any explanation of the doctrine of sacrifice which leaves out substitution and atonement. One thing seems clear from our investigation, that we have in the 'Aqiqa sacrifice as well as in the great annual feast of Islam with its day of sacrifice at Mecca, a clear testimony to the doctrine of a vicarious atonement and the remission of sin through the shedding of blood. Were St. Paul present at an 'Aqiqa ceremony or at 'Arafah on the great day of the feast, would he not preach to the assembled multitudes on the " remission of sins through His blood "? (Eph. 1: 7 — Col. 1: 14 — Rom. V: 11 — Rom. III: 25.)

Surely there is pathos as well as interest in the fact that the great Moslem world of childhood from its infancy has been consecrated to the religion of Islam by the 'Aqiqa sacrifice.

### BOOKS REFERRED TO IN THIS CHAPTER

" Al Bukhari " (Bulak, 1314).  Vol. VII, p. 83.

" Commentary on al Bukhari," Fath-ul-Bari, by El 'Ainy.  Vol. IX, p. 710.

" Commentary on al Bukhari," by al Askalany.  Vol. IX, p. 464.

" Commentary on al Muwatta," by al Zarkani.  Vol. III, p. 23.

" Badayat ul Majtahid," by El Kurtubi bin Rushd el Hafidh.  Vol. I, p. 375.

" Minhaj ut Talibin," by al Nawawi, p. 127.

" Mishkat ul Masabih (Delhi).  P. 363.

" Ihya ulum id Din," by al Ghazali.  Vol. II, p. 35.

Commentary on the same, by al Murtadhi.  Vol. V, p. 390.

" The Encyclopaedia of Islam " (Leyden).

" The Jewish Encyclopaedia " (Arts. Hair; First-born; Child; Sacrifice).

W. Robertson Smith, " Kinship and Marriage in Early Arabia " (Cambridge, 1885).  " The Religion of the Semites " (New York, 1889).

C. Snouck Hurgronje, " Mekka " (The Hague, 1888).

C. M. Doughty, " Arabia Deserta " (Cambridge, 1888).

G. A. Herklots, " Customs of the Moosulmans of India " (London, 1832).

Major W. Fitz G. Bourne, " Hindustani Mussulmans and Mussulmans of the Eastern Punjab " (Calcutta, 1914).

N. Adriani and Alb. C. Kruijt, " De Barre's-sprekende Toradja's " (Batavia, 1912).

Budgett Meakin, " The Moors " (London, 1902).

Dr. Pennell, " Among the Wild Tribes of the Afghan Frontier " (London, 1909).

Marshall Broomhall, " Islam in China " (London, 1910).

# CHAPTER VI

## THE FAMILIAR SPIRIT OR QARINA

AMONG all the superstitions in Islam there is none more curious in its origin and character than the belief in the *Qarin* or *Qarina*. It probably goes back to the ancient religion of Egypt, or to the animistic beliefs common in Arabia as well as in Egypt, at the time of Mohammed. By *Qarin* or *Qarina* the Moslem understands the double of the individual, his companion, his mate, his familiar demon. In the case of males a female mate, and in the case of females a male. This double is generally understood to be a devil, *shaitan* or *jinn,* born at the time of the individual's birth and his constant companion throughout life. The *Qarina* is, therefore, of the progeny of Satan.

The conception of the soul and the belief in a double among Moslems closely resembles the idea of the Malays and other animists. " The Malay conception of the human soul," we read, " is that of a species of thumbling, a thin unsubstantial human image, or mannikin, which is temporarily absent from the body in sleep, trance, disease, and permanently absent after death. This mannikin, which is usually invisible but is supposed to be about as big as the thumb, corresponds exactly in shape, proportion and even complexion, to its embodiment or casing, *i. e.,* the body in which it has its residence. It is of a vapory, shadowy, or filmy essence, though not so impalpable, but that it may cause displacement on entering a physical object. . . . The soul appears to men (both waking and sleeping) as a phantom separate from the body, of which it bears the likeness, manifests physical power, and walks, sits, and sleeps." [1] What this concept has become in Islam we shall see in a moment.

That the shadow is a second soul, or a semblance of the soul, is also an animistic idea. The same thing appears in Islam, for the shadow of a dog defiles the one who prays as much as does the dog himself. [2] The Javanese believe that black chickens and black cats do not cast a shadow because they come from the underworld. When one reads of this one cannot help comparing with it the Moslem belief in the *Qarina*.

There are many passages in the Koran in which this doctrine is plainly taught, and by reading the commentaries on these texts, a world of superstition, groveling, coarse, and, to the last degree, incredible, is opened to the reader. The Koran passages read as follows: [3] (Chapter of the Cave, verse 48), " And when we said to the angels, ' Adore Adam,' they adored him, save only Iblis, who was of the jinn, who revolted from the bidding of his Lord. ' What! will ye then take him and his seed as patrons, rather than me, when they are foes of yours? bad for the wrong-doers is the exchange! ' " The reference here is to the words, " Satan and his seed." (See especially the Commentary of Fahr al Din al Razi, margin, Vol. VI, p. 75.)

In speaking of the resurrection when the trumpet is blown and the day of judgment comes, we read: (Chapter Kaf, verses 20–30), " And every soul shall come — with it a driver and a witness! ' Thou wert heedless of this, and we withdrew thy veil from thee, and to-day is thine eyesight keen! ' And his mate (*qarina*) shall say, ' This is what is ready for me (to attest).' ' Throw into hell every stubborn

---

[1] " Malay Magic," by W. W. Skeat, London, 1900.

[2] I have not found this stated in the Traditions, but it is a well-known belief in Egypt and in Arabia.

[3] Palmer's translation is used throughout.

misbeliever! — who forbids good, a transgressor, a doubter! who sets other gods with God — and throw him, ye twain, into fierce torment!' His mate shall say, 'Our Lord! I seduced him not, but he was in a remote error.' He shall say, 'Wrangle not before me; for I sent the threat to you before. The sentence is not changed with me, nor am I unjust to my servants.' On the day we will say to hell, 'Art thou full?' and it will say, 'Are there any more?'"

And again we read:   (Chapter of Women, verses 41, 42), "And those who expend their wealth in alms for appearance sake before men, and who believe not in God nor in the last day; — but whosoever has Satan for his mate, (*qarina*) an evil mate has he."

Again:   (Chapter of the Ranged, verses 47–54), "... and with them damsels, restraining their looks, large eyed; as though they were a sheltered egg; and some shall come forward to ask others; and a speaker amongst them shall say, 'Verily, I had a mate (qarina) who used to say, "Art thou verily of those who credit? What! when we are dead, and have become earth and bones, shall we be surely judged?"' He will say, 'Are ye looking down?' and he shall look down and see him in the midst of hell. He shall say, 'By God, thou didst nearly ruin me!'"

(Chapter "Detailed," verse 24), "We will allot to them mates, for they have made seemly to them what was before them and what was behind them; and due against them was the sentence on the nations who passed away before them; both of *jinns* and of mankind; verily, they were the losers!"

(Chapter of Gilding, verses 35–37), "And whosoever turns from the reminder of the Merciful One, we will chain to him a devil, who shall be his mate; and verily, these shall turn them from the path while they reckon they are guided; until when he comes to us he shall say, 'O, would that between me and thee there were the distance of the two orients, for an evil mate (art thou)!' But it shall not avail you on that day, since ye were unjust; verily, in the torment shall ye share!"

To speak of only one of these passages, what Baidhawi says in regard to the Chapter of the Ranged, verse 49, leaves no doubt that the *qarina*, which has been the mate of the believer all through life, is cast into hell on the day of judgment, and that this evil spirit, which is born with every man, is determined to ruin him, but that the favor of God saves the believer, and that one of the special mercies of heaven for the believer is to behold his companion devil forever in torment.

Before we deal further with the comment as given on these verses, and the teaching in Moslem books, we consider the possible origin of this belief in teaching found in the " Book of the Dead " of ancient Egypt. " In addition to the Natural-body and Spirit-body," writes E. A. Wallis Budge (" Book of the Dead," Vol. I, p. 73), " man also had an abstract individuality or personality endowed with all his characteristic attributes. This abstract personality had an absolutely independent existence. It could move freely from place to place, separating itself from, or uniting itself to, the body at will, and also enjoying life with the gods in heaven. This was the *ka*, a word which at times conveys the meaning of its Coptic equivalent κω, and of ἔιδωλον, image, genius, double, character, disposition, and mental attributes. What the *ka* really was has not yet been decided, and Egyptologists have not yet come to an agreement in their views on the subject. Mr. Griffith thinks (Hieroglyphs, p. 15), that ' it was from one point of view regarded as the source of muscular movement and power, as opposed to *ba*, the will or soul which set it in motion.' " In September, 1878, M. Maspero explained to the Members of the Congress of Lyons the views which he held concerning this word, and which he had for the past five years been teaching in the College of France, and said, " *le ka' est une sorte de double de la personne humaine d'une matiére moins grossiére que la matiére dont est forme le corps, mais qu'il fallait nourrir et entretenir comme le corps lui-même; ce double vivait dans le tombeau des offrandes qu'on faisait aux fêtes canoniques, et aujourd'hui encore un grand nombre des génies de la tradition populaire égyptienne ne sont que des doubles, devenus démons au moment de la conversion des fellahs au christianisme, puis a l'islamisme."* [4]

Other authorities whom Mr. Budge quotes think that the *Ka* was a genius and not a double.   Mr. Breasted thinks that the *ka* was the superior genius intended to guide the fortunes of the individual in the hereafter.   But Mr. Budge goes on to say:   " The relation of the *ka* to the funerary offerings has been ably discussed by Baron Fr. W. v. Bissing (Versuch einer neuen Erklarung des Ka'i der alten Aegypter in the Sitzungsberichte der Kgl. Bayer.   Akad., Munich, 1911), and it seems as if the true solution of the mystery may be found by working on the lines of his idea, (which was published in the *Recueil,* 1903, p. 182), and by comparing the views about the ' double ' held by African peoples throughout the Sudan. The funeral offerings of meat, cakes, ale, wine, unguents, etc., were intended for the *ka;* the scent of the burnt incense was grateful for it (sic).   The *ka* dwelt in the man's statue just as the *ka* of a god inhabited the statue of the god.   In the remotest times the tombs had special chambers wherein the *ka* was worshiped and received offerings.   The priesthood numbered among its body an order of men who bore the name of ' priests of the ka ' and who performed services of honor of the *ka* in the " *Ka* chapel ! "   Although not in any sense

---

[4] *The Qarina.* The belief in the Qarina shows itself in the common speech of the people.   When an Egyptian wishes to send some one away he always uses the expression *Rukh-anta-wa-huwa,* i.e., *Go thou and he.* The latter pronoun refers to the man's demon mate or Qarina.

an Egyptologist, I believe further light may be thrown on the real significance of *ka* by what popular Islam teaches to-day.

Whatever may be the significance of *ka* in Egyptology, we are not in doubt as to what Mohammed himself thought of his *ka* or *qarina*. In the most famous volume of all Moslem books on the doctrine of *jinn*, called "Kitab akam al marjan fi Ahkam al Jan" by Abdullah-esh-Shabli (769 A. H.) we read in chapter five as follows: "It is related by Muslim and others from 'Ayesha that the Apostle of God left her one night and that she said, 'I was jealous of him.' Then she said, 'Mohammed saw me and came for me and said, "What's the matter with you, 'Ayesha? are you jealous?"' And I replied, 'Why should one like me not be jealous of one like you?' Then the apostle of God said, 'Has your devil spirit got hold of you?' Then I said, 'O Apostle of God, is there a devil with me?' Said he, 'Yes, and with every person.' Said I, 'And with you also, O Apostle of God?' Said he, 'Yes, but my Lord Most Glorious and Powerful has assisted me against him, so that he became a Moslem.'" Another Tradition is given in the same chapter on the authority of Ibn Hanbal as follows: "Said the Apostle of God, 'There is not a single one of you but has his *qarina* of the *jinn* and his qarina of the angels.' They said, 'And thou also, O Apostle of God?' 'Yes,' he replied, 'I also, but God has helped her so that she does not command me except in that which is true and good.'" The Tradition here given occurs in many forms in the same chapter, so that there can be no doubt of its being well-known and, in the Moslem sense, authentic.

Here is another curious form of the same Tradition. "Said the Apostle of God, 'I was superior to Adam in two particulars, for my devil (*qarina*), although an unbeliever, became through God's help a Moslem and my wives were a help to me, but Adam's devil remained an infidel and his wife led him into temptation.' " We also find an evening prayer recorded of Mohammed as follows: " Whenever the Apostle of God went to his bed to sleep at night he said, ' In the name of God I now lay myself down and seek protection from him against the evil influence of my devil (*qarin, shaitan*), and from the burden of my sin and the weight of my iniquity. O God, make me to receive the highest decree."

As regards the number of these companion devils and their origin, Tradition is not silent. " It is said that there are males and females among the devils, out of whom they procreate; but as to Iblis, God has created. . . . (The significance of this passage, which is not fit for translation, is that Iblis is an hermaphrodite) . . . there come forth out of him every day ten eggs, out of each of which are born seventy male and female devils. (Ibn Khallikan, quoted in Hayat al-Hawayan, article *jinn.*)

In another tradition also found in the standard collections it is said that Iblis laid thirty eggs —" ten in the west, ten in the east, and ten in the middle of the earth — and that out of every one of those eggs came forth a species of devils, such as al-Gilan, al-'Akarib, al-Katarib, al-Jann, and others bearing diverse names. They are all enemies of men according to the words of God. ' What! will ye then take him and his seed as patrons, rather than we, when they are foes of yours?' with the exception of the believing ones among them."

Al-Tabari, in his great commentary, vol. 26, p. 104, says the *qarin* or *qarina* is each man's *shaitan* (devil), who was appointed to have charge of him in the world. He then proves his statement by a series of traditions similar to those already quoted: " his *qarin* is his devil (*shaitan*) "; or, according to another authority there quoted, " his *qarina* is his *jinn.*" (The second form of the word is feminine, the first masculine.)

According to Moslem Tradition, not only Mohammed but even Jesus the Prophet had a *qarin*. As He was sinless, and because, in accordance with the well-known tradition, Satan was unable to touch Him at His birth, His *qarin* like that of Mohammed was a good one. " On the authority of Ka'ab the Holy Spirit, Gabriel, strengthened Jesus because He was His *qarin* and his constant companion, and went with Him wherever He went until the day when He was taken up to heaven." (Qusus al Anbiya," by Al Tha'alabi.)

Now while in the case of Mohammed and Jesus and perhaps also in the case of other prophets, the *qarin* or *qarina* was or became a good spirit, the general teaching is that all human beings, non-Moslems as well as Moslems, have their familiar spirit, who is in every case jealous, malignant, and the cause of physical and moral ill, save in as far as his influence is warded off by magic or religion. It is just here that the belief exercises a dominating place in popular Islam. It is against this spirit of jealousy, this other-self, that children wear beads, amulets, talismans, etc. It is this other-self that through jealousy, hatred and envy prevents love between husband and wife, produces sterility and barrenness, kills the unborn child, and in the case of children as well as of adults is the cause of untold misery.

The *qarina* is believed often to assume the shape of a cat or dog or other household animal. So common is the belief that the qarina dwells in the body of a cat at night-time, that neither Copts nor Moslems would dare to beat or injure a cat after dark.[5]

Many precautions are taken to defend the unborn child against its mate, or perhaps it is rather against the mate of the mother, who is jealous of the future child. Major Tremearne, who studied the subject in North Africa, says

[5] Many stories are related of the terrible consequences that follow beating a cat. These stories are credited even by the educated.

("Ban of the Bori," p. 97): the *qarin* "does not come until after the child has been actually born, for the sex is not known before that time." And again (p. 131): "All human beings, animals, plants and big rocks, have a permanent soul (*quruwa*) and a familiar bori of the same sex, and, in addition, young people have a temporary bori of the opposite sex, while all living things have two angels (*mala'ika*) in attendance. Small stones are soulless, and so are those large ones which are deep in the earth, 'for they are evidently dead,' else they would not have been buried. The soul has a shape like that of the body which it inhabits, and it dwells in the heart, but where it comes in and out of the body is not known. It is not the shadow (*ennuwa*), for it cannot be seen, and in fact the *ennuwa* is the shadow both of the body and of the soul. Yet the word *quruwa* is sometimes loosely used for shadow, and there is evidently some connection, for a wizard can pick the soul out of it. Neither is it the breath, for when a person sleeps his soul wanders about; in fact, it does so even when a person is day-dreaming."

All this, which is descriptive of conditions among the Hausa Moslems of North Africa, closely resembles the belief in Egypt. The *jinn* of the opposite sex, that is the soul-mate, generally dwells underground. It does not wish its particular mortal to get married. For, again I quote from Major Tremearne, "It sleeps with the person and has relations during sleep as is known by the dreams." This invisible companion of the opposite sex is generally spoken of in Egypt as "sister" or "brother." His or her abode is in quiet shady places, especially under the threshold of the house. The death of one or more children in the family is often attributed to their mother's mate, and therefore, the mother and the surviving children wear iron anklets to ward off this danger. Most people believe that the *qarina* dies with the individual; others that it enters the grave with the body. Although generally invisible there are those who have second sight and can see the *qarina*.   It wanders about at night in the shape of a cat.

I have recently taken down verbatim from Sheikh Ahmed Muharram of Daghestan and later from Smyrna an account of the popular belief.   He says that his statement represents the belief of all Turkish and Russian Mohammedans.   The *qurana* (plural of *qarina*) come into the world from the *'Alalam ul Barzakhiya* [6] at the time the child is conceived, before it is born; therefore during the act of coition, Moslems are told by their Prophet to pronounce the word " bismillah." This will prevent the child from being overcome by its devil and turned into an infidel or rascal.   The *qarina* exists with the fœtus in the womb.   When the child is born the ceremony of pronouncing the creed in its right ear and the call to prayer in the left is to protect the child from its mate.   Among the charms used against *qurana* are portions of the Koran written on leaden-images of fish or on leaden discs.   The *qurana* are invisible except to people who are idiots and to the prophets.   These often have second vision.   The *qurana* do not die with their human mates, but exist in the grave until the day of the resurrection, when they testify for or against the human being.   The reason that young children die is because Um es Subyan (the child-witch) is jealous of the mother, and she then uses the *qarina* of the child to put an end to it. " The way I overcome my *qarina*," said Ahmed Muharram, " is by prayer and fasting."   It is when a man is overcome with sleep that his *qarina* gets the better of him.   " When I omit a prayer through carelessness or forgetfulness, it is my *qarina* and not myself.   The *qarina* is not a spirit merely but has a spiritual body, and all of them differ in their bodily appearance, although invisible to us.   The *qarina* does not

[6] The unseen world, Hades, the abode of souls after death and before birth.

increase in size, however, as does the child." The Sheikh seemed to be in doubt in regard to the sex of the *qarina*. At first he would not admit that the sex relation was as indicated, thinking it improper for a man to have a female mate, but after discussion he said he was mistaken. He admitted also that all these popular beliefs were based upon the Koran and Tradition, although superstitious practice had crept in among the masses.

A learned Sheikh at Caliub, a Moslem village near Cairo, was also consulted on the subject. At first he tried to explain away the idea of popular Islam by saying that the *qarina* only referred to the evil conscience or a man's evil nature, but after a few questions he became quite garrulous, and gave the following particulars: The expectant mother, in fear of the *qarina,* visits the *sheikha* (learned woman) three months before the birth of the child, and does whatever she indicates as a remedy. These *sheikhas* exercise great influence over the women, and batten on their superstitious beliefs, often impersonating the *qarina* and frightening the ignorant. The Moslem mother often denies the real sex of her babe for seven days after it is born in order to protect its life from the *qarina.* During these seven days she must not strike a cat or she and the child will both die. Candles are lighted on the seventh day and placed in a jug of water near the head of the child, to guard it against the *qarina.* Before the child is born a special amulet is prepared, consisting of seven grains each of seven different kinds of cereal. These are sewn up in a bag, and when the infant is born it is made to wear it. The mother also has certain verses of the Koran written with musk water or ink on the inside of a white dish. This is then filled with water and the ink washed off and the contents taken as a potion. The Sheikh told me that the last two chapters of the Koran and also *Surat Al Muja-dala* were most commonly used for this purpose. One of the most common amulets against the *qarina* or the child-witch is that called the " Seven Covenants of Solomon." [7]

In Upper Egypt the bride wears a special amulet against the *qarina* fastened to her hair at the back or elsewhere on her person. It consists of a triangular bag an inch long of colored cloth containing seeds. The tongue of a donkey dried is considered a most powerful charm against the *qarina* and is used as an amulet on the house or the person.

A third amulet against the *qarina* of which I have a specimen from the village of Sirakna consists of a flat bronze ring three quarters of an inch in diameter. On this they tie threads of yellow, red, and blue silk. It is then hung in the armpit of a little child to protect it from the *qarina*.

Charms and amulets against the *qarina* abound. Books on the subject are printed by the thousands of copies. Here, for example, are the directions given for writing an amulet in the celebrated book called *" Kitab Mujaribat "* by Sheikh Ahmed Al Dirbi (p. 105): " This (twenty-fourth) chapter gives an account of an amulet to be used against *qarina* and against miscarriage. This is the blessed amulet prepared to guard against all bodily and spiritual evils and against harm and sorcery and demons and fear and terror and *jinn* and the *qarina* and familiar spirits and ghosts and fever and all manner of illness and wetting the bed, and against the child-witch (*Um es Subyan*) and whirlwinds and devils and poisonous insects and the evil eye and pestilence and plague and to guard the child against weeping while it sleeps — and the mystery of this writing is great for those children who have fits every month or every week or who cannot cease from crying or to the woman who is liable to miscarriage. And it is said that this amulet contains the great and powerful name of God — in short, it is useful for all evils. It must be

---

[7] A translation of this is given in the chapter on amulets, charms and knots.

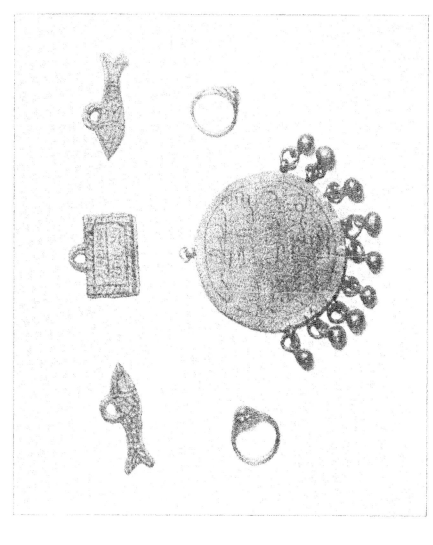

AMULETS AND "LUCKY" RINGS, USED IN LOWER EGYPT

The fish amulets are made of lead and are used against the Qarîna. These are specially manufactured at Damanhûr, a city of the Delta.

written the first hour of the first day of the week, and reads as follows: " In the name of God the Merciful, the Compassionate, there is no God but He, the Living, the Eternal, etc. (to the end of the verse on the throne).    In the name of God and to God and upon God, and there is no one victorious save God and no one can deliver him who flees from God, for He is the Living, the Self-subsisting, whom slumber seizes not nor sleep, etc.    I place in the safe keeping of God him who carries this amulet, the God than whom there is no other, who knows the secret and the open.    He is the Merciful, the Compassionate.    I protect the bearer by the words of God Most Perfect and by His glorious names from evil that approaches and the eyes that flash and the souls of the wicked and from the evil of the father of wickedness and his descendants and from the evil of those that blow upon knots and from the evil of the envier when he envies, and I put him under the protection of God the Most Holy, King of the Angels and of the Spirits, Lord of the worlds, the Lord of the great throne, Ihyashur, Ihyabur, Ihya-Adoni, Sabaoth Al Shaddai; [8] and I put the bearer under the keeping of God by the light of the face of God which does not change and by His eye which does not sleep nor slumber and His protection which can never be imagined nor escaped and His assistance which needs no help and His independence which has no equal and His eternity without end, His deity which cannot be overcome and His omnipresence which cannot be escaped, and I put him under the protection of the Lord of Gabriel and Michael and Israfil and Izrail and of Mohammed, the seal of the Prophets, and of all the prophets and apostles, and in the name of Him who created the angels and established their footsteps by His majesty to hold up His throne when it was borne on the face of the waters, and by the eight names writ-

---

[8] This portion shows Jewish origin and gives some of the Hebrew names of God — Jehovah.

ten upon the throne of God.    I also give the bearer the protection of K.H.T.S. and the seven H.W.M.'s and H.M.S.K.'s, and by the talisman of M.S. and M.R. and R. and H.W.M. and S. and K. and N. and T.H. and Y.S.[9] and the learned Koran and by the name of God Most Hidden and His noble book and by Him who is light upon lights, by His name who flashed into the night of darkness and destroyed by his blaze every rebellious devil and made those that feared trust Him; and by the name by which man can walk upon water and make it as dry land; and by the name by which Thou didst call thyself in the book which came down and which Thou didst not reveal to any but by whose power Thou didst return to Thy throne after the creation; and by the name by which Thou didst raise up the heavens and spread out the earth and createst paradise and the fire; the name by which Thou didst part the sea for Moses and sent the flood to the people of Noah, the name written on Moses' rod and by which Thou didst raise up Jesus, the name written on the leaves of the olive trees and upon the foreheads of the noble angels.    And I put the one who wears this amulet under the protection of Him who existed before all and who will outlast all and who has created all, God, than whom there is no other, the Living, He is the Knowing and the Wise; and I put the bearer under the protection of the name of God by which He placed the seven heavens firmly and the earth upon its mountains and the waters so that they flowed and the fountains so that they burst forth and the rivers so that they watered the earth, and the trees brought forth their fruit and the clouds gave rain and night became dark and the day dawned and the moon game his light and the sun his splendor and the stars went in their course and the winds who carried His messages; and I put the bearer under the protection of the name by which Jesus spoke in the cradle and by which He raised the dead

[9] These are the mystical letters which occur in the Koran text.

from the grave, and by which He opened the eyes of those born blind and cured the lepers, the name by which He made the dumb to speak.   And I protect him by the Merciful God and His great name and His perfect words, which neither riches nor the sinner can resist, from the evil which comes down from heaven or the evil that ascends to heaven and from the evil which is found upon the earth or which comes out of the earth, and from the terror of the night and of the day and from the oppression of the night and of the day; and I protect him from all powerful influences of evil and from the cursed devil and from envious men and from the wicked infidel; and I protect him by the Lord of Abraham, the friend of God, and Moses, the spokesman of God, and Jesus and Jacob and Isaac and Ishmael and David and Solomon and Job and Yunas and Aaron and Seth and Abel and Enoch and Noah and Elijah and Zecahriah and John and Hud and Elisha and Zu Kifl and Daniel and Jeremiah and Shu'aib and Ilyas and Salih and Ezra and Saul and the Prophet-of-the-fish and Lokman and Adam and Eve and Alexander the Great and Mary and Asiah (Pharaoh's wife) and Bilkis and Kharkil and Saf the son of Berachiah and Mohammed the seal of the prophets; and I protect him by God than whom there is no other, who will remain after all things have perished, and by His power and by His might and by His exaltation above all creatures and above all devils male and female, and all manner of *jinn,* male and female, and familiar spirits of both sexes, and wizards and witches, and deceivers male and female, and infidels male and female, and enemies male and female, and ghoul and demons, and from the evil eye and the envious, from the evil in things of ear and eye and tongue and hand and foot and heart and conscience, secret or open. And I protect the wearer from everything that goes out and comes in, from every breath that stirs of evil or of movement of man or beasts, whether he be sick or well, awake or sleeping, and from the evil of that which dwells in the earth or in the clouds or in the mountains or in the air or the dust or the vapor or the caves or the wells or the mines, and from the devil himself, and from the flying demons, and from those who work sorcery and from the evil of the whirlwind caused by the chief of the *jinn*, and from the evil of those who dwell in tombs and in secret places, in pools and in wells and from him who is with the wild beasts or within the wombs, and from him who is an eavesdropper of the secrets of the angels, etc., etc.' " (After this the amulet closes with the words of the Moslem creed written three times, the call to prayer twice and) " May God's blessing and peace be upon the Prophet and upon his companions forever until the day of judgment. Praise be to God the Lord of the worlds." *All this seems the height of folly to the educated Moslem. Yet it is taken from one of the best selling books on popular magic and medicine, printed in Cairo, third edition, 1328 A.H. (six years ago) 192 pages, fine print, and sold for ten cents!*

No one can read of these superstitious practices and beliefs, which are inseparable from the Koran and Tradition, without realizing that the belief in the *qarina* is a terror by night and by day to pious Moslem mothers and their children. For fear of these familiar spirits and demons they are all their life time subject to bondage. A mother never dares to leave her infant child alone in Egypt for fear of the *qarina*. The growing child must not tramp on the ground heavily for fear he may hurt his *qarina*. It is dangerous to cast water on the fire lest it vex the *qarina*. On no account must the child be allowed to go asleep while weeping. Its every whim must be satisfied for fear of its evil mate. It is the firm belief in Egypt that when a mother has a boy her *qarin* (masculine) has also married a *qarina* (feminine), who at that time gives birth to a girl. This demon-child and its mother are jealous of the human mother and her child. To pacify the *qarina* they sacrifice a chicken, which must be absolutely black and sacrificed with the proper ceremonies. It is impossible to see the *qarina* except in one way. Following a Jewish superstition (Jewish Encyclopedia, art. demonology), a man may see evil spirits by casting the ashes of the fœtus of a black cat about his eyes or by sprinkling these ashes around his bed he can trace their footsteps in the morning.

When we remember that only one-third of one per cent. of the women in Egypt are able to read, we can imagine the power that is exercised over them by the lords of this superstition, who sell amulets and prescribe treatment for the expectant mother and her child. Pitiful stories have come to me from those who were eye-witnesses of this swindle which is being carried on in every village of the Delta.

Al-Ghazali himself in his great work, " The Revival of the Religious Sciences," in speaking of the virtue of patience, says: " He who is remiss in remembering the name of God even for the twinkling of an eye, has for that moment no mate but Satan. For God has said, ' And whosoever turns from the reminder (remembrance) of the Merciful One, we will chain to him a devil, who shall be his mate (*qarina*).' "

We may perhaps appropriately close this chapter with what one of the learned men relates regarding the victory of the believer over his demon and its powers. It may lead us to a new conception of that petition in the Lord's Prayer which we offer also for our Moslem brothers and sisters: " Lead us not into temptation but deliver us from the Evil One." " ' Verily, the devil is to you a foe, so take him as a foe.' This is an order for us from Him — may He be praised! — that we may take him as a foe. He was asked, ' How are we to take him as a foe and to be delivered from him ? ' and he replied, ' Know, that God has created for every believer seven forts — the first fort is of gold and is the knowledge of God; round it is a fort of silver, and it is the faith in Him; round it is a fort of iron and it is the trust in Him; round it is a fort of stones and consists of thankfulness and being pleased with Him: round it is a fort of clay and consists of ordering to do lawful things, prohibiting to do unlawful things, and acting accordingly; round it is a fort of emerald which consists of truthfulness and sincerity toward Him; and round it is a fort of brilliant pearls, which consists of the discipline of the mind (soul). The believer is inside these forts and Iblis outside them barking like a dog, which the former does not mind, because he is well-fortified (defended) inside these forts. It is necessary for the believer never to leave off the discipline of the mind under any circumstances or to be slack with regard to it in any situation he may be in, for whoever leaves off the discipline of the mind or is slack in it, will meet with disappointment (from God), on account of his leaving off the best kind of discipline in the estimation of God, whilst Iblis is constantly busy in deluding him, in desiring for his company, and in approaching him to take from him all these forts, and to cause him to return to a state of unbelief. We seek refuge with God from that state!" [10]

[10] " Al Damiri — Hayat-ul-Hayawan." Vol. I, p. 470. (English Translation by Jayakar.)

# CHAPTER VII

## JINN

WHEN the Moslem loudly professes belief in the one true God, the second article of the creed adds that he also believes in the existence of God's angels. The word here used for angels is *mala'ikat,* derived from the Arabic root *"alaka,"* which means to carry a message. The derivation therefore is similar to that of the English word angel. The Moslem term, however, covers three distinct orders of created beings.

First, angels proper. Heavenly messengers imbued with subtle bodies and created of light. They neither eat or drink or have any distinction of sex. Their general characteristic is complete obedience to the will of God. They are included in His army of slaves. Their place is in Heaven, and their general work consists in praising and executing His commands. Their forms are beautiful and they are divided into ranks and degrees. The four archangels whose names are well-known; two recording angels, one on the right shoulder and the other on the left, constantly watch the believer; the guardian angels; the cherubim; the angels of the tomb and the special guardian of Paradise called Ridwan. Another order of spiritual beings are the devils with their chief, Satan, whose original name was Azazil. The third class of supernatural creatures find their place between men and angels. They are called Jinn.

According to Moslem tradition the Jinn were created of fire some thousands of years before Adam. The Jinn are considered to be like men, capable of future salvation and damnation; they can accept or reject God's message. They are believers or non-believers. According to the Koran Mohammed was sent to convert the Jinn to Islam as well as the Arabs. (Suras 72: 1–7 and 15: 27.) The Jinn are reported to be eaves-droppers and constantly trying to go behind the curtain of heaven in order to steal God's secrets. For this reason the good angels throw stones at them, that is shooting stars, and the common name given to these demonic transgressors is therefore "the stoned ones"— Ar-rajim. (See the commentaries on Suras 55: 14; 51: 56; 11: 120, etc.) The general abode of all of these spirits or demons is said to be the mountains of Qaf which are supposed to encircle the world.

Although Mohammed destroyed polytheism with its priest-hood and idols, the substratum of paganism remained and was incorporated into Islam by his revelations on Jinn. Well-hausen has shown how belief in Jinn was universal in Arabia before Islam. Men and Jinn are often spoken of as the *Thaqalan,* i. e., the two classes of material beings endowed with souls. The etymological derivation of the word is interesting and its cognate words such as those for garden, fœtus, shield, show the same root meaning: to hide, cover. Among the names for Jinn the following are female: *ghul, si'lat, 'aluq and 'auluq.* The male Jinn are called *'afrit* and *'azab,* etc. The word *'afrit* occurs in the Kor'an (Sur. 27: 39).

Professor Macdonald in his fascinating book, "The Religious Attitude and Life in Islam," throws considerable light on the doctrine of Jinn both before and after the rise of Islam.

He tells us how Hasan ibn Thabit, a close friend of Mo-hammed, and one who praised him in his poetry, was initiated into his verses by a female Jinn. "She met him in one of the streets of Medina, leapt upon him, pressed him down and compelled him to utter three verses of poetry. Thereafter he was a poet, and his verses came to him as the other Arab poets from the direct inspiration of the Jinn. He refers himself to his 'brothers of the Jinn' who weave for him artistic words, and tells how weighty lines have been sent down to him from heaven in the night season. The curious thing is that the expressions he uses are exactly those used of the 'sending down,' that is revelation of the Qur-an."

Dr. Macdonald points to the close parallel between the terms used in the story of Hassan ibn Thabit's inspiration and the account we have of the first revelation of Mohammed. "Just as Hassan was thrown down by the female spirit and had verses pressed out of him, so the first utterances of prophecy were pressed from Mohammed by the angel Gabriel. And the resemblances go still farther. The angel Gabriel is spoken of as the companion (qarin) of Muhammad, just as though he were the Jinni accompanying a poet, and the same word, *nafatha,* 'blow upon,' is used of an enchanter, of a Jinni inspiring a poet and of Gabriel revealing to Muhammad."

In the preceding chapter on the *Qarina* this belief in a double or twin guardian soul was fully treated. Here we deal with the subject in general as unfolded in the Koran and in orthodox tradition. The Jinn are referred to in the Koran in the following passages: Chapter VI: 100: "Yet they made the *jinn* partners with God, though he created them! and they ascribed to Him sons and daughters, though they have no knowledge; celebrated be His praise! and exalted be He above what they attribute to Him! The inventor of the heavens and the earth! how can He have a son, when He has no female companion, and when He has created everything, and everything He knows?"

Chap. VI: 127: "And on that day when He shall gather them all together, 'O assembly of the jinns! he have got much out of mankind.' And their clients from among mankind shall say, 'O our Lord! much advantage had we one from another '; but we reached our appointed time when thou hadst appointed for us.  Says He, ' The fire is your resort, to dwell therein for aye! save what God pleases; verily, thy Lord is wise and knowing!' "

Chapter VII: 36:  "He will say, ' Enter ye — amongst the nations who have passed away before you, both of jinns and men — into the fire '; whenever a nation enters therein, it curses its mate; until, when they have all reached it, the last of them will say unto the first, ' O Our Lord! these it was who led us astray, give them double torment of the fire!' He will say, ' To each of you double! but ye do not know.' And the first of them will say unto the last, ' Ye have no preference over us, so taste ye the torment for that which ye have earned!'

Chapter VII: 177:  "We have created for hell many of the jinn and of mankind."

Chapter XXIII: 70:  "Is it that they did not ponder over the words, whether that has come to them which came not to their fathers of yore?  Or did they not know their apostle, that they thus deny him?  Or do they say, ' He is possessed by a jinn?'  Nay, he came to them with the truth, and most of them are averse from the truth."

Chapter XXXIV: 45:  "Say, ' I only admonish you of one thing, that ye should stand up before God in twos or singly, and then that ye reflect that there is no *jinn* in your companion.  He is only a warner to you before the keen torment.' "

Chapter LV: 14:  "He created men of crackling clay like the potters.  And He created the jinn from smokeless fire."

Chap. LV: 32:  "O assembly of jinns and mankind! if ye are able to pass through the confines of heaven and earth then pass through them! — ye cannot pass through save by authority!"

The whole of the chapter of the Jinn — namely, Chapter LXXII. The important passages are the earlier ones: " Say, ' I have been inspired that there listened a company of the *jinn,* and they said, " We have heard a marvelous Qur'an that guides to the right direction ; and we believe therein, and we join no one with our Lord, for, verily, He — may the majesty of our Lord be exalted ! — has taken to Himself neither consort nor son. . . .

" ' And, verily, a fool among us spake against God wide of the mark ! . . .

" ' And we thought that men and *jinn* would never speak a lie against God.' . . .

" And there are persons amongst men who seek for refuge with persons amongst the *jinn,* but they increase them in their perverseness. And they thought, as ye thought, that God would not raise up any one from the dead.

" But we touched the heavens and found them filled with a mighty guard and shooting-stars ; and we did sit in certain seats thereof to listen ; but whoso of us listens now finds a shooting-star for him on guard."

And the last chapter of the Koran, one of the first chronologically, reads: " Say, ' I seek refuge in the Lord of men, the King of men, the God of men, from the evil of the whisperer, who slinks off, who whispers into the hearts of men ! — from jinns and men ! ' "

The belief in jinn among Moslems is almost the same as the belief in spiritual beings — demons, sprites, elves, etc.— in the African religions. Nassau writes (p. 50) : " The belief in spiritual beings opens an immense vista of the purely superstitious side of the theology of Bantu African religion.

All of the air and the future is peopled with a large and indefinite company of these beings. The attitude of the Creator (*Anyambe*) toward the human race and lower animals being that of indifference or of positive severity in having allowed evils to exist, and His indifference making Him almost inexorable, cause effort in the line of worship to be therefore directed only to those spirits who, though they are all probably malevolent, may be influenced and made benevolent." One has only to compare this with the popular practice of Islam to see how close is the parallel.

Jinn are called forth by whistling or blowing a pipe. This therefore is considered an omen of evil. Before Islam as now certain places were considered as inhabited by the jinn. Higar (the city of the dead from the days of Thamud), graveyards and outhouses are their special resort. When entering such places a formula must be uttered to drive them away. Jinn are specially busy at night and when the morning-star appears they vanish. Wherever the soil is disturbed by digging of wells or building there is danger of disturbing the jinn as well. Whenever Mohammed changed his camp he was accustomed to have the *Takbir* cried in order to drive them away. The whirlwind is also an evidence of the presence of jinn. When the cock crows or the donkey brays it is because they are aware of the presence of jinn (Bokhari 2: 182). They also dwell in animals and, as Wellhausen rightly says, *"The zoology of Islam is demonology."* The wolf, the hyena, the raven, the *hudhud,* the owl are special favorites in this conception. A specially close connection exists between the serpent and the jinn; in every snake there is a spirit either good or evil. Examples of the Prophet's belief in this superstition are given by Wellhausen.[1]

In the old Arabian religion the jinn were nymphs and satyrs of the desert. They were in constant connection with wild animals and often appeared in brute forms. Robertson Smith in his " Religion of the Semites," shows us the relations that were supposed to exist between these spirits of the wild and the gods. He says: " In fact the earth may be

[1] " Reste Arabischen Heidentums," Berlin, 1897, p. 153.

said to be parceled out between demons and wild beasts on the one hand, and gods and men on the other. To the former belong the untrodden wilderness with all its unknown perils, the wastes and jungles that lie outside the familiar tracks and pasture grounds of the tribe, and which only the boldest men venture upon without terror; to the latter belong the regions that man knows and habitually frequents, and within which he has established relations, not only with his human neighbors, but with the supernatural beings that have their haunts side by side with him. And as man gradually encroaches on the wilderness and drives back the wild beasts before him, so the gods in like manner drive out the demons; and spots that were once feared, as the habitation of mysterious and presumably malignant powers, lose their terrors and either become common ground or are transformed into the seats of friendly deities. From this point of view, the recognition of certain spots as haunts of the gods is the religious expression of the gradual subjugation of nature by man." To the Arabs of Mohammed's day this teaching formed the background of their supernatural world. The heathen of Mecca considered the jinn as the sons and daughters of Allah. When Islam came this relation was denied, but the existence of the jinn and their character remained unchanged. Dr. Macdonald quotes a number of instances in the history of Islam where the saints had intercourse with God through Jinn (pp. 139–152). We need not marvel at these stories of later tradition for we find in Moslem books a number of instances given where Mohammed himself held converse with jinn. The following is a typical example: " One day the Prophet prayed the morning prayer with us in the Mosque of Al-Madina. Then when he had finished, he said, ' Which of you will follow me to a deputation of the jinn tonight?' But the people kept silence and none said anything. He said ' which of you?' He said it three times; then he walked past me and took me by the hand, and I walked with him until all the mountains of al-Madina were distant from us and we had reached the open country. And there were men, tall as lances, wrapped completely in their mantles from their feet up. When I saw them a great quivering seized upon me, until my feet would hardly support me from fear. When we came near to them the Prophet drew with his great toe a line for me on the ground and said, ' sit in the middle of that.' Then when I had sat down, all fear which I had felt departed from me. And the Prophet passed between me and them and recited the Qur-an in a loud voice until the dawn broke. Then he came past me and said, ' Take hold of me.' So I walked with him, and we went a little distance. Then he said to me, ' Turn and look; dost thou see any one where these were?' I turned and said, ' O Apostle of God, I see much blackness!' He bent his head to the ground and looked at a bone and a piece of dung, and cast both to them. Thereafter he said, ' They are a deputation of the jinn of Nasibin; they asked of me traveling provender; so I appointed for them all bones and pieces of dung.' "

Al-Tabarani relates on the strength of respectable authorities, on the authority of Abu-Tha'labah al-Khushani Al-Khushati, (*Mishkat al-Masabih*) that the Prophet said, " The genii are of three kinds; the genii of one kind have wings with which they fly in the air; those of the second kind are snakes; and those of the third kind alight and journey to distant places." And again, " All the Moslems hold the opinion that our Prophet was sent for the genii as well as for men. God has said, ' (Say)' This Kur'an was inspired to me to warn you and those it reaches.' " It reached the genii, (as well as man). God has also said, ' And when we turned towards thee some of the genii listening to the Kur'an, and when they were present at (the reading of) it, they said, " Be

EGYPTIAN GEOMANCER

Seated by the roadside these fortune tellers, who are generally Moslems from North Africa, read the future from the imprint made by the petitioner's hand in dry sand. Rosary and books on magic complete his outfit

silent!"'' and when it was over they turned back to their people warning them."

Moslem tradition leaves no doubt as to the dealings which Mohammed had with these inhabitants of the air (p. 451). " It is related in (*Kitab Khair al-bushr bi-khair al-bashar*) by the Imam, the very learned Muhammed b. Dafar on the authority of Ibn-Mas'ud who said, ' The Apostle of God said to his Companions, being at the time in Mecca, " Whoever of you likes to be present to-night to see the affair of the genii, let him come with me "; so I went out with him, and when we reached the upper part of Mecca, he marked out a boundary line for me, and then going away stood up and commenced to recite the Koran, upon which he was concealed (from my view) by many bodily forms which came between me and him, so much so that I could not hear his voice; then they dissipated as clouds do, and went away, only as clouds do, and went away, only a small company of them under ten (in number) remaining behind. The Prophet then came and asked (me), " What has the small company done?" and I replied, " There they are, O Apostle of God." He then took a bone and some dung and gave them to them and prohibited the use of a bone or dung for cleaning oneself after answering the call of nature.' "

A similar tradition is found in the *Sahih* of Muslim (pp. 452–3). " We were with the Prophet one night, and we missed him; so we searched for him in the valleys and watercourses, and said (to ourselves), ' He has been either taken away quickly, as though birds have carried him away, or has been beguiled, taken away to a place, and there slain.' We spent that night in the worst way that any people could spend; but when the morning dawned, he came from the direction of Hira, and we said to him, ' O Apostle of God, we missed you and therefore searched for you, but did not find you and spent the night in the worst manner that a party could spend (it), upon which the Prophet replied, ' A caller of the genii came to me, so I went away with him and recited the Koran to them.' He then went away with us and showed us the traces of their fires; they (the genii) then asked him for traveling provisions and he said (to them), ' For you is every bone over which the name of God has been taken (at the time of slaughtering), which you may take and which will fall into your hands with the largest quantity of flesh (over it), and all the globular dung as fodder for your animals.' The Prophet then said (to us), ' Do not clean yourselves with them for they are the food of your brethren.' ' "

Again (p. 455), " Al-Bukhari, Muslim, and an-Nasa'i relate, on the authority of Abu-Hurairah, that the Prophet said, ' An Afrit (a wicked genius) out of the genii came suddenly upon me last night, desiring to disturb me in my prayer, so I strangled him and wished to tie him to one of the columns of the mosque, but I remembered the words of my brother, (the prophet) Sulaiman.' "

The following story reminds us somewhat of the Wandering Jew and is also related on good authority. It is given by Damiri (p. 461). " I was with the Apostle of God outside the mountains of Mecca, when an old man approached leaning on a staff. The Prophet said, ' The walk is that of a genius and so is his voice,' and he replied, ' Yes,' The Prophet then asked him, ' From what kind or tribe of genii ? ' and he replied, ' I am Hamah b. al-Himmor b. Him b. Lakis b. Iblis,' upon which the Prophet said, ' I see that only two generations (fathers) have passed between you and him (Iblis),' and he replied, ' I have eaten (lived through) the (whole) world excepting a little of it; during the nights when Cain (Kabil) killed Abel (Habil) I was only a boy, a few years old, and used to ascend high hills to look down, and used to incite discord between mankind.' The Apostle of God thereupon said, ' Wretched was the action ! ' but he replied,

'O Apostle of God, leave off reproaching me, because I am one of those who believed in Noah and repented through him'; I then reproached him for his prayer (against his people — al-Kur'an LXXI: 27), upon which he cried and made me cry, and said, 'I am by God, verily one of those who have repented and I take refuge with God from being one of the ignorant ones. I then met Hud and believed in him, and I met Abraham with whom I was in the fire when he was thrown into it, and I was with Joseph when he was thrown into the well, preceding him to the bottom of it; I met Jethro (Shu'aib), and Moses, and Jesus the son of Mary, who told me, " If you meet Mohammed greet him with my salutation," and now I have delivered to you his message and have believed in you.' The Prophet thereupon said, 'Salutation to Jesus and to you! What is it you want, O Hamah?' and he replied, 'Moses taught me the Pentateuch, and Jesus taught me the Gospel and now teach me the Koran.'" In another version, it is said that the Prophet taught him ten chapters out of the Koran.

So firm is the belief in jinn that long disputes have arisen regarding the question of 40 people being present in the Friday congregation. Some authorities hold that they are counted among them and others will not accept the testimony of those who claim to see them. Special sections are also devoted in books of Moslem law regarding marriage of Jinn with human beings and their rights of inheritance!

We also learn that jinn do not enter a house in which there is a citron. " It has been related to us regarding the Imam Abu'l-Husain 'Ali b. al-Hasan b. al-Husain b. Mohammed al-Khila'i — he was so surnamed on account of his selling robes of honor and was one of the disciples of al-Shafi'i; his grave is a well-known one at al-Karafah, and prayers addressed in its name are answered; he was called the kadi of the jinn,— as having informed that they (the genii) used to come to him and recite the Koran (for the purpose of learning it) ; one Friday they kept away from him, and when they came again he asked them the reason of that, and they replied, " There was in your house a citron, and we do not enter a house in which that fruit is." [2]

Similar precautions against evil germs of the spirit world are common in India and Egypt to-day.   In Egypt as in Morocco the belief in jinn includes such things as setting aside dishes of food at dusk to propitiate them.   Others keep loaves of bread under their mattresses with a similar idea; while meal and oil are thrown into the corner of new houses for the jinn.   The placing of knives and daggers under the pillows of the sick is for the same purpose.

Skeat in his book " Malay Magic" gives a complete account of the Malay pantheon and shows how the jinn, good and bad, dominate the thought of the masses.   There is an interesting account of the origin of the jinn according to Moslem belief, and he speaks of how they may be bought at Mecca at a fixed price.   He gives a picture of the black and white jinn mentioned:

" The White Genie is said to have sprung, by one account, from the blood-drops which fell on the ground when Habil and Kabil bit their thumbs; by another, from the irises of the snake Sakatimuna's eyes (benih mata Sakatimuna), and is sometimes confused with the White Divinity ('Toh Mambang Puteh), who lives in the sun.

" The name of his wife is not mentioned, as it is in the case of the Black Genie, but the names of three of his children have been preserved, and they are Tanjak Malim Kaya, Pari Lang (lit. kite-like, i.e., ' winged ' Skate), and Bintang Sutan (or Star of Sutan).

" On the whole, I may say that the White Genie is very

[2] All   page   references   are   to   Ad-Damiri's   Hayat   al-Hayawan (Jayaker).

A facsimile reproduction, one-half reduced, of a Chinese Moslem
amulet sold at Shanghai in the leading mosques. The central character is the Arabic for *Bismillah* "*In the name of God.*"  At the four
corners are the names of the archangels, Gabriel, Michail, Azrail and
Asrafil.  On the right side of the central monogram is the call to
prayer in the usual form.  On the left side is the first chapter of the
Koran followed by the six articles of the orthodox creed.  On the
outer edge beginning at the upper right hand corner is the Verse of
the Throne.  This amulet is used to defend the possessor against Jinn
and other evil influences and to produce good health and prosperity.

seldom mentioned in comparison with the Black Genie, and that whereas absolutely no harm, as far as I can find out, is recorded of him, he is, on the other hand, appealed to for protection by his worshipers."

"A very curious subdivision of Genii into Faithful (Jin Islam) and Infidel (Jin Kafir) is occasionally met with, and it is said, moreover, that Genii (it is to be hoped orthodox ones) may sometimes be *bought* at Mecca from the 'Sheikh al Jin' (Headman of Genii) at prices varying from $90 to $100 apiece." [3]

One may almost say of popular Islam what Dr. Warneck does of the heathen Battaks of Sumatra: "The worship of spirits, with the fear underlying it, completely fills the religious life of the Battaks and of all animistic peoples. Their whole daily life in its minutest details is saturated with it. At birth, name-giving, courting, marriage, house-building, seed-time and harvest, the spirits must be considered." [4] What the Moslem belief in jinn involves can best be indicated by giving here the table of contents of one of the standard works on the subject called *Akam ul Mirjan fi Ahkam al Jann* by Mohammed ibn Abdallah al-Shibli who died 789 A. H. It is for sale in every Moslem city throughout the world. I follow the chapter headings without note or comment: the reader will pardon its literalisms:

Introduction: Proof of the existence of Jinn.

Moslems, People of the Book and the infidels of the Arabs agree on the existence of jinn.

Great philosophers and physicians proclaim their existence —

Beginning of creation of jinn.

The origin of jinn is fire as the origin of man is earth.

Bodies of jinn.

---

[3] Skeat's "Malay Magic," pp. 95–96.
[4] "Living Christ and Dying Heathenism," p. 80.

Kinds of jinn.

Residence of jinn.

Diversification of jinn.

Demons' ability of diversification.

God gave different forms to angels, jinn and men.

Some dogs are of the jinn.

Jinn look at the private parts of man when exposed.

What prevents demons from sleeping at men's houses.

Man's Companion of the jinn, the Qarina.

Jinn eat and drink.

Some traditions concerning this subject.

The Devil eats and drinks with his left hand.

What prevents jinn from taking the food of man.

Jinn marry and beget children.

That jinn have responsibilities.

Were there any prophets of jinn before the Prophet? The jinn are included in the mission of the Prophet.

The jinn went to the Prophet and heard him.

Sects of jinn.

Worship of jinn with man.

Reward of jinn.

Infidels of jinn enter the Fire.

Believers of jinn enter Paradise.

Do the believers of jinn see God in Paradise? Prayers behind a jinni.

A jinn passed between the hands of a praying man.

A man kills a jinni.

Marriage of jinn.

Jinn expose themselves to women.

Some jinn prevent others from exposing themselves to women.

If a jinn cohabited with a woman must she purify herself? The hermaphrodites are the sons of the jinn.

What if a jinn robs a woman of her husband?

Prohibition of eating and burnt offerings of jinn.

Jinn give *fatwas*.

Jinn preach to men.

Jinn teach medicine to men.

Jinn and men quarrel before men.

Jinn fear men.

Jinn obey men.

How to get refuge against jinn.

The influence of the Koranic verses on the bodies of jinn.

Why jinn obey amulets.

Solomon was the first man who took servants of Jinn.

What must be written for the sick.

Jinn reward men for good and evil.

How jinn cast down men.

How jinn enter men's bodies.

Are the motions of the epileptic due to jinn?   How to heal him.

The plague is of jinn.

The passions caused by Satan.

The evil eye caused by Jinn.

Its effect on men.

Jinn are bound with chains in the month of Ramadan.

The worship of jinn by men.

Jinn foretell the mission of the Prophet.   Heaven is guarded from them by shooting stars.

Jinn told of the Prophet's attack.

Jinn told of his converts.

Jinn told of Badr story.

Jinn told of the murdering of Said ibn Ebada.

It is allowed to ask jinn concerning the past, not the future.

Testimony of jinn on the day of Judgment.

Jinn lament and eugolize several dead Moslems.

Was Satan of the angels?

Did God speak to Satan?

Satan's fault in saying he is better than Adam.

Satan's whispering.

God's name drives away the whisper.   Stories concerning that.

Satan's call to man.

Evil-doing is desired by Satan.

How Satan seduces man.

Satan is always with the one who contradicts others.

The learned man is stronger than the pious before Satan.

Satan weeps at the death of the believer for being unable to seduce him.

Angels wonder at the escape of the believer's heart from Satan.

The four wailings of Satan.

Satan's throne is over the sea.

Satan's place.

Satan gave his five children five positions.

The presence of Satan at cohabitation.

The presence of Satan at the birth of every child.

Satan runs through man's veins.

Satans expose themselves to boys at night.

What diverts Satan from boys.

Satan sleeps on the vacant bed.

Satan never takes a siesta.

Satan ties three knots over the head of the sleeping.

Bad dreams are from Satan.

Satan never imitates the Prophet.

The Sun arises and sets betwen the two horns of Satan.

The sitting-place of Satan.

Satan flees at prayer call.

Satan accompanies the unjust judge.

Satan walks in one shoe.

Satan flees if man repeats El-Sajäda.

Yawning, sleeping and sneezing are from Satan.

Haste is from Satan.

A donkey brays when he sees a demon.

Satan exposes himself to the people of the mosques.

Satan's pride not to have knelt down to Adam and to have seduced him to eat from the tree.

Is Eden in heaven or on earth?

Satan showed himself to Eve.

Satan showed himself to Noah in the ark.

Satan showed himself to Abraham when he was about to offer up Isaac.

Satan showed himself to Moses.

Satan showed himself to Zul Kifl.

Satan showed himself to Job.

Now all this — and nearly every chapter is a door to a world of groveling superstition and demonolatry — finds its parallel in the beliefs of the animist. Among them the earth, air and water are supposed to be peopled with spirits. They are most numerous in the forest and in the waste fields, where they lie in wait for the living, and afflict them with disease and madness, or drag them away to an awful death. " They prowl round the houses at night, they spy through the crevices of the partitions or come into the house in the form of some man or beast. Sometimes in epidemics they can even be seen. There are men who have the spiritual gift of being able to see spirits and souls. Sometimes these men see the spirit of the dead stepping behind the coffin and perching the soul of a living man upon it — the inevitable result of which is, that the man must die. The number of dangerous spirits to which human misery is traced back is legion. Names are given and attributes ascribed to spirits of particularly bad repute, such as the spirit who causes cholera: he is of a terrific size, and carries a mighty club with which he smites his victim to the earth." [5]

The spirits are mostly mischievous and ill-disposed. They lurk in tree-tops and all sorts of places and cause disease, misfortune and death. It is much more important to keep the hurtful ones in good humor than to honor the kindly disposed, who are, therefore, practically ignored.

There are all sorts of legends current among animists of India as to the origin of these ghosts or spirits, but most of them have some admixture proving their comparatively late date. A clear distinction must be made between gods and spirits. There are no gods in Animism proper. The word god implies a higher degree of personality, and where that is attributed to these spirits the influence of some more advanced creed can generally be traced. The impersonal element in Animism must strike any one who tries to investigate it. Undefined shadowy powers with no settled habitation sigh in the wind, whisper in the rustling leaf and lurk in silence in the tree-tops. They may attach themselves for longer or shorter periods to a particular object. Any striking natural feature such as a blasted or lonely tree, a waterfall, a mountain peak, is sure to be thus inhabited. But the primeval forest is their special domain, and as this is cleared little sacred groves must everywhere be left standing. Constantly one is told of some tree or grove, " a very strong spirit lives there," but if you ask its name or origin none can be assigned. Its existence and power are undoubted, and many tales of the mischief it has caused will be quoted in proof. In every particular the popular Moslem doctrine of jinn is Animistic, *except their belief in Allah as Lord of jinn,* as well as the Lord of men. He is over all, God blessed forever and yet for fear of the jinn the Moslem masses are all their lifetime subject to fear and dread and bondage.

[5] " The Living Christ and Dying Heathenism," Warneck, p. 68.

What Warneck writes of the pagan tribes in Malaysia is not less true of their Moslem neighbors and of Moslem women and children in Arabia and the villages of the Delta. "Except in case of necessity," he says, "no one leaves the house after sunset or in moonlight, when the spirits swarm in great numbers. Houses and villages are shifted here and there to escape the influence of evil spirits. Sick people are carried secretly by night into another house to get away from the tormenting spirit. They prefer to deceive the spirits. During harvest loud singing and whistling are avoided, lest the spirits should suppose that men were rejoicing at an abundant harvest, and out of envy take their share." [6]

When I traveled in Yemen nothing so distressed my Arab companions as the awful habit of whistling. There are traditions to prove that Mohammed forbade any one to blow a pipe or whistle especially at night-time.

In regard to devil-worship and the fear of evil spirits, Wilkinson says that in Malay "the upper stratum is, of course, Moslem; the Malays accept the whole demonology of the Persians and Arabs and have even added to it by assuming mere demon-epithets such as "accursed" (mala'un) or "misbegotten" (haramzadah, jadah) to be the names of new varieties of devils. The next stratum is Hindu because Hanuman is still vaguely remembered as a dog-faced or horse-faced demon, meteors are described as the ghostly arrows of Arjuna, and the legends of the Indian Ramayana have become folk-lore in the Northern States. The ancient literature of the Malays is also full of references to Hindu mythology." His concluding words are significant:

"It is comparatively easy to identify those portions of Malay demonology which owe their existence to the historic Moslem or Hindu influenecs, but below these upper strata of beliefs we find further strata belonging to primeval religions

[6] "The Living Christ and Dying Heathenism," p. 79.

of whose character we know very little. We are here dealing with a very mixed race of people who have probably preserved traditions handed down to them from several distinct sources. A few facts stand out fairly distinctly. The fishermen along the coast of the Peninsula sacrifice to four great spirits of the sea who go by many names but whose scope of authority is always the same; one is the Spirit of Bays, another that of Banks or Beaches, another that of Headlands, and the last and fiercest is the Spirit of Tideways or Mid-currents. Most of the designations given to these ancient divinities are merely descriptive of their functions. So long as things go well, the names of the four Moslem Archangels are considered sufficient; if things go badly Sanscrit words are used; if matters become desperate, the fisherman throws prudence to the winds and appeals to the spirits in pure Indonesian terms which they cannot fail to understand." [7]

[7] "Malay Beliefs," pp. 26–27.

# CHAPTER VIII

## PAGAN PRACTICES IN CONNECTION WITH THE PILGRIMAGE

WHEN we consider Mecca, Mohammed's words of prophecy in the second chapter of his book seem to have been literally fulfilled: "So we have made you the center of the nations that you should bear witness to men." The old pagan pantheon has become the religious sanctuary and the goal of universal pilgrimage for one-seventh of the human race.

From Sierra Leone to Canton, and from Tobolsk to Cape Town, the faithful spread their prayer carpets, build their houses (in fulfillment of an important tradition, even their outhouses!) and bury their dead toward the meridian of Mecca. If the Moslem world could be viewed from an aëroplane, the observer would see concentric circles of living worshipers covering an ever-widening area, and one would also see vast areas of Moslem cemeteries with every grave dug toward the sacred city.

The earliest settlements at Mecca were undoubtedly due to the fact that the caravan trade from South Arabia northward found here a stopping place near the spring of Zem Zem, long before the time of Mohammed, just as the early Roman settlements at Wiesbaden and other places in Germany were so located because of the medicinal waters.

The sacred Mosque, Masjid al Haram, with the Ka'aba as its center, is located in the middle of the city. Mecca lies in a hot, sandy valley, absolutely without verdure and surrounded by rocky, barren hills, destitute of trees or even shrubs. The valley is about 300 feet wide and 4,000 feet long, and slopes towards the south. The Ka'aba or House of God (*Beit Allah*) is located in the bed of the valley. All

146

the streets slope toward it, and it occupies, as it were, the pit of a theater.

The Ka'aba proper stands in an oblong space 250 paces long and 200 broad, surrounded by colonnades, which are used as schools and as a general meeting place for pilgrims. The outer enclosure has nineteen gates and six minarets; within the enclosure is the well of Zem Zem, the great pulpit, the staircase used to enter the Ka'aba door, which is high above the ground, and two small mosques called al Kubattain. The remainder of the space is occupied by pavements and gravel, where prayers are said by the four orthodox sects, each having its own allotted space.

In the southeast corner of the Ka'aba, about five feet from the ground, is the famous Black Stone, the oldest treasure of Mecca. The stone is a fragment resembling black volcanic rock, sprinkled with reddish crystals, and worn smooth by the touch of centuries. It was undoubtedly an aërolite and owes its reputation to its fall from the sky. Moslem historians do not deny that it was an object of worship before Islam. In Moslem tradition it is connected with the history of the patriarchs, beginning as far back as Adam.

The word Ka'aba signifies a cube, although the measurements, according to Ali Bey, one of the earliest writers who gives us a scientific account of the pilgrim ceremonies, do not justify its being so called. Its height is thirty-four feet four inches, and the four sides measure thirty-eight feet four inches, thirty-seven feet two inches, thirty-one feet, seven inches, and twenty-nine feet. The cloth covering is renewed every year. At present it is made of silk and cotton tissue woven at Khurunfish, the factory site in Cairo. The time of departure of the annual procession which takes it to Mecca is one of the great feast days in Cairo.

Formerly, we are told, the whole of the Koran text was woven into the Ka'aba covering. Now the inscription contains the words, " Verily, the first house founded for mankind to worship in is that at Mecca, a blessing and a direction to all believers." Seven other short chapters of the Koran are also woven into this tapestry, namely, the Chapter of the Cave, Miriam, Al Amran, Repentance, T.H., Y.S., and Tabarak.

The final duty of righteous Moslems and the most important ceremony of the Moslem religion is the pilgrimage to Mecca. The pilgrimage (Hajj) to Mecca is not only one of the pillars of the religion of Islam, but it has proved one of the strongest bonds of union and has always exercised a tremendous influence as a missionary agency. Even to-day the pilgrims who return from Mecca to their native villages in Java, India and West Africa are fanatical ambassadors of the greatness and glory of Islam. From an ethical standpoint, the Mecca pilgrimage, with its superstitious and childish ritual, is a blot upon Mohammedan monotheism. But as a great magnet to draw the Moslem world together with an annual and ever-widening *esprit de corps,* the Mecca pilgrimage is without a rival. . . . For the details of the pilgrimage one must read Burckhardt, Burton, or other of the score of travelers who have risked their lives in visiting the forbidden cities of Islam. The record of their heroism has been compiled in one short volume by Augustus Ralli under the title " Christians at Mecca " (Heinemann, London, 1909). The earliest European pilgrim was Ludovico Bartema who reached Mecca in 1503. The most accurate in his description of the ceremonies of the *Hajj* is Burckhardt (1814–5), the most fascinating, Burton (1853), and it remained for a Hollander, Christiaan Snouck Hurgronje, to give us a history of Mecca, a photographic atlas of the city, and a philosophical dissertation on the pilgrimage.[1] " It is

[1] " Het Mekkaansche Feest," Leiden, 1880 and Mekka 2 vols. in German. The latter book is accompanied by a photographic atlas.

possible," says Ralli, " to divide Christian pilgrims to Mecca into three groups. First come those from Bartema to Pitts, inclusive, whom I have already compared to a cloud of light skirmishers. They are followed by the votaries of science — Badia, Seetzen, Burckhardt, Hurgronje. In a parallel column advance those impelled by love of adventure or curiosity — von Maltzan, Bicknell, Keane, Courtellemont. Burton belongs to both the latter groups; Wallin to the first, but he fell on evil days; and it is hard to classify Roches.

"It would tax the ingenuity of most of us to find such another heterogeneous collection of men devoted to one theme. It is a far cry from the humble Pitts to the princely Badia, from the scientific Burckhardt to the poetical Courtellemont, from the impersonal Hurgronje to the autobiographical Roches, from the obscure Wild to the world-famous Burton. Such contrasts might be pursued in the written records that remain; between Burckhardt's orderly accumulation of facts and Keane's rollicking narrative. But suffice it that the members of this select company, differing in time and country, aim and temperament, are united by the single bond of a strange adventure." This strange adventure led them all to observe the pagan rites of the great monotheistic faith of Islam, of which the ceremonies in brief are as follows: After donning the garb of a pilgrim and performing the legal ablutions, the *Hajji* visits the sacred mosque and kisses the Black Stone. He then runs around the Ka'aba seven times — thrice very rapidly and four times very slowly — in imitation of the motions of the planets. Next he offers a prayer: " O Allah, Lord of the Ancient House, free my neck from hell-fire, and preserve me from every evil deed; make me contented with the daily food Thou givest me, and bless me in all Thou hast granted." At " the place of Abraham " he also prays; he drinks water from the sacred well of Zem Zem and again kisses the Black Stone. Then the pilgrim runs

between the hills of Safa and Marwa. He visits Mina and
Arafat, a few miles from Mecca, and at the latter place
listens to a sermon. On his return he stops at Mina and
stones three pillars of masonry known as the " Great Devil,"
the " middle pillar " and the " first one " with seven small
pebbles. Finally, there is the sacrifice of a sheep or other
animal as the climax of the pilgrim's task. Snouck Hurgronje and Dozy have given us the theory of the origin of
these strange ceremonies in their monographs. The whole
pilgrimage is, in the words of Kuenen, "*a fragment of incomprehensible heathenism taken up undigested into Islam.*"
And as regards the veneration for the Black Stone, there is a
tradition that the Caliph Omar remarked: " By God, I
know that thou art only a stone and canst grant no benefit
or do no harm. And had I not known that the Prophet
kissed thee I would not have done it." (Nisai, Vol. II,
p. 38.)

There are two books that may be considered authoritative
on the ceremonies of the pilgrimage: Wellhausen's " Reste
Arabischen Heidentums," pp. 68–249, and Burton's " Pilgrimage to Al Medina and Mecca."

Burton's description of the ritual is complete:

" We then advanced towards the eastern angle of the
Ka'abah, in which is inserted the Black Stone; and, standing
about ten yards from it, repeated with upraised hands,
' There is no god but Allah alone, Whose Covenant is Truth,
and Whose Servant is Victorious. There is no god but
Allah, without Sharer; His is the Kingdom, to Him be
Praise, and He over all Things is potent.' After which we
approached as close as we could to the stone. A crowd of
pilgrims preventing our touching it that time, we raised our
hands to our ears, in the first position of prayer, and then
lowering them, exclaimed, ' O Allah (I do this), in Thy
Belief, and in verification of Thy Book, and in Pursuance of

Thy Prophet's Example — may Allah bless Him and preserve! O Allah, I extend my Hand to Thee, and great is my Desire to Thee! O accept Thou my Supplication and diminish my Obstacles, and pity my Humiliation, and graciously grant me Thy pardon!' After which, as we were still unable to reach the stone, we raised our hands to our ears, the palms facing the stone, as if touching it, recited the various religious formulæ, the Takbir, the Tahlil, and the Hamdilah, blessed the Prophet, and kissed the finger-tips of the right hand. The Prophet used to weep when he touched the Black Stone, and said that it was the place for the pouring forth of tears. According to most authors, the second Caliph also used to kiss it. For this reason most Moslems, except the Shafa'i school, must touch the stone with both hands and apply their lips to it, or touch it with the fingers, which should be kissed, or rub the palms upon it, and afterwards draw them down the face. Under circumstances of difficulty, it is sufficient to stand before the stone, but the Prophet's Sunnat, or practice, was to touch it. Lucian mentions adorations of the sun by kissing the hand.

"Then commenced the ceremony of *Tawaf,* or circumambulation, our route being the *Mataf* — the low oval of polished granite immediately surrounding the Ka'abah. I repeated, after my *Mutawwif,* or cicerone, 'In the Name of Allah, and Allah is omnipotent! I purpose to circuit seven circuits unto Almighty Allah, glorified and exalted!' This is technically called the Niyat (intention) of Tawaf. Then we began the prayer, 'O Allah (I do this), in Thy belief, and in Verification of Thy Book, and in Faithfulness to Thy Covenant, and in Perseverance of the Example of the Apostle Mohammed — may Allah bless Him and preserve!' till we reached the place Al-Multazem, between the corner of the Black Stone and the Ka'abah door. Here we ejaculated, 'O Allah, Thou hast Rights, so pardon my transgressing them.' Opposite the door we repeated, ' O Allah, verily the House is Thy House, and the Sanctuary Thy Sanctuary, and the Safeguard Thy Safeguard, and this is the Place of him who flies to Thee from (hell) Fire! At the little building called Makam Ibrahim, who took Refuge with and fled to Thee from the Fire! — O deny my Flesh and Blood, my Skin and Bones to the (eternal) Flames!' As we paced slowly round the north or Irak corner of the Ka'abah we exclaimed, ' O Allah, verily I take Refuge with Thee from Polytheism, and Disobedience, and Hypocrisy, and evil Conversation, and evil Thoughts concerning Family, and Property and Progeny!' When fronting the Mizab, or spout, we repeated the words, ' O Allah, verily I beg of Thee Faith which shall not decline, and a Certainty which shall not perish, and the good Aid of Thy Prophet Mohammed — may Allah bless Him and preserve! O Allah, shadow me in Thy Shadow, on that Day when there is no Shade but Thy Shadow, and cause me to drink from the Cup of Thine Apostle Mohammed — may Allah bless Him and preserve! that pleasant Draught after which is no Thirst to all Eternity, O Lord of Honor and Glory!' Turning the west corner, or the Rukn al-Shami, we exclaimed, ' O Allah, make it an acceptable Pilgrimage, and a Forgiveness of Sins, and a laudable Endeavor, and a pleasant Action (in Thy sight), and a store which perisheth not, O Thou Glorious! O Thou Pardoner!' This was repeated thrice, till we arrived at the Yamani, or south corner, where the crowd being less importunate, we touched the wall with the right hand, after the example of the Prophet, and kissed the finger-tips. Finally, between the south angle and that of the Black Stone, where our circuit would be completed, we said, ' O Allah, verily I take refuge with Thee from Infidelity, and I take Refuge from the Tortures of the Tomb, and from the Troubles of Life and Death. And I fly to Thee from Ignominy in this World and the Next, and I implore Thy Pardon for the Present and for the Future. O Lord, grant to me in this Life Prosperity, and in the next Life Prosperity, and save me from the Punishment of Fire.'

"Thus finished a Shaut, or single course round the house. Of these we performed the first three at the pace called Harwalah, very similar to the French *pas gymnastique,* or Tarammul, that is to say, 'moving the shoulders as if walking in sand.' The four latter are performed in Ta'ammul, slowly and leisurely, the reverse of the Sai, or running. These seven Ashwat, or courses, are called collectively the Usbu." (Burton's "Pilgrimage to Al Madinah and Mecca," pp. 164–167.)

He continues (p. 169): "Having kissed the stone we fought our way through the crowd to the place called Al-Multazem. Here we pressed our stomachs, chests, and right cheeks to the Ka'abah, raising our arms high above our heads and exclaiming, 'O Allah! O Lord of the Ancient House, free my Neck from Hell-fire, and preserve me from every ill Deed, and make me contented with that daily bread which Thou has given to me, and bless me in all Thou hast granted!' Then came the Istighfar, or begging of pardon: 'I beg Pardon of Allah the Most High, who, there is no other God but He, the Living, the Eternal, and unto Him I repent myself!' After which we blessed the Prophet, and then asked for ourselves all that our souls most desired."

Prayer is granted at fourteen places besides Al-Multazem, all of them connected, as we shall see, with the old idolatry of Arabia. Viz.:

1. At the place of circumambulation.
2. Under the Mizab, or spout of the Ka'aba.
3. Inside the Ka'aba.
4. At the well Zem Zem.

5. Behind Abraham's place of prayer.
6. On Mt. Safa.
7. On Mt. Marwah.
8. During the ceremony called " Al-Sai."
9. Upon Mount Arafat.
10. At Muzdalifah.
11. In Muna.
12. During the devil-stoning.
13. On first seeing the Ka'aba.
14. At the Hatim of Hijr.

" Muna," says Burton (Vol. II, p. 180), " more classically called Mina, is a place of considerable sanctity. Its three standing miracles are these: The pebbles thrown at ' the Devil' return by angelic agency to whence they came; during the three Days of Drying Meat rapacious beasts and birds cannot prey there; and lastly, flies do not settle upon the articles of food exposed so abundantly in the bazars. During pilgrimage houses are let for an exorbitant sum, and it becomes a 'World's Fair' of Moslem merchants. At all other seasons it is almost deserted, in consequence, says popular superstition, of the Rajm or (diabolical) lapidation. Distant about three miles from Meccah, it is a long, narrow, straggling village, composed of mud and stone houses of one or two stories, built in the common Arab style. Traversing a narrow street, we passed on the left the Great Devil, which shall be described at a future time. After a quarter of an hour's halt, spent over pipes and coffee, we came to an open space, where stands the Mosque ' Al-Khayf.' Here, according to some Arabs, Adam lies, his head being at one end of one long wall, and his feet at another, whilst the dome covers his omphalic region. After passing through the town we came to Batn al-Muhassir, 'The Basin of the Troubler' (Satan) at the beginning of a descent leading to Muzdalifah (the Approacher), where the road falls into the valley of the Arafat torrent.

"At noon we reached the Muzdadifah, also called Masha al-Haram, the 'Place dedicated to religious Ceremonies.' It is known in Al-Islam as 'the Minaret without the Mosque,' opposed to Masjid Nimrah, which is 'the Mosque without the Minaret.' Half-way between Muna and Arafat, it is about three miles from both."

Burton: (Vol. II, pp. 180–7): "Arafat, anciently called Jabal Ilal, 'the Mount of Wrestling in Prayer' and now Jabal al-Rahmah, the 'Mount of Mercy' is a mass of coarse granite split into large blocks, with a thin coat of withered thorns."

(Pp. 188–9): "The Holy Hill owes its name and honors to a well-known legend. When our first parents forfeited Heaven by eating wheat, which deprived them of their primeval purity, they were cast down upon earth. The serpent descended at Ispahan, the peacock at Kabul, Satan at Bilbays (others say Semnan and Seistan), Eve upon Arafat and Adam at Ceylon. The latter, determining to seek his wife, began a journey, to which earth owes its present mottled appearance. Wherever our first father placed his foot — which was large — a town afterwards arose; between strides will always be 'country.' Wandering for many years, he came to the Mountain of Mercy, where our common mother was continually calling upon his name, and their recognition gave the place the name of Arafat. Upon its summit, Adam, instructed by the archangel Gabriel, erected a Mada'a, or place of prayer: and between this spot and the Nimrah Mosque the couple abode till death."

Burton: (Vol. II, pp. 203–205): "We found a swarming crowd in the narrow road opposite the 'Jamrat-al-Akabah,' or, as it is vulgarly called, the Shaytan al-Kabir — the 'Great Devil.' These names distinguish it from another pillar, the 'Wusta,' or Central Place (of stoning), built in the middle of Muna, and a third at the eastern end, 'Al-Aula' or the 'First Place.'

" The 'Shaytan al-Kabir' is a dwarf buttress of rude masonry, about eight feet high by two-and-a-half broad, placed against a rough wall of stones at the Meccan entrance to Muna. Finding an opening, we approached within about five cubits of the place, and holding each stone between the thumb and forefinger of the right hand, we cast it at the pillar, exclaiming, 'In the name of Allah, and Allah is Almighty! (I do this) in Hatred of the Fiend and to his Shame.' After which came the Tahlil and the 'Sana' or praise to Allah. The seven stones being duly thrown, we retired, and entering the barber's booth, took our places upon one of the earthen benches around it. This barber shaved our heads, and, after trimming our beards and cutting our nails, made us repeat these words: 'I purpose loosening my Ihram according to the Practice of the Prophet, Whom may Allah bless and preserve! O, Allah, make unto me in every Hair, a Light, a Purity, and a generous Reward! In the name of Allah, and Allah is Almighty!'"

After following all these details of the ceremony with Burton for our guide, we are ready to ask the why and wherefore of the performances.

If the Jews and Christians had hearkened to the call of Mohammed at Medina when he made the Kibla, Jerusalem, the course of Moslem history might have been that of an oriental Unitarian sect. But when the Prophet changed the Kibla from Jerusalem to Mecca he compromised with idolatry and the result was that *Islam at its very center has remained pagan.* The transformation of the old Pantheon of the Arabs into the house of God which Abraham rebuilt and which Adam himself founded was the legend to justify the adoption of these pagan practices. Other ceremonies which had noth-

THE CITY OF MECCA; IN THE CENTER, THE KA'ABA

Once the central shrine of Arab Paganism, now of the Mohammedan Faith, it stands in the *Harem* or sacred court

ing to do with the Ka'aba but which were performed at certain places near Mecca were also adapted to the new religion. In the tenth year A. H. Mohammed made his pilgrimage to Mecca, the old shrine of his forefathers, and every detail of superstitious observance which he fulfilled has become the norm in Islam. As Wellhausen says the result is that " we now have the stations of a Calvary journey without the history of the Passion." Pagan practices are explained away by inventing Moslem legends attributed to Bible characters, and the whole is an incomprehensible jumble of fictitious lore.

The Ka'aba itself in its plan and structure is a heathen temple. The covering of the Ka'aba goes back to old heathenism. The Temple was the Bride and she received costly clothing. The building stands with its four corners nearly to the points of the compass; not the sides of the building, but the corners point N.S.E. and W. We may therefore expect, as is the case, that the holy objects were at the corners of the building. The Black Stone is in the E.S.E. corner; the other four corners also had sacred stones which are still places of special worship. The front of the Ka'aba is the N.E. side, and the door is not in the middle but near the Black Stone. Between the Stone and the door is the *Multazam,* the place where the pilgrim presses himself against the building, hugs the curtain and calls upon God. On the N.W. side there is an enclosure in the shape of a half-circle called the *Hajr,* or the *Hatim.* Wellhausen has a note (p. 74) to show that this enclosure was formerly a part of the Ka'aba but that shortly before Mohammed's time the building was restored on a smaller foundation. This enclosure, therefore, marks the original size of the heathen temple. There seems to be no doubt that the Black Stone was the real idol of the Ka'aba. *Bait Allah* and *Masjid,* according to Wellhausen, originally signified " the stone " and not " the temple." In ancient days there was an empty well inside the Ka'aba to receive votive offerings. In front of the well stood a human image, that of the god Hobal. One may still see a similar worship at the tomb of Eve, near Jiddah, where there is a well for offerings under the middle dome which is over the navel of Mother Eve. It has been thought that Hobal, the main god of the Ka'aba, was perhaps "Allah" himself. Others say that the word has connection with Baal the sun-god. When we remember the circumambulation of the Ka'aba seven times, three times rapidly and four times more slowly in imitation of the inner and outer planets, it is not strange to find Baal the sun-god chief of the temple. The present place called *Maqam Ibrahim* (Sura 2: 119) was originally a stone for offerings. A short distance outside of Mecca are the two hills Al Safa and Al Marwa; both of these names signify "a stone," i. e., an idol. The road between them runs almost parallel with the front of the Ka'aba and directly east is the well of Zem Zem, originally also a place for sacred offerings. It contained two golden gazelles among other things. There are many other sacred places in the vicinity formerly associated with idol-worship now transformed by Moslem legend into graves of the saints, etc. Arafat and Muzdalifa are at present only stations where one stops on the pilgrimage. No offerings are brought there. Formerly Muzdalifa was a place of fire-worship. Wackidi says: "Mohammed rode from Arafat towards the fire kindled in Muzdalifa; this is the hill of the holy fire." The mountain was called Quzah and Wellhausen thinks it may have been the place of the thunder-god whose sign was the rainbow. (Quzah.)

The early history of Mecca shows that it was a place of pilgrimage long before Mohammed. The battle of Islam for the conquest of Arabia was determined at Mecca. This was the capture of the Pagan center. In conquering it Islam was itself conquered. "There is no god but Allah"— and the old idol-shrines at Mecca? Dozy has shown that Mecca was an old Jewish center, but his conclusions have been disputed by later writers.[4]

Not only the pilgrimage itself, but its calendar goes back to paganism. The names of the Arabic months have many of them a pagan significance. Of course the calendar was solar, but Mohammed changed it into a lunar calendar. Moharram was the month of the great feast. Tree worship and stone worship as we shall see later belong to the old heathenism. In Nagran a date-palm served as god. A number of sacred trees or groves between Mecca and Medina which formerly were idol temples, are now visited because "Mohammed resided there, prayed there, or had his hair cut under them." (See Bokhari, 1 : 68–3 : 36.)

Prof. A. J. Wensinck in writing on the Hajj in the Encyclopedia of Islam (Vol. II, p. 22 ff.) gives it as his opinion that "great fairs were from early times associated with the Hadjdj which was celebrated on the conclusion of the date-harvest. These fairs were probably the main thing to Muhammed's contemporaries, as they still are to many Muslims. For the significance of the religious ceremonies had even then lost its meaning for the people." Nevertheless the significance of the various rites and ceremonies although no longer understood clearly, point to a pagan origin. Snouck Hurgronje thinks he sees a solar rite in the *wukuf* ceremony. Wensinck says: "The god of Muzdalifa was Quzah, the thunder-god. A fire was kindled on the sacred hill also called Quzah. Here a halt was made and this *wukuf* has a still greater similarity to that on Sinai, as in both cases the thunder-god is revealed in fire. It may further be presumed that the traditional custom of making as much noise as possible and of shooting was originally a sympathetic charm to call forth the thunder."

[4] "De Israeliten te Mekka van David's tyd enz," Dozy (Leiden).

As soon as the sun was visible, the *ifada* to Mina used to begin in pre-Islamic times. Mohammed therefore ordained that this should begin before sunrise; here again we have the attempt to destroy a solar rite. In ancient times they are said to have sung during the ifada, "*ashrik thabir kaima nughir.*" The explanation of these words is uncertain; it is sometimes translated: "Enter into the light of morning, Thabir, so that we may hasten." And again we know from a statement in Ibn Hisham (ed. Wustenfeld, p. 76, et seq.), that the stone throwing only began after the sun had crossed the meridian. Houtsma has made it probable that the stoning was originally directed at the sun-demon; important support is found for this view in the fact that the Pilgrimage originally coincided with the autumnal equinox as similar customs are found all over the world at the beginning of the four seasons. With the expulsion of the sun-demon, whose harsh rule comes to an end with summer, worship of the thunder-god who brings fertility and his invocation may easily be connected, as we have seen above at the festival in Muzdalifa. The name *tarwiya*, "moistening," may also be explained in this connection as a sympathetic rain-charm, traces of which survive in the libation of Zem Zem water. Other explanations of the stone-throwing are given. Van Vloten connects it with snake-worship or demonolatry and as proof gives the expression used in the Koran so frequently, *As Shaitan ar rajim* — "the pelted devil." Chauvin finds in it "an example of *scopelism* (sic) the object being to prevent the cultivation of the ground by the Meccans." Both theories have been refuted by Houtsma.[5] Regarding the throwing of the pebbles in the pilgrimage ceremony we may compare what Frazer says in his chapter on the transference of evil to stones and sticks among pagans and animists ("The Scapegoat," pp. 23–24):

[5] See Art. "Hadjdj in the Encyclop. of Islam," Vol. II, p. 200.

" Sometimes the motive for throwing the stone is to ward off a dangerous spirit; sometimes it is to cast away an evil; sometimes it is to acquire a good. Yet, perhaps, if we could trace them back to their origin in the mind of primitive man, we might find that they all resolve themselves more or less exactly *into the principle of the transference of evil.* For to rid themselves of an evil and to acquire a good are often merely opposite sides of one and the same operation; for example, a convalescent regains health in exactly the same proportion as he shakes off his malady. And though the practice of throwing stones at dangerous spirits, especially at mischievous and malignant ghosts of the dead, appears to spring from a different motive, yet it may be questioned whether the difference is really as great to the savage as it seems to us." . . . " Thus the throwing of the sticks or stones would be a form of ceremonial purification, which among primitive peoples is commonly conceived as a sort of physical rather than moral purgation, a mode of sweeping or scouring away the morbid matter by which the polluted person is supposed to be infected. *This notion perhaps explains the rite of stone-throwing observed by pilgrims at Mecca;* on the day of sacrifice every pilgrim has to cast seven stones on a cairn, and the rite is repeated on the three following days. The traditional explanation of the custom is that Mohammed here drove away the devil with a shower of stones; but the original idea may perhaps have been that the pilgrims cleanse themselves by transferring their ceremonial impurity to the stones which they fling on the heap."

Dr. Snouck Hurgronje gives, in addition, the following pagan practices of the pilgrimage. It is commonly supposed that in the time of ignorance two idols were worshiped on Safa and Marwa, and the names of these idols are mentioned. In the second chapter of the Koran, Verse 153, the pagan custom observed by the Arabs before Islam is sanctioned.  Prof. Hurgronje thinks that the existence of the small sanctuaries around the Ka'aba are due to the existence of sacred trees, stones and wells, which formerly were pagan places of worship, but were afterwards Islamized by stating that under such a tree the Prophet sat down — this stone spoke to him — on that stone he sat down — and certain wells even were made sacred because Mohammed spat in them. (Azraqi, p. 438, quoted in Hurgronje, p. 123.)

A little south of the valley of Arafat there is a small hill called the Hill of Grace, on the top of which there was formerly a small building with a dome.  At present it is connected with Um Salima, but its origin is lost in obscurity. When the Wahhabis came to Mecca and desired to purify it of idolatry, they destroyed these places.  Prof. Hurgronje concludes that while the general ritual of the pilgrimage is Mohammedan, there are many practices that now are condemned as innovations, which are in reality old Arabian and pagan in their character.  His conclusion at the end of his learned paper is this:  " Should Sprenger's hope ever be fulfilled,— and it is not probable — that a school of Tübingen critics should arise in Islam, then surely the feast at Mecca and the pilgrim ceremonies would be the first to disappear among the practices which belong to the heart of the Moslem religion."

# CHAPTER IX

## MAGIC AND SORCERY

In no monotheistic religion are magic and sorcery so firmly entrenched as they are in Islam; for in the case of this religion they are based on the teaching of the Koran and the practice of the Prophet. In one celebrated passage [1] we read: " they follow that which the devils recited against Solomon's kingdom;— it was not Solomon who misbelieved, but the devils who misbelieved, teaching men sorcery,— and what has been revealed to the two angels at Babylon, Harut and Marut, yet these taught no one until they said, ' We are but a temptation, so do not misbelieve.' Men learn from them only that by which they may part man and wife; but they can harm no one therewith, unless with the permission of God, and they learn what hurts them and profits them not. And yet they knew that he who purchased it would have no portion in the future; but sad is the price at which they have sold their souls, had they but known. But had they believed and feared, a reward from God were better, had they but known."

In the commentaries we have a long account of how these two angels, Harut and Marut, had compassion on the frailties of mankind and were sent down to earth to be tempted. They both sinned, and being permitted to choose whether they would be punished now or hereafter, chose the former and are still suspended by the feet at Babel in a rocky pit, where they are great teachers of magic.[2] There are other passages

[1] "The Qur'an," E. H. Palmer, Part I, Sura 11:96 ff.

[2] Hughes' *Dictionary of Islam*, p. 168. In a beautifully illustrated Persian book of Traditions found in the Sultaniah Museum, Cairo, there is a picture of these culprits.

in the Koran dealing with magic, in fact the book itself, as we have already seen, has magical power. The superstitions that obtained in Arabia before Islam have been perpetuated by it. No orthodox Moslem doubts that men are able to call forth the power of demons and Jinn by means of magic (*sihr*). Everywhere there are professional magicians, wizards and witches. The popular belief in them to-day in Arabia is well described by Doughty (Vol. II, p. 106). "Wellah," he said, "Sheykh Khalil, one of them sitting on such a beam, may ride in the night-time to Medina and return ere day, and no man know it; for they will be found in their houses when the people waken." "How may a witch that has an husband gad abroad by night, and the goodman not know it?" "If she take betwixt her fingers only a little of the ashes of the hearth, and sprinkle it on his forehead, the dead sleep will fall upon him till the morning. But though one knew his wife to be a witch, yet durst he not show it, nor put her away, for she might cause him to perish miserably! yet the most witches are known, and one of them, he added darkly, is a neighbor of ours. When it is the time to sleep they roam through the village ways: and I warn thee, Sheykh Khalil! for a thing which we looked not for may happen in a moment! have a care in thy coming home by night." "I would willingly see them." "Eigh! speak not so fool-hardily, except thou know some powerful spells to say against them. I have heard that *Dakhilallah* (a menhel, or man of God), once meeting with the witches did cry against them words which the Lord put into his heart, out of the Koran, and they fled from him shrieking that the pairs of hell were come upon them." "The witches," said the melancholy Imam, "are of all ages: they have a sheikh, who is a man, and he also is known." "And why are they not punished?" "Wellah, it is for fear of their malice. The hags assemble in dead hours of the night, and sitting in a place of ordures, they strip off their smocks, and annoint their bodies with cow milk (which in Arabia is esteemed medicinal), and then the witches cry, 'We be issued from the religion of Islam.' So they gad it in the dim streets, and woe worth any man returning lateward if they meet with him! For they will compel him to lie with them; and if he should deny them, they will change him into the form of some beast — an ox, a horse, or an ass: and he shall afterward lose his mind, and in the end perish miserably. But they eat, *wellah*, the heart (and he is aware of it) of him who consents to them, and suck the blood of his living body; and after this he will become a fool, and be a dazing man all his days."

The sorcerer who desires to exercise his magic art begins by sacrificing a black cock. He then reads his spell, ties his knots, or flings his magical readings into the wells. All this is done in the same fashion to-day as was customary before Mohammed. To such practices the last two chapters of the Koran refer. Much more important and more widespread than the magic of producing demonic influence is the magic of acting against them — what might be called " anti-magic." Illness, especially in the case of children, is caused by Jinn. The one remedy is therefore magic. And consists in stroking or rubbing, the tying of knots, or spitting and blowing. I have seen an educated *kadi* in Arabia solemnly repeat chapters from the Koran and then blow upon the body of his dying child, in order to bring back health again. The Rev. Edwin E. Calverley tells this story: " What do you suppose I have just seen? " exclaimed an excited Jew to a Christian in a Moslem city of Arabia.

" What was it? Where did you see it? "

" There was a whole group of Arab women standing outside the big door of the mosque and they all had cups or glasses in their hands."

" Oh, they were beggars, and they were waiting for the men to get through reciting their prayers."

" But no, they were not beggars, because I saw the beggars at another door, and besides, I watched the men as they came out of the mosque, and, it is hard to believe it, they spat right into the cups and glasses and bowls that the women and children and even men held out to them. Some of the Moslems spat into one cup after another,— into every cup that was put near them. I never saw the like in all my life ! "

" That is indeed most strange and revolting ! What were they doing it for ? I'm sure I don't know. Why don't you go and ask some Moslem about it ? "

Soon he came back, utterly disgusted.

" Did you find out what the purpose is ? "

" Yes, and that is the most repulsive thing of all ! I wouldn't have believed it about them if anybody but one of their own religion had told it to me. Those people with the cups and bowls have some friend or some one in their family who is sick, and they are collecting the spittle of the men who have just finished their prayers for their sick ones at home."

My Moslem friends could not give me the religious authority supporting their unhygienic custom, but such authority exists nevertheless. Al Bukhari (Sahih VII, p. 150) gives two traditions reporting Mohammed's sanction for the practice. After recording the usual " chain of witnesses, Al Bukhari relates that " Aisha (May Allah be pleased with her) said that the Prophet (Allah bless him and give him peace) told a sick man, ' In the name of Allah the earth of our land and the saliva of some of us cure our sick, by the permission of our Lord.' "

Spitting is used for all difficult performances, for example, to open locks that will not otherwise yield to the key. (See

Doughty Vol. I, p. 527 and Vol. II, p. 164.) In this way they cure sick camels. Doughty says (Vol. II, p. 164): " Another time I saw Salih busy to cure a mangy *thelûl;* he sat with a bowl of water before him, and mumbling thereover he spat in it, and mumbled solemnly and spat many times; and after a half-hour of this work the water was taken to the sick beast to drink. Spitting (a despiteful civil defilement) we have seen to be some great matter in their medicine. Is it that they spit thus against the malicious jinn? Parents bid their young children spit upon them: and an Arabian father will often softly say to the infant son in his arms, ' Spit upon babu! spit, my darling.' "

Another case he gives as follows: (Vol. I, p. 527): " A young mother yet a slender girl, brought her wretched babe, and bade me spit upon the child's sore eyes; this ancient Semitic opinion and custom I have afterward found wherever I came in Arabia. Meteyr nomads in el-Kasim have brought me, some of them bread and some salt, that I should spit in it for their sick friends. Their gossips followed to make this request with them and when I blamed their superstition they answered simply, that ' such was the custom here from time out of mind.' "

In regard to blowing and spitting as methods of healing or conferring a blessing, it is important to note the Arabic distinction between *nafakha* and *nafatha,* the latter means to *blow with spittle.* A Moslem correspondent in Yemen points out this distinction and says that there is no real healing power or hurting power in the dry breath. It is the spittle or soul-stuff that transfers good or ill.

Among the animistic tribes of West Africa spitting is one of the means of conferring a blessing. The same thing is true among the Barotse of South Africa. Mr. Nassau writes: " The same Benga word, *tuwaka,* to spit, is one of the two words which mean also ' to bless.' In pronouncing a blessing there is a violent expulsion of breath, the hand or head of the one blessed being held so near the face of the one blessing that sometimes in the act spittle is actually expelled upon him." [3]

Concerning South Africa he quotes a testimony of Wilson: " Relatives take leave of each other with elaborate ceremony. They spit upon each other's faces and heads, or rather, pretend to do so, for they do not actually emit saliva. They also pick up blades of grass, spit upon them, and stick them about the beloved dead. They also spit on the hands: all this is done to ward off evil spirits. Spittle also acts as a kind of taboo. When they do not want a thing touched they spit on straws, and stick them all about the object."

In India, we are told, many women with their little children go to the mosques at the prayer hour and stand near the door. After prayers as the people come out from the mosques still repeating their *wazifas* they breathe on these children. Often in case of sickness in the family some one is sent for (such as an Imam) who repeats some *suras* or verses of the Koran and either directly breathes on the sick or on a little water which is given to the sick to drink. Sometimes he touches his tongue with his forefinger and then the tongue of the sick, and in this way saliva is used for healing purposes."

" In Yemen," writes a Moslem correspondent, " it is common to blow on the sick or use saliva for healing. But it is necessary that the one who blows or uses spittle should be a pious man, and that before he does it the *Fatiha* be repeated. This practice is in accordance with the example of the Prophet as he worked miracles in this way and his Companions did likewise."

In Tabriz, Persia, a holy man often is asked to say prayers for the sick and breathe on them.

" Some people," says Mr. Gerdener of South Africa, " who

[3] " Fetichism in West Africa," p. 213.

have been to Mecca are supposed to possess the power to breathe on the face of the sick and cure them. Passing the hand in front of the face is also resorted to, especially for children."

In Bahrein, Arabia, saliva mixed with oil, is used as an ointment and is also taken internally. It is collected in a cup from various contributors!

The Mullah's breath is supposed to be efficacious in sickness. He receives a fee for this treatment. "Mrs. D. called on the women of Sheikh J——'s household, and he was in the room doctoring a sick boy. He sat beside him," writes Miss Kellien, "muttering pious phrases supposedly from the Koran, and punctuating every few words by spitting towards the child's face, and then watching her to see how she took it. She said his wives were convulsed with laughter which they were careful to hide, and had apparently little faith in the virtue of such treatment."

To cure headache in Algeria the *taleb* will take hold of the patient's head with the first finger and thumb across the brow and gently blow upon the patient's face until the pain has disappeared. A *taleb* will spit in the mouth of a patient supposed to be possessed by *jinn,* knock him sharply on the back between the shoulder-blades, and the evil spirit will leave him.

In Tunis if a person is ill, some one is brought who spits on his own hands and wipes them over the sick person's face and hands.

Among Moslems everywhere sneezing has an evil significance and may have bad results. To ward these off, those who are present utter a pious formula. This was the custom before Islam as well as to-day. Gaping is of the devil (Bukhari 2:180), therefore it is followed by the expression, " I take refuge in God (from Satan)."

The chief danger, however, always present to the Semitic

mind, is that of the "evil eye" — not only of him who envies but also of him who admires. It is also feared in the glance of the *Jinn* and the *'afrit*. Mohammed was a believer in the baneful influence of the evil eye. Asma Bint 'Umais relates that she said, " O Prophet, the family of Ja'far are affected by the baneful influences of an evil eye; may I use spells for them or not?" The Prophet said, " Yes, for if there were anything in the world which would overcome fate, it would be an evil eye." [4]

Again we read,[5] " Anas says: ' The Prophet permitted a spell (*ruqyah*) being used to counteract the ill effects of the evil eye; and on those bitten by snakes or scorpions.' " (Sahih Muslim — p. 233.)

Um Salmah relates " that the Prophet allowed a spell to be used for the removal of yellowness in the eye, which, he said, proceeded from the malignant eye." (Sahih Al-Bokhari, p. 854.)

" 'Auf ibn Malik says ' The Prophet said there is nothing wrong in using spells, provided the use of them does not associate anything with God.' " (Mishkat, Book XXI, ch. I.)

The magic resting in *knots* is also referred to in the Koran. In the Chapter of the Daybreak [6] we read: " Say, I seek refuge in the Lord of the Daybreak, from the evil of what He has created; and from the evil of the night when it cometh on; and from the evil of the *blowers upon knots.*" That the custom is animistic is clear from Frazer's description of it in his work on Taboo [7]: " At a difficult birth the Battaks of Sumatra make a search through the possessions of husband and wife and untie everything that is tied up in a bundle.

[4] *Mishkat*, XXI, C. I., Part 2.
[5] Hughes' *Dictionary*, p. 303.
[6] Surah 113.
[7] Vol. II, pp. 296–7 and 300.

In some parts of Java, when a woman is in travail, everything in the house that was shut is opened, in order that the birth may not be impeded; not only are doors opened and the lids of chests, boxes, rice-pots, and water-buts lifted up, but even swords are unsheathed and spears drawn out of their cases. Customs of the same sort are practiced with the same intention in other parts of the East Indies." He goes on to say, "We meet with the same superstition and the same custom at the present day in Syria. The persons who help a Syrian bridegroom to don his wedding garments take care that no knot is tied on them nor buttoned, for they believe that a buttoned or a knot tied would put it within the power of his enemies to deprive him of his nuptial rights by magical means."

Among the Jews also knots played an important part in magic. " Even to-day among the children of Kiev one of the ways of determining who shall be ' it ' is to tie a knot in a handkerchief; the children pick out the corners, and the one selecting the knotted corner is ' it.' In Kovno, when a wart is removed a knot is tied around it with a thread and this knot is placed under the threshold." [8]

Commentators on the Koran relate that the reason for the revelation of the chapter quoted above was that a Jew named Lobeid, had, with the assistance of his daughters, bewitched Mohammed by tying eleven knots in a cord which they hid in a well. The Prophet falling ill in consequence, this chapter and that following it were revealed; and the angel Gabriel acquainted him with the use he was to make of them, and told him where the cord was hidden. The Khalif Ali fetched the cord, and the Prophet repeated over it these two chapters; at every verse a knot was loosed till on finishing the last words, he was entirely freed from the charm.[9]

[8] The Jewish Encyclopedia, article Knot.
[9] See " Al Razi," Vol. VIII, pp. 559–564. Here we also learn that an

In Malay magic, heathen practices are so thoroughly mixed up with Mohammedan prayers that it is hard to disentangle the threads of superstition. Skeat tells us that in order to injure an enemy the method followed is as follows:

" Take parings of nails, hair, eyebrows, saliva, etc., of your intended victim (sufficient to represent every part of his person), and make them up into his likeness with wax from a deserted bees' comb. Scorch the figure slowly by holding it over a lamp every night for seven nights and say:

" ' It is not wax that I am scorching.

" ' It is the liver, heart and spleen of So-and-so that I scorch.' After the seventh time burn the figure, and your victim will die." [10]

The following prayer is also used in burying a wax image of one's enemy after piercing it with the thorn of the palm tree:

"Peace be to you!  Ho, Prophet 'Tap, in whose charge the earth
      is,
  Lo, I am burying the corpse of Somebody,
  I am bidden (to do so) by the Prophet Mohammed,
  Because he (the corpse) was a rebel to God.
  Do you assist in killing him or making him sick;
  If you do not make him sick, if you do not kill him,
  You shall be a rebel against God,
  A rebel against Mohammed,
  It is not I who am burying him,
  It is Gabriel who is burying him.
  Do you too grant my prayer and petition, this very day that has
      appeared,
  Grant it by the grace of my petition within the fold of the Creed
      La ilaha." [11]

*afrit* used to tease Mohammed, so Gabriel taught him to repeat this chapter at bed-time. It was also given him as a charm against the evil eye.

[10] " Malay Magic," p. 570.
[11] " Malay Magic," p. 571.

In this way the one who performs magic absolves himself from blood-guiltiness by shifting the burden of his guilt to the shoulders of the Angel Gabriel.

The teaching of the Koran is to blame for other forms of magic; is it not the inspired word of God? Among the Moslems Solomon is a great historic figure. He is still looked upon as the ruler of the animal world; the very trappers in the jungle address their prey in the name of " God's prophet, Solomon." His adventures with the Queen of Sheba are recorded in romance, his seal (the pentacle) is drawn by sorcerers on talismans and gives its name to the five-pointed starfish, and his wealth, like the treasure of Korah, is much sought for by local magicians.

Miss Holliday says that one of the most prevalent forms of magic in Persia is filling a metal bowl with water, holding money or some metallic object between the thumb and forefinger and stirring the water with it; they divine by looking in the water. Sometimes a cloth is placed in the bowl and chirping sounds, like the voices of sparrows are heard. I have heard of a woman in Urumia who has a familiar spirit, who is sometimes visible and whose answers to questions have a muttering or chirping sound. Sometimes a metal plate is used with letters on the rim from which answers are deduced. " The family of my Moslem cook," writes Miss Holliday, " have a singular distinction, their house being what is known as an ' ojock,' literally, a hearthstone, or fireplace. This is a rare thing; women bring their small infants to him and making a noose of a handkerchief round his gun, pass the child three times through it, which is supposed to protect it from the evil eye. All the sons of this clan have this power of blessing and protecting which is unknown to other Moslems. They have peculiar customs; one is, that after the birth of a child all in the house must abstain from all food of animal origin for a week, till the mother has gone to the bath. The majority are monogamists and divorce is rare among them. My cook thinks there is but one other clan in this city which has the power of being an 'ojock.' Women here wishing to avert the evil eye from a young child, will bring it to my cook and give it to him as his own, then will give him money, with which he hires the mother, as the child's nurse, and she takes it away to her home."

She continues: "Two or three onions were pierced by a spit because the woman said the evil spirits did not like the odor or the looks of the sharp iron. Three eggs were put in a bowl at the pillow and stayed there till the mother was taken to the bath. When they left the house, one was broken and thrown out to attract the attention of the *jinns* to that, another when half way to the bath and the last when they reached the door, so that she could enter while their curiosity detained them without. A copy of the Koran was usually tied in a headkerchief and laid at the pillow.

"One must not come in 'on top of the baby' till the forty days are expired. So they would hold the baby over the door and I would enter the room under it. This was only for one who was not present at the birth."

"One form of magic very common in Cape Town," says Mr. Gerdener, "is the casting of dice, also human bones and pebbles of varied color. In fact all through the country even by Europeans, Moslem magic is believed in and they send for 'Malay doctors,' paying them large sums for humbug. The term Malay is synonymous in local newspaper circles with 'Moslem.' Amber beads, dried dates, flowers, Zem Zem water and sand or earth from Mohammed's grave are all used for good luck; dates and flowers for sickness, the flower being put into water and the newly born child bathed in it. The flower is subsequently taken out, dried and kept among the child's garments, until the next arrival. The sand or earth is worn in a rag round the neck to ward off sickness or to keep off evil spirits, of which the Moslem world seems to swarm. These rags are also worn by criminals to escape the police."

Mekkeya, a Moslem convert at Bahrein, Arabia, says that people who deal in magic often take the head of a sheep, bury it in the cemetery and every night for seven days go to the place, where they first curse father and mother forty times, and then open the grave. If the head salutes him for each of these seven nights he digs it up and takes it home with him where it is kept in state and gives an answer regarding all the owner's intended magic. Should it fail to answer during one of the seven nights, it cannot be used.

For magic purposes pieces of the Kaaba-covering, Zem Zem water, earth which is mixed with water and used as medicine, date stones from Mecca, etc., are kept in a box in the house because of the blessing they are supposed to contain.

The following is one form of magic prevalent in Algeria. A dish of *semoule* is placed before a dead body dug out of its grave and placed in an upright position before the dish, while some one takes the dead hand and presses it over the *semoule;* it is then made into little figures of various descriptions and sold as charms.

Sometimes words are written on paper which is then pounded up and given to some one in their coffee or food.

Writing is also put into the mouth of a toad. The mouth is then sewn up, the toad's limbs are bound together and the toad is put into a hole in the ground. As the toad pines and dies the person for whom the charm is bought also pines and dies.

Sometimes a *ketuba* is tied to the neck of a tortoise and the tortoise put at the doorstep of the person hated with his or her name attached, who will then also pine away and die.

Sometimes a viper's head is cut off, dried in the sun and

pounded up and mixed with the food or drink of the victim, who dies. All these things are the work of *talebs*. There are numerous other forms of magic of the same sort for bringing about the illness or death of some one, or as love-charms.

Many animistic customs are in vogue among Moslems in connection with their marriage ceremonies. The reader is referred to a complete treatise on the subject by Edward Westermarck ("Marriage Ceremonies in Morocco," Macmillan, London, 1914), from which we quote one example: "As a protection against magic the gift removed from the wheat which is to be used for the wedding is thrown into a river, water-course or spring, or buried in the ground; the bridegroom steps three times over the bundle of old clothes containing *his shaved-off hair;* the bride is carefully guarded by women on her way to the bridegroom's place, particularly for fear lest some malevolent person should in a magical manner deprive her of her virginity; she shakes out the henna powder from her slippers and throws it into water; and when the young wife pays her first visit to her parents she goes and comes back in the evening, being still very susceptible to the evil eye."

One has only to compare these practices with the marriage customs of pagan tribes to see how much of animism lies back of them. The whole question of sexual pollution in Islam can be explained best of all by animistic belief. To refer once more to Westermarck: — "The Moors say that a scribe is afraid of evil spirits only when he is sexually unclean, because then his reciting of passages of the Koran — the most powerful weapon against such spirits — would be of no avail. Sexual cleanness is required of those who have anything to do with the corn,[12] for such persons are otherwise supposed to pollute its holiness, and also, in many cases, to do injury to themselves."

[12] Cf. Frazer, The Corn Spirit, in his "The Golden Bough."

In another place he shows how the bride brings blessing to others just as she does among the pagan races of Malaysia. " When milk is offered to the bride on her way to the bridegroom's place, she dips her finger into it or drinks a few drops and blows on the rest, so as to impart to it a little of her holiness, and the milk is then mixed with other milk to serve as a charm against witchcraft, or poured into the churn to make the butter plentiful; or when, on her arrival at the bridegroom's place, his mother welcomes her with milk, she drinks of it herself and sprinkles some on the people. She hurls the lamb, which is handed her, over the bridegroom's tent so that there shall be many sheep in the village."

Astrology with its belief that the sun, the moon and the planets preside over the seven days of the week and govern by their good or bad influences, is generally prevalent among the uneducated classes. Books on astrology are among the best sellers even in the shops near the Azhar in Cairo. The following invocations taken from the " Book of Treasures " of the celebrated physician and philosopher, Ibn Sina (died A.D. 1035), are still used and published widely (one would hardly call the prayers monotheistic) :

*Invocation to Venus.* O blessed, moist, temperate, subtle, aromatic, laughing and beautiful Princess, who art the mistress of jewels, ornaments, gold, silver, amusements, and of social gatherings; O Lady of sports and jokes, conquering, alluring, repelling, strengthening, love-inspiring, matchmaking! O Lady of joy, I pray thee to grant my wishes by the permission of God the Most High!

*Invocation to Mercury.* O veracious, excellent, just, eloquent Prince who art pleasant to look at, a writer, an arithmetician, a master of wickedness, fraud, trickery and helper in all stratagems! O truthful, noble, subtle and light one, whose nature and graciousness are unknown, as they are boundless, because thou art boding good the well-boding ones, and boding evil with the evil-boding; a male with males, a female with females, diurnal with diurnals, and nocturnal with nocturnals, accommodating thyself to their natures, and assimilating thyself to their forms. Everything is thine. I ask thee to do my will, by the permission of God.[13]

In astrology it is generally believed that Saturn presides over Saturday, and his color is black; the Sun presides over Sunday and his color is yellow; the moon presides over Monday and his color is green; Mars presides over Tuesday and his color is red; Mercury presides over Wednesday and his color is blue; Jupiter presides over Thursday and his color is sandal; Venus presides over Friday and her color is white. There are also seven angels, one for each day of the week, and special perfumes which are to be burned in connection with these incantations. The *modus operandi* in the books on this subject is to take the first letters of the names of the persons concerned and use them with the tables of astrology. We then take the first letter of the planet relating to the person or thing asked for, writing them, and putting the sign of the accusative case on a hot letter, that of the nominative on a dry one, and that of the genitive on a moist one, and the thing is done. E.g. if we wish to join the letters of Mahmud and Fatimah with the letter of the planet representing the thing asked for, namely Venus (Zuhrah), we take the first letter of Mahmud, the first of Fatimah, and the first of Venus. Then we operate with them, fumigating them with the appropriate perfumes; you must however have your nails cut, put on your best clothes, and be alone; and your wish will be granted by the permission of God. It is still customary to get the horoscope of new-born children from astrologers. We can also learn the future by Geomancy which is called in Arabic *Ilm ar raml* (sand) because the figures and dots were

[13] From the article on Magic by E. Rehatsek, M.C.E., in the *Journal of the Asiatic Society*, Vol. XIV, No. 37.

formerly traced on that material, instead of on paper as at present; the operator is called *Rammal,* and he not seldom calls in astrology to aid him in his vaticinations and prognostications. Books on Geomancy are numerous enough, but the actual *modus operandi* must be learned from a practitioner. See the illustration on page 185.

Of many other magical practices in vogue among Moslems to-day we cannot write at length. I may mention, however, the use of magic bowls or cups, which goes back to great antiquity. Generally speaking the cups are of two kinds. One is called *Taset al Khadda* from the Arabic root *khadda* which means " to shake your cup." [14] This kind is also called *Taset al Turba.* These all are used for healing, and to drive away the ills of the body. A specimen of this sort, so carefully kept by old families, may be seen in the Arab Museum, made by an engraver called Ibrahim in 1581 A.D. According to a Coptic writer the owners of such goblets often lend them to others who need them. The right manner to use the goblet is to fill it with water in the early morning, place some ordinary keys in it and leave them until the following day, when the patient drinks the water. This operation is repeated, three, seven, or forty consecutive nights until the patient gets rid of the evil effects of his fright. It would not be strange if the oxide of iron acted on the patients.

The Moslem goblets generally contain Koran inscriptions and the keys spoken of are suspended by wires from the inner cup which rests in the center of the *Taseh.* This is fastened to the cup by a screw allowing the inner cup to revolve so that the keys reach every position of the outer goblet. Two magic cups which I purchased, the smaller one at Alexandria, the larger at Cairo, are both made of brass, the larger measuring a little over eight inches in diameter and two inches in

[14] See Lane's *Dictionary.*

height; the smaller one five inches and a quarter in diameter and one and a half in height. The inner cup or basin in both cases is two inches in diameter. The keys are suspended from perforations numbering thirty in the case of the larger cup and twenty in that of the smaller. (See illustration opposite.)

To begin with the larger cup; on the inside we have round the rim certain numerical signs equivalent to the number 1711 — which may have magical significance — but the numbers are not distinct nor are they uniform. Then follows the inscription taken from the chapter " Y.S." of the Koran (Surah XXXVI) " In the name of the Merciful and Compassionate God. Y.S. By the wise Quran, verily, thou art of the apostles upon a right way. The revelation of the mighty the Merciful! That thou mayest warn a people whose fathers were not warned, and who themselves are heedless. Now is the sentence due against most of them, for they will not believe. Verily, we will place upon their necks fetters, and they shall reach up to their chins, and they shall have their heads forced back; and we will place before them a barrier, and behind them a barrier; and we will cover them and they shall not see; and it is all the same to them if thou dost warn them or dost warn them not, they will not believe. Thou canst only warn him who follows the reminder, and fears the Merciful in the unseen; but give him glad tidings or forgiveness and a noble hire."

The remainder of this section of the Koran is given on the outside of the cup on the outer circle and reads as follows: " Verily we quicken the dead, and write down what they have done before, and what vestiges they leave behind; and everything we counted in a plain model.

" Strike out for them a parable: the fellows of the city when there came to it the apostles; when we sent those two and they called them both liars." The outside of the cup

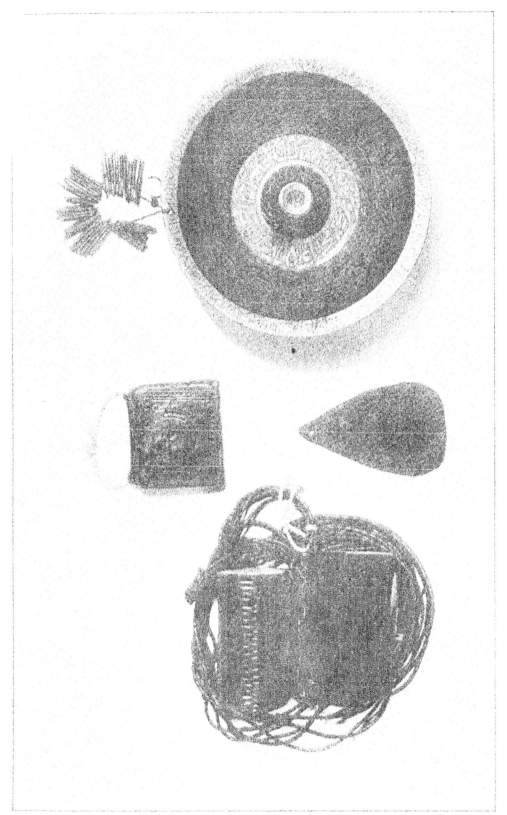

MAGIC BOWL AND AMULETS.

The Magic Bowl is described in Chapter Nine. The amulets contain portions of the Koran, either folded flat or in a round cylinder. The leather amulet in the middle of the picture is used for infants and protects them from the Evil Eye. It has the names of angels and jinn.

also contains in bold characters five of the beautiful names of God, namely, " O Healer, O Sufficient One, O Thou Who Carest, O Thou Who Givest Health, O Thou Who Judgest." Here also we have a number of mystical symbols, Arabic numbers, etc.

The smaller cup also has on the inside the first portion of the chapter already indicated and in addition the following verse from the twenty-fourth chapter of the Koran: " God is the Light of the Heavens and the Earth; His light is as a niche in which is a lamp, and the lamp is in the glass, the glass is as though it were a glittering star," and a portion of the seventeenth chapter, " The Night Journey ": " And we will send down of the Koran that which is a healing and a mercy to the believers." There is no inscription on the outside of the smaller cup. Each of the keys is inscribed with the words, " *Bismillahi ar Rahman ar Rahim.*" [15]

Another cup is used for evil purposes. It is manufactured at Medina and bears the inscription in Arabic, " Al Medina the Illuminated. In the year 1305 A.H." It is made of aromatic wood with a yellow tinge and a bitter taste, turned by hand and with no verses from the Koran. This cup is called *Al Kubaiya al Kimiya,* or " the cup of Alchemy." Its strange use is to separate husband and wife or by sorcery to injure a woman or draw her away into unlawful love. Two verses of the Koran are written backward with *semen humanis* on the inside of the cup and it is filled with water and the woman is made to drink it secretly. The verses are the following: " And the whoremonger shall marry none but a whore or an adultress; and the whore shall none marry but an idolater; God has prohibited this to the believers." And also a verse from the sixty-fifth chapter: " O Thou Prophet! when ye divorce women, then divorce them at their term, and calculate the term and fear God your Lord. Do

[15] In the name of God the merciful, the compassionate.

not drive them out of their houses unless they have committed manifest adultery."

That this cup also is in common use is established by the fact that the person who gave it to me said that his father in Ramleh (near Alexandria) used to let it out and receive one pound a night for its use. Apparently these cups are manufactured in large quantities at Medina by the Moslems and the virtue consists not only in the power of the Koran chapters but in the material of the cup and the place of its manufacture.

Ahmed Zaki Pasha, an Arabic scholar and secretary of the Council of Ministers in Cairo, read a paper before the Egyptian Institute recently with regard to one of the healing cups now kept at the old Coptic Church as a relic.[16] From this paper we learn the following particulars:

Magic Cups fall into two categories — those which cure the sufferings caused by violent and sudden emotions which the Arabs call " Cups of Terror," and those which serve to cure maladies, physical as well as moral, and even domestic troubles. The " Cups of Terror " are jealously preserved by those who possess them, and are in general use to this day in Egypt. The owners willingly lend them to their suffering fellow mortals; one condition, however, attaches to such loans, non-compliance with which will cause the cup to lose its charm forever — the borrower must make a monetary deposit. Zeki Pasha related that in the case of one of these cups, which he produced, he had had to pay the sum of £75 to the mother of the head of the family possessing it.

The following is the procedure that must be followed to work the charm of the " Cup of Terror." The cup has to be filled with water at the hour when the Faithful proceed to the mosque for the dawn prayer. A bunch of keys and other

[16] A full account of another cup of this character was given by E. Rehatsek, M.C.E., in the *Journal of the Royal Asiatic Soc.*, Vol. XIV, No. 37. Our illustration is taken from this article.

metal trinkets, all of them rusty, are then dipped in the water, which is left out in the open, and which the person to be cured has to drink the next morning. This ceremony, repeated three, seven, or forty consecutive nights, as the case may be, invariably cures any one suffering from the effects of strong emotions.

The other category, which is far more interesting from both the superstitious and the historic point of view, falls into two classes, those that are anonymous,— i.e. undated, and those that bear either the name of a distinguished personage or a definite date. It is to the second class of this category that the cup forming the subject of the paper belongs.

This cup Zeki Pasha calls the Saladin Cup, because of the dedication which is inscribed upon it. The inside, made of white brass, bears a circular inscription consisting of mystic and cabalistic letters, which, albeit several Arabic letters and cyphers are distinguishable, are so intermingled that it is quite impossible to make anything out of them. Above this inscription are sixteen medallions, identical in form but with alternating Koranic and mystic inscriptions, on them. The Koranic medallions contain the formula: " In the name of God, the Merciful and All-Forgiving." The original bottom of the cup has disappeared, and has been replaced by a curious piece of copper, on which there are no inscriptions. On the outside of the cup, which is made of red copper, is the dedicatory formula, which is worth reproducing. It runs as follows:

" Honor to our Lord, the Sultan King, the defender of the cause of God, who is supported (by Him) the victorious, Abu-l-Mouzaffar, Yusef, the co-sharer of the Commander of the Faithful! (This cup) has been proved by experience (to be a cure for) viper and scorpion bites, fever, to bring about the return of her husband to the divorced and abandoned woman, to cure (the bite of a) mad dog, intestinal pains, colic, headache . . . to destroy the effects of witchcraft, (to stop) bleeding, to exorcise the evil eye, to drive away sadness and heart qualms, and all ills and infirmities except death . . . to prevent the vexations caused by troublesome children. (It should be) placed at the head (of the patient) and be used as a bath by the old maid (to help her get a husband)."

Below this inscription are ten medallions, alternately round and trapezoid in form. All are covered with mystic signs entirely incomprehensible to us to-day. Underneath the medallions is a circular inscription in Arabic characters, some of which are obliterated, but from which with the help of contemporary cups in the Arab Museum, it has been possible to reconstruct the following text:

" Made after astrological observations reproduced and engraved during the apogee of the star and according to the horoscopes derived from the astral tables. This has been agreed upon and adopted by the principal religious heads of the Rashidite Caliphs in order to safeguard the Moslem community. Executed at Mecca in the year . . . for all ills and infirmities."

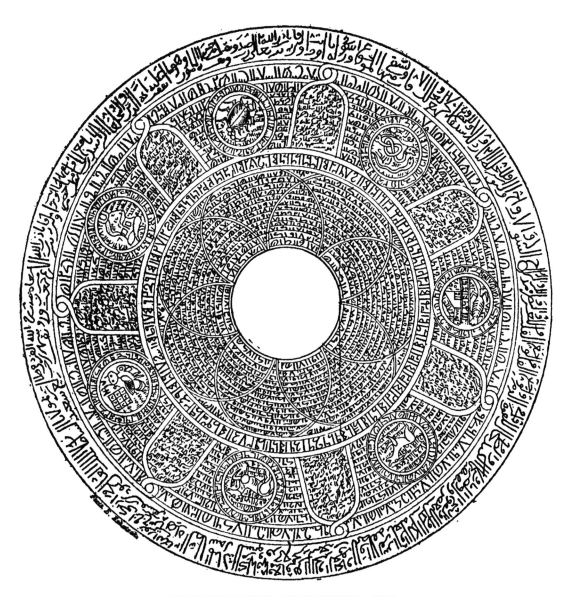

TALISMANIC MEDICINE CUP

*From Rehatsck's Article " Magic "— Jour. Asiatic Soc., Vol. XIV: 37.*

# CHAPTER X

THE belief in the magic effect of inanimate objects on the course of events seems to belong to a condition of the intellect so low as to be incapable of clear reasoning regarding cause and effect. Yet it is so early a form of belief or super-belief (i.e. superstition) that it survives the rise of knowledge and reasoning among most peoples. The lowest of mankind — the Tasmanians — had great confidence in the power of amulets, the Shilluks of the Sudan wear them in a bunch, the Arabs have always had great faith in charms, and Southern Italy — in our own as in Pliny's time — abounds in amulets. In ancient Egypt they were even more common than they are to-day. "On examining the two hundred and seventy different kinds of amulets found in Egypt," says Dr. Flinders Petrie, "there are only about a dozen which remained unclassed, and without any known meaning. The various ascertained meanings may be completely put in order under five great classes. These are (1) the amulets of Similars, which are for influencing similar parts, or functions, or occurrences, for the wearer; (2) the amulets of Powers, for conferring powers, and capacities, especially upon the dead; (3) the amulets of Property, which are entirely derived from the funeral offerings, and are thus peculiar to Egypt; (4) the amulets of Protection such as charms and curative amulets; (5) the figures of gods, connected with the worship of the gods and their functions."[1] All these classes of amulets, except the last, are in use among Moslems to-day, in many

[1] "Amulets of Ancient Egypt," p. 6.

cases of the same form and material as in the days of the Pharaohs. Metal discs, animal shapes, etc., similar to those that were used in the days of Isis are still in use by the Egyptians, as is shown by Mr. Budge. The ancient Egyptians used magical figures made of wax just as they do to-day. The names of the gods were inscribed in magical fashion then as now, and the ceremonies used for purification, sacrifice and horoscopes are strangely like those we find in modern Moslem books.

Not only in Egypt but in all the lands of the East and wherever Islam has carried its stern monotheistic creed the use of animistic charms and amulets has persisted or been modified or in many cases been introduced by Moslem teaching. Moslem amulets are made of anything that has magical power. Everything that attracts the eye (even the tattoo marks or the mole on the face) is useful for this purpose. Amulets are used on horses, camels and donkeys as well as for men, women and children. The ringing noise of metal charms drives away the demons. Amulets are worn round the neck and as rings, anklets, girdles, etc. The amulet which hangs around the neck was universal in pre-Islamic days and was called *tamima*. When the boy reaches puberty the *tamima* is cut off. The following names are given to amulets and talismans in Arabic:

> *audha* — root signifies to protect — take refuge.
> *hijab* — root signifies to shield as with a curtain.
> *hirz* — root signifies to guard against evil.
> *nafra* — root signifies to flee from, *i. e.,* make demons flee.
> *wadh* — root signifies to make distinct.
> *tamima* — root signifies to be complete (oldest name given).

Has this word *tamima* any connection with the Urim and Thummim of the Old Testament? No doubt Moslem religious magic owes much to later Jewish sources.   The character and even the shape of amulets is often borrowed from Judaism, *e. g.,* we have in Islam something very similar to " ABRACADABRA," a magic word or formula used in incantations, especially against the intermittent fever or inflammation, the patient wearing an amulet upon his neck, with the following inscription:

A B R A C A D A B R A  
A B R A C A D A B R  
A B R A C A D A B  
A B R A C A D A  
A B R A C A D  
A B R A C A  
A B R A C  
A B R A  
A B R  
A B  
A  

The underlying idea was to force the spirit of the disease gradually to relinquish its hold upon the patient.[2]

The vain search for the supreme name of God, a name which Solomon is said to have used, is common among those who write talismans.   The Gnostics in their magic used the word ABRAXAS as that of the highest being; the value of the letters in this name equal 365, the number of the days in the year.   Many derivations are given for the word and it became a common magical term in Judaism.

Conjuring spirits or exorcising demons in Islam is by the use of certain prayer-formulas.   These formulas compel God to do what is requested and indicate a belief in the fetish power of the words themselves.   It is especially the use of the

---

[2] Has this any relation to *Abraka* and *dabra,* i. e. " Most blessed word "? or " I will bless the Word "?

names of God and the great name of God that produce these results.

The number 99 for the names of God is a hyperbole for any large number. The Arabs were accustomed to say 33, 44, 99, 333, etc., for any large number and the significance of the saying " God has 99 names," indicates simply that his names are manifold. The number 99 is not given by Bukhari nor Muslim. According to Goldziher it was first given by Tirmadhi and Ibn Maja, and the latter even states that there is no good authority for this tradition.

There are many different lists of the names. Kastallani points out no less than twenty-three variants. In later days under the influence of the *Sufis* the number of God's names increased to one thousand and one. One of the most popular books of common prayer, by 'Abdallah Mohammed Gazali (died 870 A. H.), illustrates this magical use of God's names and often uses such expressions as " I beseech Thee by Thy hidden and most Holy Name which no creature understands, etc., etc." There are many books on the magical use of the names of God, especially one called *Da'wa al juljuliyeh (i. e., Jalla jallalahu).*

These names of God are used not only for lawful prayer but for strength and power to execute unlawful acts. This shows that they have a magical rather than a holy character. In the notoriously obscene book *Rajua, al Sheikh ila Saba,* written by a " pious " Moslem, these names of God are recommended to be used for immoral purposes.[3]

The terms used in magic are *Da'wah; 'azima* or Incantation; *Kahana* — Divination; *Ruqya* — Casting a Spell; and *Sihr* — Magic. The two former are considered lawful, the latter are considered forbidden by many authorities.[4]

[3] A vast literature on the use of God's names and the magic of numbers has grown up called *Kutub al Ruhaniyat* on Geomancy, Orithomancy and dreams.

[4] Hughes' *Dictionary,* p. 304.

According to a statement of the Prophet, what a fortune-teller says may sometimes be true; because if one of the jinn steals away the truth he carries it to the magician's ears; for the angels come down to the regions next the earth (the lowest heaven), and mention the words that have been pre-ordained in heaven; and the devils, or evil jinn, listen to what the angels say, and hear the orders predestined in heaven, and carry them to the fortune-tellers. It is on such occasions that shooting stars are hurled at the devil. It is also said that the diviner obtains the services of the devil (*Shaitan*) by magic arts, and by names invoked, and by the burning of perfumes, and other practices he informs him of secret things. For the devils, before the mission of the Apostle of God, used to ascend to heaven, and hear words by stealth. That the evil jinn are believed still to ascend sufficiently near to the lowest heaven to hear the conversation of the angels, and so to assist magicians, appears from many traditions and is asserted by all Moslems.

For all of the Arabic terms mentioned above the English word is Amulet, concerning the derivation of which there has been much dispute. Formerly it was supposed to be derived from the Arabic word *Hamala,* but it really is an ancient Latin word of unknown etymology. Moslem amulets may be classified as of Pagan, Jewish, or Christian origin. In Egypt, for example, a common amulet used on children consists of a small leaden fish, similar to the fish amulets found in the catacombs which represented the initials of the Greek words for Jesus Christ, Son of God, Saviour.

The use of amulets was very extensive among the Jews in the Rabbinical period and we can clearly trace many of the amulets in use to-day by Moslems to these Jewish practices. The amulet itself, it appears, might consist either of an article inscribed with the name of God, with a Scripture passage or the like, or of the root of some herb. Grains of wheat wrapped in leather sometimes served as amulets. The most frequent form of amulet, however, was a small pearl wrapped in leather. To protect a horse from evil influence, a fox's tail or a crimson plume was fastened between its eyes. Children owing to their feeble powers of resistance, were held to be much exposed to the danger of magic fascination; they were, therefore, protected by means of knots, written parchments, etc., tied round their necks. Furniture and household belongings were protected by inscribing the name of God upon foot-rests and handles. Usually, at least among men, amulets were worn on the arm; but exceptionally they were carried in the hand. Women and children wore them especially on neck-chains, rings, or other articles of jewelry. An amulet would sometimes be placed in a hollow stick, and would be all the more efficacious because no one would suspect its presence; it was a species of concealed weapon. Figuratively, The Torah is said to be such an amulet for Israel. The priestly benediction (Num. vi, 24–26) protected Israel. against the evil eye. . . . Upon an amulet said to be potent in curing the bite of a mad dog, was written, " Yah, Yah, Lord of Hosts." Medicine did not disdain the use of amulets. Abraham they taught wore a jewel on his neck which healed every person he looked upon. A " stone of preservation " was said to protect women from miscarriage.[5] This stone of preservation is still a common superstition in Egypt among Moslems; it is called in Arabic *Hajr an Naqdha* and is loaned by different families in a neighborhood to rub on the limbs of a convalescent, to protect children against contagion, etc.

The later science of amulets and their use seems to be almost wholly borrowed from Judaism. Moslem works on the subject follow the Cabila. We read that in the Middle Ages Christians employed Jews to make amulets for them.

[5] The Jewish Encyclopedia, Vol. I, art. Amulet.

At present in Cairo, Baghdad and Damascus Jewish silversmiths carry on a large trade in Moslem amulets, in fact an amulet is supposed to have special power if it has not only Arabic but Hebrew letters on it.

The sale of amulets of every description is carried on within a stone's throw of Al Azhar University, and some of the professors, as well as many of the students, promote the industry. A favorite amulet, printed by the thousands and sent from Cairo throughout all North Africa and the Near East, is entitled *The Amulet of the Seven Covenants of Solomon.* It consists of a strip of paper seventy-nine inches in length and four inches in breadth, lithographed, and with portions of it covered with red, yellow, green, or gold paint. The whole is then rolled up, tied, put into an amulet case of leather and silver, and worn by men as well as by women and children. The specimen which is translated herewith was purchased from Mohammed el Maliji, a bookseller near Al-Azhar and renowned for his controversial writings and anti-Christian poems. As typical of the real character of popular Islam this translation, which is verbatim except where indicated, will interest the reader:

## THE SEVEN COVENANTS OF SOLOMON

*What God wills will be*

There is no god but God, Mohammed is the Apostle of God.

| Abu Bakr | | Omar |
|----------|-----------|-------|
| | God Most High | |
| Hassan | | Hussein |
| | Mohammed | |
| | Peace upon him | |
| Othman | | 'Ali |

Gabriel, Peace upon him; Michael, Peace upon him; Israfil, Peace upon him; 'Azrail, Peace upon him.

An amulet for jinns and payment of debts, and a preserver from all secret diseases, and for traveling by land and sea, and for meeting governors, and for winning love, and for selling and buying, and for traveling by day and night: Certainly my prosperity is through God and Mohammed. Him alone I have trusted and to Him I repent.

The Seven Covenants against all evils and to preserve men and cause blessings.

Talha, Zobeir, Abd-al-Rahman, El Haj.

It is useful for the sting of scorpions, serpents, and all other insects. The one who carries this (amulet) gains by its blessing all desires.

(Here a picture is given of a scorpion and a snake.)

Certainly every person attains to what he purposes. This is the amulet of great power and might and proof.

## "IN THE NAME OF GOD THE MERCIFUL, THE COMPASSIONATE

" Thanks be to God the Lord of the worlds, and prayer and peace be upon the noblest apostle, our Lord Mohammed, and upon his family and Companions. But after this it is related of the prophet of God Solomon, son of David, (peace upon both), that he saw an old woman with hoary hair, blue eyes, joined eyebrows, with scrawny limbs, disheveled hair, a gaping mouth from which flames issued. She cleaved the air with her claws and broke trees with her loud voice. The prophet Solomon said to her, ' Art thou of the jinn or human ? I have never seen worse than you.' She said, ' O prophet of God, I am the mother of children (*Um-es-Subyan*). I have dominion upon sons of Adam and daughters of Eve, and upon their possessions. I enter houses and gobble like turkeys and bark like dogs, and low like cows, and make a noise like camels, and neigh like horses, and bray like donkeys, and hiss like serpents, and represent everything. I make wombs barren and destroy children. I come to women and close their wombs and leave them, and they will not conceive, and then people say they are barren. I come to a woman in pregnancy and destroy her offspring. It is I, O prophet of God, who come to the woman engaged and tie the tails of her garments, and announce woes and disasters. It is I, O prophet of God, who come to men and make them impotent. (The expressions here used are too indecent for translation.) It is I, O prophet of God, who come to men and oppose their selling and buying. If they trade, they do not gain, and if they plow they will not reap. It is I, O prophet of God, who cause all these.' Then Solomon (peace be upon him), seized her in anger and said to her, 'O cursed one, you shall not go before you give me covenants for the sons of Adam and daughters of Eve, and for their wombs and their children, or I will cut you with this sword.' She then gave the following:

## " ' *The First Covenant*

" ' By God, there is no God but He, the Profiter, the Harmful, the Possessor of this world and the next, the Life-giver, the Guide to the misbelievers, the Almighty, the Dominant, the Grasper, from whom no one can escape, and whom no one can overcome nor defeat. I shall not come near the one upon whom this amulet is hung, neither in travel nor in sleep, nor in walking, nor in loneliness, and God is witness to what I say, Here is its seal,

## " ' *The Second Covenant*

" ' In the name of God, the Merciful, the Compassionate. By God, there is no God but He, the Knower of secrets, the

Mighty. . . . I will not touch the one who carries this, neither in his humors, nor in his bones, nor in flesh nor blood nor skin nor hair; nor by any evil as long as earth and heavens exist, and God is witness to what I say, and this is the seal.

### " ' *The Third Covenant*

" ' In the name of God, the Merciful, the Compassionate. By God, who is God but He, the Living, the Self-subsisting. I will not touch the one who carries this, neither in his prosperity nor his children . . . (etc., as before).

### " ' *The Fourth Covenant*

" ' In the name of God, etc. (Attributes to God differ). I will not touch the one who carries this neither in his walking nor sitting, (etc.).

### " ' *The Fifth Covenant*

" ' In the name of God, etc. I will not touch the one who carries this neither in his property, nor trade, etc., etc.

### " ' *The Sixth Covenant*

" ' In the name of God, etc. I will not touch . . . neither secretly nor openly, etc., etc.' "

Then follow the Koranic verses called *Al Munajiyat.*

### " *Special Information and Benefit for Securing Love and Friendship*

" O Thou who dost unite the hearts of the sons of Adam and daughters of Eve by love, we ask you to make the bearer accepted and loved by all, and give him light and favor. God is the Light of Heaven.

### " *Light Verse*

" God is the Light. The similitude of His Light is as a

niche in a wall wherein a lamp is placed and the lamp enclosed in a case of glass. The glass appears as it were a shining star. It is lighted with the oil of a blessed tree, and olive neither of the east nor of the west. It wanteth little but that the oil thereof would give light although no fire touched it.

### " Throne Verse

" God! There is no god but He, the Living, the Eternal. Slumber doth not overtake Him, neither sleep. To Him belongeth whatsoever is in heaven and on earth. Who shall intercede with Him except by His permission? He knows what is between their hands and behind them; and they cannot encompass aught of His knowledge except as He please. His throne is as wide as heaven and earth. The preservation of both is no weariness to Him. He is the High, the Mighty."

Perhaps the most celebrated amulet in the world of Islam is that called *Al Buduh,* a magic square supposed to have been revealed to Al Ghazali and now known by his name. It has become the starting-point for a whole science of talismanic symbols. Some of the Moslem authorities say that Adam invented the square. It is so called from the four Arabic letters which are key to the combination. To the popular mind this word *buduh* has become a sort of guardian angel, invoking both good and bad fortune. The square is used against stomach pains, to render one's self invisible, to protect from the evil eye, and to open locks; but the most common use is to insure the safe arrival of letters and packages.

A description of a common Moslem amulet in silver is given by Prof. D. B. Macdonald in the " Festschrift of Ignaz Goldziher " edited by Carl Bezold (Strassburg, 1911, p. 267). It was bought at Damascus and is about two inches

long, pear-shaped, of silver metal.   On one side is *Ya Hafiz*
and the names of the Seven Sleepers of the Cave and their
dog *Qitmir* are written in circular fashion to form a hexagon
or Solomon's Seal.   On the other side is a magic square with
the names of the four archangels around its sides.   All the
elements of the charm are of great talismanic value.   According to Lane these names of archangels, the sleepers and their
dog are sometimes engraved in the bottom of a drinking-cup,
and more commonly on the round tray of tinned copper which
placed on a stool forms the table for dinner, supper, etc.
Another charm supposed to have similar efficacy is composed
of the names of those common articles of property which the
Prophet left at his decease.   These relics were two *subhahs*
(or rosaries), his *mushaf* (or writings) in unarranged frag-
ments, his *mukhulah* (or the vessel in which he kept the black
powder with which he painted the edges of his eyelids), two
*seggadehs* (or prayer carpets), a hand-mill, a staff, a tooth-
pick, a suit of clothes, the ewer which he used in ablution,
a pair of sandals, *a burdeh* (or woolen covering), three mats,
a coat of mail, a long woolen coat, his white mule, *ed-duldul,*
and his she-camel, *el'adba.*[6]

We need not be surprised at these modern relic worshipers
for according to Tradition even the Companions carried hair
of the Prophet in their head-gear on the field of battle and
Hasan and Hussein, the grand-sons of the Prophet, wore small
amulets filled with the down of the feathers of the angel
Gabriel.[7]

In addition to the amulets mentioned we give the translation of an amulet from Upper Egypt written on ordinary
paper with black ink in running hand.   At the end there are
some marks and symbols including the usual so-called Seal
of Solomon.

[6] "Manners and Customs of the Modern Egyptians," Lane, p. 255.
[7] Wackidi 429, Aghani 14:163; Buchari 4:33.

"O! the Blessedness of ' In the Name of God the Merciful, the Compassionate '— Peace and Prayers of God are upon our Master Mohammed, family and companions." Your God and ours is One. No God but He the Merciful, the Compassionate. God, there is no God but He, the Living, the Eternal. Slumber doth not overtake Him, neither sleep. To Him belongeth whatsoever is in heaven and on the earth. Who shall intercede with Him except by His permission? He knows what is between their hands and behind them; and they cannot encompass aught of His knowledge except as He please. His throne is as wide as Heavens and the earth. The preservation of both is no weariness to Him, He is the High, the Mighty. The Apostle believeth in what hath been sent down from His Lord, as do the faithful also. Each one believeth in God and His Angels and His Scriptures and His apostles; we make no distinction between any of His Apostles, and they say we have heard and we obey. Thy mercy Lord for unto Thee must we return! God will not burden any soul beyond its power. It shall enjoy the good which it hath acquired, and shall bear the evil for the acquirement of which it labored. O our Lord punish us not if we forget, or fall into sin: O our Lord, and lay not on us a load like that which thou hast laid on those who had been before us, O our Lord; and lay not on us that for which we have not strength: but blot out our sins and forgive us, and have pity on us. Thou art our Protector: help us then against the unbelievers. Now hath an apostle come to you from among yourselves: your iniquities press heavily upon him. He is careful over you, and towards the faithful, compassionate, merciful. And if they turn away, then say: God sufficeth me; there is no God but He. In Him put I my trust. And He is the Lord of the Glorious Throne.

"H. S. Sh. M. In the Name of the Living, the Eternal, who never dies, I have preserved you from all evil. No power and no strength except in the Great One. In His name nothing can hurt you in earth or in heaven. He is the All Hearer, the All Knowing. I take refuge in the Face of God the Gracious, and in the Words of God being full, which no body, believer or unbeliever, can comprehend, of any evil from heaven, and what happens in it, and what is in earth, or comes out of it, or the events of day or night. Let all events be good. In the name of God the Creator, the Greatest. This amulet is a refuge against what I fear." (Names of some Jinn — illegible.) He is the All Hearer, the All Knower.

"Had we sent down this Koran on some Mountain, thou wouldst certainly have seen it humbling itself, and cleaving as under for the fear of God. Such are the parables we propose to men in order that they may reflect. He is God beside whom there is no other God, He is the King, the Holy, the Peaceful, the Faithful, the Guardian, the Mighty, the Strong, the Most High. Far be the Glory of God from that which they unite with him. He is God the Producer, the Maker, the Fashioner, to whom as ascribed excellent titles. Whatever is in the heavens and in the earth praiseth Him; and He is the Mighty, the Wise. In the name of God the Compassionate, the Merciful. Say He is one God, God the Everlasting. He begetteth not, and is not begotten, and there is none like unto Him. In the Name of God, etc. . . . I betake me for refuge to the Lord of the Daybreak, against the mischief of His creation, and against the mischief of the first darkness when it overspreadeth and against the mischief of any enchantress, and against the mischief of the envier when he envieth. In the Name of God, etc. . . . Say I betake me for refuge to the Lord of men, the King of men, the God of men, against the mischief of the stealthily withdrawing whisperer, who whispereth in man's breast — against Jinn and men.

"In the Name of God the Compassionate the Merciful.    I bewitch thee (charm thee against) every evil, every envying soul.    Praise be to God, the Lord of men, the King of men, the God of men, against the mischief of the stealthily withdrawing whisperer, who whispers in man's breast — against Jinn and men.    Prayers of God and his peace are on our master Mohammed."

In East Arabia superstitions and charms are almost as common as in Egypt although the Wahabi reformers made strong protest in their day.    "In Bahrein," writes Mrs. Dykstra, "a black kettle, turned upside down and placed on a pole, guards the owner of the house or compound from evil. To refer to the plague or any other epidemic is to bring it on, for that is blaming God and He will become angry, and the epidemic is then His punishment upon them.    A mother must not weep over the death of a child less than eight years, for her tears will be as fat in the fire to her child to continue his pain in the other world.    A dirty face and black clothes are a baby's protection against jinns.    A new-born baby must be spat on to secure its health and preservation.    Amulets and charms are worn by all to protect from evil and sickness."

In Persia, blue beads, and turquoises are used and little metal hands called the hand of Ali.    A large hand of 'Ali fastened to the top of a pole is worshiped in a mountain village near Tabriz; it was brought to the city, but not liking it, says the legend, went back by itself.    It is taken on a yearly pilgrimage to Mecca.

Mr. Gerdener of Cape Town tells us the most common amulets among Moslems there are bits of rag, containing herbs or some drug.    But more frequently they contain a small bit of paper with certain Arabic writings,— verses from the Koran and mysterious looking squares with letters and figures in the corners are also used.    These they call their *power*.

In Tunis the most common amulets are little leathern bags in which are sewn written charms, bits of incense, white caraway seeds, also shells of snails, and " Fatima's hand "; the latter being often hung round the neck of cows or donkeys to keep them from disease.  One also sees the tails of fish over house doors and the skull and horns of cattle.

It would not be an exaggeration to say of Moslems in Egypt, Persia and Morocco what is stated by Nassau of pagans in West Africa; the only difference between the pagan talisman and the Moslem one is that the pagan connects his magic with the gods of the bush; the Moslem connects his with Allah and the Koran:

" For every human passion or desire of every part of our nature, for our thousand necessities or wishes, a fetish can be made, its operation being directed to the attainment of one specified wish, and limited in power only by the possible existence of some more powerful antagonizing spirit.  This amulet hung on the plantation fence or from the branches of plants in the garden is either to prevent theft or to sicken the thief; hung over the doorway of the house, to bar the entrance of evil; hung from the bow of the canoe, to insure a successful voyage; worn on the arm in hunting, to ensure an accurate aim; worn on any part of the person, to give success in loving, hating, planting, fishing, buying and so forth, through the whole range of daily work and interests." [8]

According to Tradition, Mohammed sanctioned the use of spells and magic so long as the names were only the names of God or of good angels.[9]  It is, therefore, lawful to use charms and amulets of this character.  The system of incantation used is called *Al Da'wa;* this science is used to establish friendship, to cure sickness, to accomplish desire, to obtain

[8] " Fetishism in West Africa."
[9] Mishkat, 21:1.

victory in battle. It is an occult science and is divided into four heads: [10]

(1) *The qualifications necessary for him who practices it:* When any one enters upon the study of the sciences, he must begin by paying the utmost attention to cleanliness. No dog or cat or any stranger is allowed to enter his dwelling place, and he must purify his house by burning wood aloes, pastiles, and other sweet-scented perfumes. He must take the utmost care that his body is in no way defiled, and he must bathe and perform the legal ablutions constantly. A most important preparation for the exercise of the art is a forty-days' fast (*chilla*), when he must sleep on a mat spread on the ground, sleep as little as possible, and not enter into general conversation.

Exorcists not infrequently repair to some cave or retired spot in order to undergo complete abstinence. The diet of the exorcist must depend upon the kind of *asma,* or names of God he intends to recite. If they are the *asma ul-jalaliyah,* or "terrible attributes" of the Almighty, then he must refrain from the use of meat, fish, eggs, honey, and musk. If they are the *asma ul-jamaliyah,* or "amiable attributes," he must abstain from butter, curds, vinegar, salt and ambergris. If he intends to recite both attributes, he must then abstain from such things as garlic, onions, and assafoetida.

(2) *The use of the tables required by the performer:* This contains an arrangement of the alphabet of which we give an example on the next page.

To use the table one takes the initial letters of say Ahmad (A) and Daniel (D) and copies out in double column the result. The future is then read by discerning the agreement or discord of the planets, the elements, the perfumes, etc. In addition to this the perfumes mentioned are burnt during the incantation. This science is almost universally practiced in

[10] See Hughes' *Dictionary of Islam,* art. "Da'wa."

| Letters of the Alphabet arranged according to the Abjad (ABJAD) with their respective numbers..... | 1 | 2 | 3 | 4 | 5 |
|---|---|---|---|---|---|
| The special Attributes or names of God.. | Allah | Baqi | Jami | Dayyan | Hadi |
| The number of the Attribute ........... | 66 | 113 | 114 | 65 | 20 |
| The Meaning of the Attribute ......... | God | Eternal | Assembler | Reckoner | Guide |
| The Class of the Attribute ......... | Terrible | Amiable | Terrible and Amiable Combined | Terrible | Amiable |
| The Quality, Vice or Virtue of the Letter | Friendship | Love | Love | Enmity | Enmity |
| The Elements (Arba'ah' Anasir) ........ | Fire | Air | Water | Earth | Fire |
| The Perfume of the Letter ........ | Black Aloes | Sugar | Cinnamon | Red Sandal | White Sandal |
| The Signs of the Zodiac (Buruj) ........ | Hamal Ram | Jauza Twins | Saratan Crab | Saur Sun | Hamal Ram |
| The Planets (Kawakib) ........ | Zuhal Saturn | Mushtari Jupiter | Mirrikh Mars | Shams Sun | Zuhrah Venus |
| The Genii (Jinn) ........ | Qayupush | Danush | Nulush | Twayush | Hush |
| The Guardian Angels (Muwakkil) ........ | Israfil | Jibrail | Kalka'il | Darda'il | Durba'il |

One of a Series of Da'wa Tables

Moslem lands and there are hundreds of books on the subject. The most celebrated is that called " Shems al Ma'arif al Kubra " of Ahmed ibn Ali Al Buni, who died 622 A. H. Among the subjects treated in this book of magical practices are the following: to drive away demons, to strengthen memory, to increase property, to gain love, to cure inflammation, to hear the speech of Jinn, to increase crops. He gives us the names on the seal of Solomon, the names on the rod of Moses, the names which Jesus used to perform his miracles, etc., etc., etc. There is not a Moslem village from Tangier to Teheran where this encyclopedia of magic can not be found in daily use by some Sheikh.

Among the most common amulets in use in India are magic squares based upon the well-known magic square of Al-Ghazali. [12]

| 8 | 11 | 14 | 1 |
|---|---|---|---|
| 13 | 2 | 7 | 12 |
| 3 | 16 | 9 | 6 |
| 10 | 5 | 4 | 15 |

| 14 | 4 | 1 | 15 |
|---|---|---|---|
| 7 | 9 | 12 | 6 |
| 11 | 5 | 8 | 10 |
| 2 | 16 | 13 | 3 |

| 15 | 1 | 4 | 14 |
|---|---|---|---|
| 10 | 8 | 5 | 11 |
| 6 | 12 | 9 | 7 |
| 3 | 13 | 16 | 2 |

| 1 | 14 | 15 | 4 |
|---|---|---|---|
| 8 | 11 | 10 | 5 |
| 12 | 7 | 6 | 9 |
| 13 | 2 | 3 | 16 |

| 7 | 13 | 19 | 25 | 1 |
|---|---|---|---|---|
| 20 | 21 | 2 | 8 | 14 |
| 3 | 9 | 15 | 16 | 22 |
| 11 | 17 | 23 | 4 | 10 |
| 24 | 5 | 6 | 12 | 18 |

[12] " Qanoon-e-Islam," by Herklots, London.

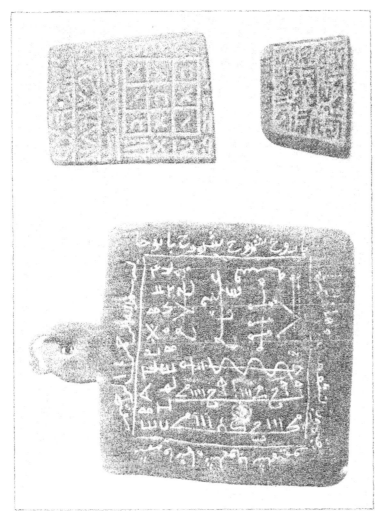

TALISMANS AND MAGICAL SQUARES FROM EGYPT

The two smaller ones are made of sandstone; be use to the left is of bronze and has the usual introductory formula together with the names of angels and jinn.

These magic squares are written on a white porcelain plate, or on paper, the inscription is then washed off with water and the latter drank; or they are worn upon the person; or they are burnt, and the individual is smoked with their fumes; or they are kept suspended in the air; or having been made into charms by being enveloped in cotton, they are dipped in odoriferous oils, and burnt in a lamp; or they are engraved on rings and worn on the fingers. " Some persons write the *taweez* or *ism* on *bhoojputur,* or have it engraved on a thin plate of silver, gold, etc., roll it up or fold and form it into a *taweez* or *puleeta,* cover it with wax, and sew some superior kind of cloth or brocade over it; or they insert it into a square hollow case or tube of gold or silver, seal it hermetically, and wear it suspended to the neck, or tie it to their upper arms or loins, or stick it into their turbans or tie it up in a corner of their handkerchiefs and carry it about their persons. People very generally have empty *taweezes* made, and suspend them to the necks of their children, together with *nadulec* [13] in the center, as well as some *baghnuk* (tiger's nails) set in silver, etc., and when they obtain a *taweez* from any renowned *mushaekh* or *mulla,* or can procure a little of any sacred relic offered on shrines, such as flowers, sundul, etc., they put these into them."

It is by such magic that people find out the hour and day of the month most propitious for undertaking a journey, for wearing new clothes, for trimming the beard, etc., for bathing, shaving, etc. The character of these superstitions may be judged from a single example which Herklots gives:

" If a person have an enemy on whom he has not the power to be revenged, though he is constantly distressed and harassed by him the following is what people, in the habit of doing these things, perform, either for themselves or for others, for a reward. However, it is not every one that succeeds

[13] *I. e.,* an amulet with the name of *Ali.*

in performing these; and practitioners only undertake them for those actually in need of relief; and the Almighty again, on His part, will only hear the supplications of those who are really distressed. He is to read the *tubut-maqoos,* or the *chayhul qaf* morning and evening daily, for twenty-one days, at each period forty-one times. Or, with some earth taken out of a grave, or the earth of the Hindoo *musan,* he is to make a doll about a span long more or less; and repeating the *soora-e-ullum-turkyf* — with the name of its accompanying demon, or the tubut reversed, or the *chayhul qaf* over twenty-one small thin wooden pegs, and repeating it three times over each peg, he is to strike them into different parts of the body of the image; such as one into the crown of the head, one into the forehead, two into the two eyes, two into the two upper arms; two into the two arm-pits, two into the two palms of the hands, two into the two nipples, two into the two sides of the body, one into the navel, two into the two thighs, two into the two knees, and two into the two soles of the feet. The image is then to be shrouded in the manner of a human corpse, conveyed to the cemetery, and buried in the name of the enemy who (it is believed) will positively die after it."

In all these charms and performances we can see animism and Islam strangely mingled, theism and paganism side by side. The prayer is made to the Almighty, the chapters read are from the Koran (*i. e.,* 9th Chapter " Tauba " is to be read backwards and the chapter called *Qaf* is to be read 40 times), but the whole character of the rite is pagan. The spiritual power or the spirit itself, the benefit of the blessing is directly connected with the charm. We may again use words in regard to Islam that Nassau uses regarding the charms of the pagans in West Africa (p. 76):

" Over the wide range of many articles used in which to confine spirits, common and favorite things, are the skins and especially the tails of bush-cats, horns of antelopes, nut-shells, snail-shells, bones of any animal, but especially human bones; and among the bones are specially regarded portions of skulls of human beings and teeth and claws of leopards. But, literally, anything may be chosen,— any stick, any stone, any rag of cloth. Apparently, there being no limit to the number of spirits, there is literally no limit to the number and character of spirits, there is literally no limit to the number and character of the articles in which they may be localized."

In the villages of the Delta, where ninety-nine per cent of the people are Moslems, and in the back streets of Cairo, the intellectual capital of Islam, I have collected amulets made of bone, shell, skin, horns of animals, teeth, claws, mud from the tombs, etc., etc. Islam and Animism live, in very neighborly fashion, on the same street and in the same mind.

# CHAPTER XI

PRIMITIVE worship in all parts of the world is connected with sacred trees and sacred stones. Paradise had its tree of knowledge and the tree of life. The Patriarchs pitched their tents under special groves and worshiped Jehovah without blame. They saw God in nature, yet did not deify nature and were charged over and over not to follow the abominations of those who worshiped under every grove. The *Ashera* or sacred poles (trees) were connected with idolatrous and orgiastic worship of the Baalim. Egyptologists speak of Osiris as a tree-god with tree-demons and on Babylonian cylinders we find pictures of sacred trees. A lordly oak or elm is so beautiful that our poet, Joyce Kilmer, who gave his life in France, wrote:

> "I think that I shall never see
> A poem lovely as a tree.
>
> A trees whose hungry mouth is prest
> Against the earth's sweet flowing breast.
>
> A tree that looks at God all day
> And lifts her leafy arms to pray. . . .
>
> Poems are made by fools like me,
> But only God can make a tree."

The account in the Book of Genesis of the Tree of Life together with that of the trees of the River of Life in the book of Revelation find their parody in what Moslems teach concerning the Lotus-tree of Paradise. (See Commentary on

Surah 97.)    It is said to be at the extremity or on the most
elevated spot, in Paradise, and is believed by Moslems to have
as many leaves as there are living human beings in the world;
and the leaves are said to be inscribed with the names of all
those beings; each leaf bearing the name of one person, and
that of his father and mother.    This tree, Moslems believe, is
shaken on the *Lailat al Qadr* (night of Destiny) a little after
sunset; and when a person is destined to die in the ensuing
year, the leaf upon which his name is written, falls off on this
occasion; if he is to die very soon his leaf is almost wholly
withered, a very small portion only remaining green; if he is
to die later on in the year, a larger portion remains green;
according to the time he has yet to live, so is the proportion
of the part of the leaf yet green.    This therefore is a very
awful night to the serious and considerate Moslems, who, accordingly, observe it with solemnity and earnest prayer.

A whole world of superstition and tradition is connected
with this tree of Paradise and pictures of it are sold as amulets in Cairo.    It is also common to find the genealogy of the
Prophet Mohammed traced back to Adam and forward to the
saints of Islam depicted as a sacred tree.    I have seen such
pictures hanging for good luck as well as for instruction in
mosques at Saigon, Indo-China and in Honan and Singapore.
But this is beside our subject.

The special veneration of trees, however, exists in all Moslem lands and has the closest possible resemblance to pagan
tree-worship, as we shall see.    In pagan belief because of
their theory of universal life all weird or abnormal objects are
sacred and have special soul-qualities.    Trees of unusual size,
rocks of peculiar shape, animals with strange deformities,—
all such things are sacrosanct.    A Moslem dares not injure
them; to do so would bring down upon himself the wrath of
unseen powers.

" Of course it is not to be supposed that the Malay peasant

is fully aware of the animistic character of his belief. He acts as his ancestors acted before him; he does not reason why. He is satisfied with the fact that a tree has a spirit attached to it; he does not stop to enquire whether that spirit is the soul of the tree or merely a ghost that has taken up its abode in the tree; all he is certain about is that some unseen power is connected with the tree." [1]

In West Africa tree-worship is common among the pagans and such trees are famous haunts of spirits. Large, prominent trees are inhabited by spirits. "Many trees in the equatorial West Africa forest throw out from their trunks," says Nassau, "at from ten to sixteen feet from the ground, solid buttresses continuous with the body of the tree itself, only a few inches in thickness, but in width at the base of the tree from four to six feet. These buttresses are projected toward several opposite points of the compass, as if to resist the force of sudden wind-storms. They are a noticeable forest feature and are commonly seen in the silk-cotton trees. The recesses between them are actually used as lairs by small wild animals. They are supposedly also a favorite home of the spirits."

In Islam the same beliefs and practices exist and go back to Arabian paganism or were adopted by Moslems in their local or national environment and Islamized. The subject was treated by Goldziher in a brief paper translated for the Moslem World (July, 1911, p. 302). Other facts have since come to our notice and all travelers in the Near East witness to the wide prevalence of this superstition. Special veneration to holy trees is offered in Syria, Palestine, and all North Africa. The Bedouins inhabiting the tracts of land traversed by Doughty look upon certain trees and shrubs as *manhals,* or abodes of angels and demons. To injure such trees or shrubs, to lop their branches, is held dangerous.

[1] "Malay Beliefs," pp. 20–21.

Misfortune overtakes him who has the foolhardiness to perpetrate such an outrage, and as may be imagined, the Arabs have many delectable stories calculated to win over the skeptic. The holy tree is hung with a variety of buntings and like ornaments. The diseased and maimed of the desert resort to it, offer it a sheep or goat, and besprinkle it with the blood of the sacrificed animal. The flesh is cooked and distributed among the friends present, a portion being left suspended from a branch of the magic tree; and the patient returns tranquil in the faith that the angel will appear in a dream and instruct him with a view to his cure. But again it is the patient only who may sleep in the shades of the sacred tree; to a healthy man the attempt would involve ruin. Professor Sachu's attention was arrested in the rocky land Jabal-ul-Amiri, southeast of Aleppo, by a stunted desiccated thorny tree of a man's height which he beheld hung on all sides with variegated rags. " Stones were heaped around its stem, and all manner of stones, large and small, were placed in the branches. Such a tree, called *zarur,* is the altar of the desert. When a woman yearns for a child, when a peasant longs for rain, or when he yearns for the restoration to health of his horse or camel he takes a stone and deposits it at the foot of the *zarur,* or fixes it somewhere between its two branches." Again, on either side of the Jordan religious veneration for sacred trees which has dominated there from times immemorial and which evoked stern Biblical enactments has still perpetuated in unaltered shape. " In no country," says the Rev. Mr. Mills, " have men greater reverence for trees than in Palestine. There we encounter a considerable number of holy trees, which are hung with pieces of cloth and garments of pilgrims who have journeyed thither to do homage to the trees. We notice on other trees rags for purposes of superstitious enchantments. Many a tree is the resort of evil spirits, but what is more weird, a place abounding in tender oaks is usually dedicated to a species of beings denominated 'Daughters of Jacob.'" Abbé Barges tells of a lotus-tree in the garden of an Arab in Jaffa to which special veneration was offered. From the branches of the tree depended lamps and strips of cloth of a variety of colors. The proprietor, explaining the strange worship, said that the seed of the tree had descended from heaven. That was why it was dedicated to the Prophet who visited the tree from time to time in the shades of the night. All good Mohammedans show the same awe-struck respect for a holy tree. The practice is noticeable in other countries too, where popular worship finds expression in veneration accorded to singular representatives of the vegetable kingdom. Schumacher recording his experiences in Jolan describes how the *butmi* tree is sometimes seen standing solitary in the midst of a field shading the final resting-place of a Moslem saint. It receives the distinctive appellation of "fakiri," the indigent, and is so secured from all outside interference, being allowed unchecked to attain to a great height. No Moslem dare break a single one of its branches or even remove a dry twig, for, as the legend has it, no man can ever bend its bough but must call down upon himself the justice of divine vengeance.

Goldziher further states: "We may glance at a few more of the diverse aspects which the cult of trees assumes in Islam. Alongside of immutable heathen forms we come upon such as have been subjected to the moderating influencing of Mohammedanism. An umbrageous tree in Wadi ul-sirar, not far from Mecca, which used to be worshiped in pre-Islamic ages, is adored as the one under which seventy prophets had their umbilical cord severed. (Al-Muwatta II, p. 284; Yakut III, p. 75.). The Abbaside Abd-ul-Samad-ibn-Ali, Governor of Mecca, built a mosque at this place. A sacred tree is either associated with the memory of Mohammed or its shadow covers a Wali's tomb. In the desert the holy tree is

TOMB OF MOSLEM SAINT AND SACRED TREE NEAR ALGIERS

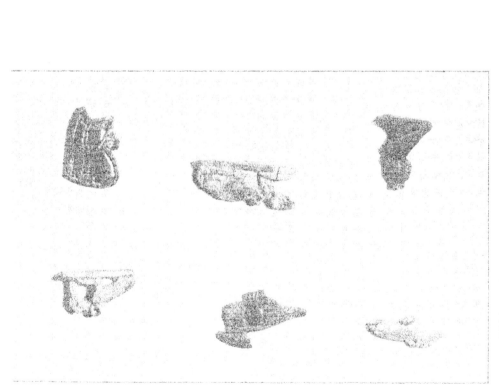

ANCIENT AMULETS FROM THE EGYPTIAN TOMBS

These are very similar in shape to those worn today

adored in all its pagan aspects; in the city the veneration is transferred to a convenient saint. And without such props the heathen cult would certainly have been uprooted. In the mosque of Rabia in Kazwin there was a tree regarded sacred by the vulgar. The Caliph ul-Mutawakkil ordered its destruction ' so that the people may no more fall into temptation.' (Beladhuri, p. 322.) It is imperative among austere Mohammedan environment to find out a dead pious man upon whom to transpose the homage really done to the tree, and when no tomb is forthcoming nigh at hand, the tree itself becomes the recipient of the worship in the shape of the habitation of a Wali. At the corner of a street in Damascus there is an olive-tree, to which pilgrimages are made, chiefly by women, among whom it is celebrated as the Holy Lady Olive (Sitti Zaytun). A dervish collects the sacrificial gifts of the pious devotees in whose behalf he offers prayers. The olive was considered an individual with a personal name. Zeytun grew into Zaytun. Morocco actually boasts of a like ' Notre Dame d'Olive' in a gigantic tree which is the center of crowded pilgrimages. A masculine counterpart of Lady Zaytun we meet in the Sheikh Abu Zeytun whose mausoleum is situated in Palestine. By an analogous process the Mohammedans have personified a venerable stone column into Sheikh-ul-Amud, or the Reverend Pillar. Objects previously looked up to as sacred continue to be so in Moslem times, only they are connected with some pious man whose existence the worshipers ever are at a loss to establish." So far the investigations of Professor Goldziher. In Yemen the Moslems give the following tradition to explain how the custom arose. I have not been able to trace it to its source. They say that the polytheists of the Koreish used to pay high honor to sacred trees and accept good and ill from their influences. They used to drive nails into the trees and hang bits of their clothing upon them, but when Islam came this practice was forbidden to the extent that one day when Omar-ibn-el-Kha-tab saw certain people going to a particular tree mentioned in the Koran where the oath of allegiance to the Prophet was taken by the Companions, he greatly feared that the people would go back to idolatry and sent some one to cut down the tree and it was cut down. This clearly shows that whatever tree-worship persists in Arabia it is due to pre-Islamic practice and is admittedly contrary to their own conception of the demands of pure theism. Yet in spite of this tradition and the loud assertion in the mosque that Allah is God alone and that all polytheism is of the devil, we find tree-worship almost universal. Sacred trees are very common in Morocco. About twenty miles distant from Mogador there is a large argan tree. Large numbers of Moors visit the spot every year. They hang upon it bits of rag, broken pottery or nails, believing that any of these things have power to unloose the hidden virtue which lies concealed within and which flowing to the donor will make this way prosperous until next visit. While hanging these things upon the tree they give utterance to desires which fill the heart. Moslems in India respect a tree called Brimje which does not bear fruit and the leaves of which are like those of a poplar tree but a little darker. This tree is often planted on their tombs and in mosques; the pilgrims then tie up a strip of cloth on the branches of the tree vowing to untie it on the fulfillment of some desire when they offer a sacrifice.

In Algeria trees become holy and are worshiped because some saint has sat under them or dreamed about them, etc. They partake of the holiness of the saint and of the special virtues belonging to him, such as healing children's illnesses, child-bearing, etc. Strips of material are hung on them as offerings to the saint. These rags then become blessed and are frequently stolen and torn by other worshipers who place the piece in their waist belts or in the folds of their head-dress.

"Anatolia," writes Dr. George E. White, "is emphatically full of sacred trees and groves, each of which usually owes its sanctity to a holy grave, and often is in close proximity to a sacred spring and a sacred stone.  Riding through the country one often spies a clump of trees, larger or smaller, on a hill top, or in some valley nook, of which even before inquiring he may be quite sure that they are regarded as sacred. Men fear to cut the wood except for a mosque or a coffin. They believe that if one were to fell a tree or lop off a bough, he would anger the spirit of the place and some 'stroke' would overtake him in consequence.  They often say that if one cut the wood it would fly back to the forest before morning. More firmly do they believe that the woodman's house would burn, or some accident befall one or more of the inmates.  At Ipejik a visitor told the people that devils would not get them if they cut down the trees.  Near Arabkir is a cave beside a holy tree, where cocks are shut up as votive offerings to starve and so propitiate the spirit of the place; the willows are accounted sacred and can heal on Palm Sunday.  Near Van the Seer rock and tree cure fever in exchange for the tying of a rag; near Harpout is a thorn-bush nearly buried in stones which cures fever; again a forty branched tree at Goganz rests on a hill top, and is visited by Armenians who have a spring festival there.  The Striker tree is feared by both Turks and Armenians, who pray as they pass it, lest some ill-luck overtake them in its vicinity.  At St. Sapanz is a tree which no one dares climb; Kurds and Armenians worship there every Sunday.  It is remarkable that Kurds should observe the Christian Sabbath in this way, and suggests that they may sometimes have changed their connection from nominal Christianity to nominal Mohammedanism, while remaining really Pagan for the most part all the time. At Agunjik a Kurd shot at a bird on a holy tree, and died eight days (that is a week) afterward. Rushdonienz has a famous walnut tree to which the sick resort, and where they remain in all sorts of weather to offer sacrifices, for at certain times or in certain stages of the weather a peculiar halo surrounds the tree and the sick are then miraculously healed. At Morenik a Sun Pole was burned in 1907 and thousands of nails were found in the ashes, the remains of years of worshipers. This tree was called the Censor, and cured all diseases for Turks or Armenians impartially. They would beat the roots with stones, burn candles before it, cast eggs into the pool hard by, or drive nails into the pole, crying ' from me to you, from you to another ' in the hope of thus expelling the disease."

In Kerbela there are trees supposed to belong to 'Ali and other Shiah saints. There are two palm trees near Kerbela under which Mary is believed to have sat when Jesus was born. Women visit these trees, eat the fruit and drink a mixture of the earth and water. Pilgrims carry a collection of hair and tie it on the trees in Kerbela, believing that on the day of resurrection they will have hair the length of the trees. Finger-nails are also tied in a bit of rag to the trees; teeth are washed, wrapped in white cloth and hung on the trees with a little salt, believing that this will keep them pure and whole until they come to claim them on the day of resurrection.

" In Persia," writes Miss Holliday, " I had a cook who found near a village two fine saplings growing from the root of an old tree; as they would be fine for walking sticks he cut them, but was reproved by his host for the night. ' If the village knew they would be very angry. Don't you know these are persons?'" Another incident is given of a tree that had fallen down in a cemetery to which rags were tied, for communion with the spirit of the tree, lights were burnt and offerings made and which had even been walled off as a protection.

The method of communion, the awe of dread consequences to those who injure the tree, and the details of worship are practically the same everywhere.

How trees are regarded and worshiped to-day in Arabia is related by Doughty (Vol. I, p. 365). " Returning one of those days I went out to cut tent-pegs at the great solitary acacia tree which stands nigh the kella; here the goats and sheep of the garrison lie down at noon after the watering. Clear gum-arabic drops are distilled upon the small boughs; that which oozes from the old stock is pitchy black, bitter to the taste, and they say medicinal: with this are caulked the Arab coasting boats which are built at Wejh. Hither I saw Doolan leading his flock, and waited to ask him for his bill, or else that he would cut down the sticks for me. He answered: ' Wellah, O son of mine uncle, ask me anything else, but in this were mischief for us both. No! I pray thee, break not, Khalil, nor cut so much as a twig of all these branches, thou art not of this country, thou art not aware: Look up! seest thou the cotton shreds and the horns of goats which hang in these boughs, they are of the Beduw, but many fell in the late winds. And seest thou these nails! certain of the Haj knock them into the stem whilst they pray!' As I laid hand anew on a good bough and took my knife, Doolan embraced me. ' No, Khalil, the man who cuts this tree,' he said, ' must die.' ' What is this folly! are you afraid of trees?' ' Ah me! she is possessed by a jinn; be not so foolhardy. Wellah, I tell thee truth, a Beduwy broke but a bough and he died within a while and all his cattle perished. Khalil, the last evening a little girl of the booth that is newly pitched here gathered some of these fallen sticks, for her mother's fire, and as they kindled, by-thy-life! the child's arm stiffened; they carried her immediately into the kella, where Haj Nejm hanged some charms about her, and by the mercy of God the child recovered.'"

And here is a pen-portrait equally pathetic of how a mother with her babe in Turkey seeks help at a holy-tree. The writer, Victoria de Bunsen, has gazed deeply into the soul of a Turk: "As my eyes wandered over the green branches, I saw that low down they were ragged and bare, and all stripped of their leaves. Instead the dry twigs were hung with objects which by much travel had grown familiar to me, the objects one learns to associate with all sacred mysterious places in the East. There were the dirty rags, the wisps of twisted hair, the little strings of beads or common charms — all the worthless cast-off things which mean so much to those who cast them off for such a purpose, and are mere rubbish to everybody else. . . . I saw a woman stoop to pass beneath them, and she came into the shade. She did not see me, and she need not, for I was close to the tomb, and evidently that was not the object of the visit. Some tall rank weeds and grass trees hid me from her sight, though I could still watch her. The woman I watched was tall and young. She wore the blue loose dress of the Lebanon women and the long coarse white veil. In her arms she carried a baby. She came swiftly and with decision in her movements. There was trouble in her face and great perplexity, but there was no doubt of the reason she had come to the tree. Kneeling down on the ground she unwinds the baby from its long thick wrappings and lays it on the ground beside her. I cannot see its face but it must be very little and weak, for I can hear its wailing cry, and it is feeble and struggling. When the swaddling clothes are loosened, the wailing ceases for a minute and I see one tiny toe kick weakly in the air. . . . While the baby lies there on the ground and feebly stretches its wasted limbs I watch with anxious sympathy, this last attempt to save the life that means so much. The baby still wears a ragged little cotton shirt under the swaddling bands, and from this the mother carefully tears a rag. Then, rising, she scans anxiously the dry, leaf-stripped branches around her. She holds the polluted discolored thing — the holy thing — the little rag in her hand. All the fever and the pain and the weakness of her child is concentrated and bound up in that rag. For her was the duty of bringing that concentrated evil — that heavy-laden rag — into contact with the holy, life-giving tree. The rag must be bound to it, cast off upon its branches. Choosing the place the woman fastens the rag to a branch with steady deliberate fingers, and then sits down again by her baby and contemplates it dangling from a twig. Who shall say what hope, what agony of suspense, fills her troubled mind ? " [2]

Stone- as well as tree-worship persists in Islam and Mohammed himself sanctioned it when in destroying all the idols of the Ka'aba he spared the Black-stone and left it in its place of honor, an object of adoration. The Meccans before Islam used to carry with them on their journeys pieces of stone from the Ka'aba, and paid reverence to them because they came from the Haram or Holy Temple. Herodotus mentions the use of seven stones by the Arabs when taking solemn oaths. The honor, almost amounting to worship, paid the meteoric *Hajuru'l Aswad* or Black Stone, is one of the many Islamic customs which have been derived from those of the Arabs who lived long before Mohammed's time. The kiss which the pious Mohammedan pilgrim bestows on it is a survival of the old practice, and was a form of worship in Arabia as in many other lands. The various gods of the ancient Arabs were represented by images or stones. It is interesting to know that some of these are still preserved as witness to Mohammed's triumph over idolatry. Doughty says: " On the morrow I went to visit the three idol-stones that are shown

[2] "The Soul of a Turk," Victoria de Bunsen, p. 242.

at Tayif-El-'Uzza, which I had seen in the small (butchers') market place. It is some twenty feet long; near the end upon the upper side is a hollowness which they call *makam er-ras,* the head place; and this, say they, was the mouth of the oracle. Another and smaller stone, which lay upon a rising-ground, before the door of the chief gunner, they call *el-Hubbal:* this also is a wild granite block, five or six feet long and cleft in the midst ' by a sword-stroke of our lord Aly.' " . . . " A little without the gate we came to the third reputed bethel-stone. This they name *el-Lata* (which is Venus of the Arabs, says Herodotus): it is an unshapely crag; in length nearly as the 'Uzza, but less in height, and of the same gray granite." (Vol. II: 515).[3] Even to-day among the Shiahs in Bahrein, Arabia, there are ancient stones which are objects of worship because they are supposed to have jinn in them that have the power to come to life. Offerings of food are made to them on Tuesday night and sometimes on Thursdays. The person making the offering always salaams the jinn and after hoping that he may " eat in health " the food is placed on the stone. In the morning the dish is found empty. Women often take a piece of silk for a garment in payment of a vow and leave it on the stone. Each stone seems to have its " *seyyida* " who is responsible for the removal of the silk, as the women say.

In Tabriz, Persia, there is a large marble tomb-stone before which candles are burnt. When children have whooping cough both Moslem and Christian mothers scrape off some of the marble dust and give it to the children as a cure.

Another form of stone-worship very common throughout

[3] Our chief authority for the ancient Arabian idolatry is the celebrated *Kitab al-Asnam* by Ibn al Kalbi. The book itself is lost, but is widely quoted by Jaqut. The best summary on the subject is found in Wellhausen's " Reste Arabischen Heidentums," and it is fully treated in W. Robertson Smith's " The Religion of the Semites," New York, 1889.

the Moslem world is that of raising up stone heaps on sacred places: "In Syria it is a common practice with pious Moslems when they first come in sight of a very sacred place, such as Hebron or the tomb of Moses, to make a little heap of stones or to add a stone to a heap which has been already made. Hence every here and there the traveler passes a whole series of such heaps by the side of the track. In Northern Africa the usage is similar. Cairns are commonly erected on spots from which the devout pilgrim first discerns the shrine of a saint afar off; hence they are generally to be seen on the top of passes. For example, in Morocco, at the point of the road from Casablanca to Azemmour, where you first come in sight of the white city of the saint gleaming in the distance, there rises an enormous cairn of stones shaped like a pyramid several hundreds of feet high, and beyond it on both sides of the road there is a sort of avalanche of stones, either standing singly or arranged in little pyramids. Every pious Mohammedan whose eyes are gladdened by the blessed sight of the sacred towns adds his stone to one of the piles or builds a little pile for himself." [4]  The custom of passers-by putting stone on a heap is a form of fetish worship. This is clear from what we read concerning the practice in West Africa.

"All day we kept passing trees or rocks," writes Nassau, "on which were placed little heaps of stones or bits of wood; in passing these, each of my men added a new stone or bit of wood, or even a tuft of grass. This is a tribute to the spirits, the general precaution to insure a safe return. These people have a vague sort of Supreme Being called Lesa who has good and evil passions; but here (Plateau of Lake Tanganyika), as everywhere else, the Musimo, or spirits of the ancestors, are a leading feature in the beliefs. They are pro-

[4] Frazer's "The Scapegoat," pp. 21, 22.

pitiated, as elsewhere, by placing little heaps of stones about their favorite haunts." [5] The stoning of " The Three Devils " at Mecca may be some form of ancestor worship if it is not in memory of the old idols.

We turn finally to Serpent-worship in Islam. Here also we are surprised to find how much animism remains in Moslem lands and lives and literature; all covered of course with the charitable mantle of their creed. The Arabic dictionary gives two hundred names for snakes. As-Suhaili says that when God caused the serpent to come down to the earth, He caused it to alight in Sijistan which is the part of God's earth abounding most in serpents, and that if it were not for the *'Irbadd* — (the male viper) eating and destroying many of them, Sijistan would (now) have been empty of its people owing to the large number of them (in it).

Ka'b-al-Ahber states that " God caused the serpent to alight in Ispahan, Iblis in Jeddah, Eve on Mount 'Arafah, and Adam on the mountain Sarandib (Ceylon) which is the land of China in the Indian Ocean." The curious may find much on serpent lore in Damiri (Vol. I, p. 631). The most common belief is that serpents are often human beings in the form of snakes. The serpent has a place also in the story of Creation which is given as follows: " Al-Kurtubi relates in the commentary on the XL chapter of the Kuran on the authority of Thawr b. Yazid, who had it from Khalid b. Ma'dan regarding Ka'b al-Ahbar as having said, ' When God created the Throne, it said, ' God has not created anything greater than myself,' and exulted with joy out of pride. God therefore caused it to be surrounded by a serpent having 70,000 wings; each wing having 70,000 feathers in it, each feather having in it 70,000 faces, each face having in it 70,000 mouths, and each mouth having in it 70,000 tongues, with its mouths ejaculating every day praises of God, the

[5] Nassau's " African Fetichism," p. 91.

number of drops of rain, the number of the leaves of trees, the number of stones and earth, the number of days of this world, and the number of angels,— all these numbers of times.   The serpent then twisted itself round the Throne which was taken up by only half the serpent while it remained twisted round it.   The Throne thereupon became humble." [6]

The following story is told on the authority of one of the Companions of Mohammed:   " We went out on the pilgrimage, and when we reached al-'Ari, we saw a snake quivering, which not long afterwards died.   One of the men out of us took out for it a piece of cloth in which he wrapped it up, and then digging a hole buried it in the ground.   We then proceeded to Makkah and went to the sacred mosque, where a man came to us and said, ' Which of you is the person that was kind to 'Amer b. Jabir?'   Upon which we replied, ' We do not know him.'   He then asked, ' Which of you is the person that was kind to the *Jann?*' and they replied, ' This one here,' upon which he said (to him), ' May God repay you good on our account!   As to him (the serpent that was buried) he was the last of the nine genii who had heard the Koran from the lips of the Prophet?'"

In Java the Moslems speak of the holy serpent found in the rice fields which must not be killed.   They relate legends in this respect that are undoubtedly of pre-Moslem origin. When the peasant finds such a sacred snake in his fields he takes it home and cares for it in order that the rice fields may have the blessing.

The Shiahs in Bahrein believe serpents are jinn in human forms and they should not be killed.   Small ones, however, are killed, placed in the sun with a little salt, and when the flesh is thoroughly dry it is cut up, put in bags and worn as an amulet against the evil eye.   Rich people have their am-

[6] P. 638, Damiri (English translation by Jayakar).

ulets placed in gold cases while poor people content themselves with leather bags.

Serpents, lizards and frogs that frequent the marabout buildings in Algeria are supposed to be inhabited by demons subdued by the dead marabout (a holy person) and it is forbidden to kill them on pain of death or subsequent ill luck. The snakes are drawn out of their lairs by the beating of tom-toms while certain Morocco sorcerers are supposed to have the power to bring them out by a few spoken words. On the occasion of an epidemic among the sheep near Reliyane the shepherds threw their sticks under a certain marabout tree and left them there for two or three days, then they made their flocks to pass by that tree, after repeating which two or three times they were healed.

In spite of the fact that Egypt is the intellectual center of Islam many forms of the serpent worship of the ancient Egyptians are still widely found, and in one case it is practiced with the sanction of the Moslem faith.

The superstitious idea that every house has a serpent guardian is pretty general throughout the country, and many families still provide a bowl of milk for their serpent protector, believing that calamity would come upon them if the serpent were neglected. This is undoubtedly a survival of the ancient belief that the serpent was the child of the earth — the oldest inhabitant of the land, and guardian of the ground.

The serpent is used very frequently by sorcerers in their incantations, and also in the preparation of medicines and philtres which are used for the cure of physical and emotional disturbances suffered by their clients.

The religious sanction given to serpent worship occurs in the case of Sheikh Heridi whose tomb or shrine, with that of his " wife," is to be seen in the sand-hills of Upper Egypt some distance from the town of Akhmim. Sheikh Heridi is really a serpent supposed to occupy one of the tombs. The birthday festival of this serpent saint takes place during the month following Ramadhan, and lasts about eight days. This festival is attended by crowds of devotees, including large numbers of sailors who encamp about the shrine during the festivities.

At other times pilgrimages on behalf of those suffering from certain ailments are made to come to the tomb. Professor Sayce in an article on the subject published in the *Contemporary Review* for October, 1893, quotes at length from various travelers who have mentioned this serpent-saint of Islam in their writings.

Professor Sayce then describes in detail the immediate surroundings of the two domed shrines, one of which belongs to the " wife " of the serpent. Near the shrines is a cleft of the rock which was probably the " grotto " inhabited by the " saint " before the shrine was erected.

Sheikh Heridi occupies as high a place in the esteem of the native to-day as he did in the days of Paul Lucas and Norden. His birthday festival is attended by crowds of devout believers. Many stories are still told of the miraculous powers of the Saint, who is declared to be a serpent as " thick as a man's thigh." If treated with irreverence or disrespect, it breathes fire into the face of the offender, who forthwith dies. It is very jealous of its wife's good name; those who show her disrespect are also put to death by the saint. The belief that if the serpent is hacked to pieces each piece will rejoin, still survives, and it is held that any one clever enough to note the place where the blood flowed, would become wealthy, because there he would find gold.

The professor points out that Sheikh Heridi may be regarded as the successor of Agathodaemon — the ancient serpent-god of healing. Belief in his miraculous powers is as strong to-day as it was in the days of the Rameses or Ptolemies.

At the entrance to the quarry through which pilgrims have to pass on their way to the shrine, Professor Sayce discovered engraved in large Greek letters in the stone the words επ'αγαθω which, he says, indicate that during the Greek period, the place was sacred, and that a divinity must have been worshiped here. It may be safely assumed that that divinity was none other than the sacred serpent now Sheikh Heridi under another name.

# CHAPTER XII

## THE ZAR: EXORCISM OF DEMONS

"WITHIN only a comparatively short period of years," says Professor Macdonald, "quite easily within thirty years, I should say — we have come to know that practically all through the Moslem world there is spread an observance exactly like the Black Mass in Christendom. That is to say, it is a profane parody of a sacred service. Among the older travelers you will find no reference to this. Lane apparently knew nothing of it, nor did even Burton, in spite of his curious knowledge of the most out-of-the-way and disrespectable sides of Islam. What it travesties is the Darwish *zikr*. . . . Now, practically throughout all Islam there is a kind of a parody of this, in which the beings whose intervention is sought are what we would broadly call devils. Yet when we speak of Moslem devils, we must always remember their nondescript character and that they are continually confused with the *jinn,* and so come to be on a dividing line between fairies, brownies, kobolds, and true theological devils. Devil-worship, then, in Islam and in Christendom are two quite different things. In Islam there is no precise feeling of rejection of Allah and of blasphemy against his name. It is, rather, akin to the old Arab 'taking refuge with the *jinn*' (Qur. lxxii, 6), denounced, it is true, by Mohammed as a minor polytheism, but compatible with acceptance and worship of Allah. Perhaps it might be described most exactly as a kind of perverted saint-worship. But its form is certainly a parody of the *zikr,* though with curious addi-

tions of bloody sacrifice, due to its African Voodo origin." [1]
The exorcism of demons is a universal desire where the belief in their power and malignity is so strong as we have seen it to be in Moslem lands, but the particular form of this belief, called the *Zar,* is unique in other ways than those pointed out by Dr. Macdonald. Evidence continues to accumulate that we deal here with a form of Animistic worship which although so long and so often concealed from western, i.e., infidel observation, is found in Morocco, Algeria, Tunisia, Tripoli, Egypt, the Soudan, East and West Arabia, Persia, Malaysia, and India. No direct witness to the existence of this superstition among Chinese Moslems has come from travelers or missionaries, but it would not surprise me to find it also in Yunan and in Kansu provinces.

> " Three things good luck from the threshold bar —
> A wedding, a funeral, and the *Zar* "—

So runs an Egyptian ditty on the lips of suffering womanhood which links these together as a trinity of evil.

The origin of the word is disputed. Dr. Snouck Hurgronje says that it is not Arabic and has no plural.[2] But in Eastern Arabia, especially in the province of Oman, the word has a plural and the plural form, *Zeeran,* is preferably used. Moreover I have been told that the word *is* Arabic and denotes " A (sinister) *visitor* " (*zara yezuru*) who makes his or her abode and so possesses the victim. " All Moslem nationalities in Mecca," he says, " practice the *Zar.* Even if they gave it another name in their own country they very soon adopt the word *Zar,* although the national differences continue."

The best account of its origin and character is that given

---

[1] " Aspects of Islam," pp. 330–332.
[2] " Mekka," Volume II, p. 124.

by Paul Kahle, although he deals mainly with Egypt.³ To his account and the fuller experiences related by women missionaries in Egypt and Arabia I am indebted for the particulars given in this chapter. One of the best accounts of the actual ceremony is that given by Miss Anna Y. Thompson of the American Mission in Egypt.⁴ She writes:

"There are places where women go to have these *Zar* spirits appeased, but generally a woman who can afford the expense of the occasion will have the performances in her own house. Formerly, I thought that only hysterical women were 'possessed,' but men also may have demon possession, and even children. Indeed, in some parts of the city of Cairo the little girls have this as a performance in their play in the streets.

"There are different kinds of demons, and it is the business of the *sheikhas* to determine which sort (or sorts) are in their patient. Yawning and lassitude go with possession, also palpitation, a stinging sensation, and sometimes rheumatism and nausea. Instead of going to a doctor for medicine, the patient goes to a *sheikh,* who takes a handkerchief belonging to the sick person and puts it under her pillow at night. The *sheikh* or *mashayikh* (plural), who appear to her during the night, are those who are making the trouble. A day is appointed, a bargain is made about the kind and expense of the ceremony, and all friends who are afflicted by these particular demons are invited to assist in the festivities.

"One of our Bible-women was permitted to attend a *Zar* in one of the houses where she was accustomed to read the Bible, so a number of the missionaries went with her to the place, which was an old building near the Bab-el-Shaa'rieh quarter. Women were sitting round on mats in the court,

³ Paul Kahle, " Zar-Beschwörungen in Egypten " in Der Islam, Band III, Helt 1, 2. Strassburg, 1912.
⁴ See *Moslem World,* July, 1913.

and the first part of the performance was the *Nass-el-Kursy,*
or preparation of the high, round table which had a large
copper tray on it.   Different kinds of nuts were brought and
spread on the outer part, and some of each were given to
us.   Then followed parched peas, sesame seed, parsley, coffee in a paper package, two heads of sugar, two bowls of
sour milk, two pieces of soap, a plate of oranges, one of feast
cakes, another of Turkish delight, candy and sugared nuts,
cucumbers and apples, all of which were covered with a
piece of red tarlatan.   Three small candles (an uneven
number) were brought, and two large ones were placed on
the floor in tin stands.   These were all lighted, and the
woman (after a bath) began to dress for the performance
which casts out sudanese spirits.   The woman was dressed
in white, and she and others were ornamented with blue and
white Sudan charms, silver chains, anklets, bracelets, etc.,
which had cowries or shells that rattled.   One woman said
to me, ' All these are a redemption for us.'   Then the *sheikha*
and her women began to get their musical instruments ready,
by heating them over a few burning coals in a little earthen-
ware brazier.   They had two *darabukka,* or wedding drums,
two drums the shape of sieves and one barrel drum.

" The demon in one person of the family is a Christian
demon, and the possessed woman wears a silver cross and
crucifix to keep him happy.[5]   If she were to take these off
she would suffer.   She also wears a silver medallion with
bells on it, and silver rings on each finger, one having a cross
on it.   Her child danced with the drums.   A curious thing
was that this woman spent a few months in a mission school

[5] Before I heard of Miss Thompson's story I discovered in the bazaar
at Cairo silver crosses engraved and sold to Moslem women by Jewish
dealers.   One shows Christ upon the cross, while the other represents
the Virgin, and has " the verse of the Throne," from the Koran, on
the reverse side.   They are used to cast out Christian devils by the
dreaded power—*i.e.,* the cross of the Christians.

years ago, and she promised to send her daughter to be educated by us in the same building.

"The performance began when the patient was seated on
the floor, by the *sheikha* drumming vigorously and chanting
over her head.  One elderly relative, who was standing, began to sway back and forth, and was followed by the patient
and others.  After a period of rest, during which some
smoked, the woman was told to rise, and the *sheikha* held her
head, then each hand, the hem of her dress, and each foot,
over the incense which had been burned before the food on
the tray.  Ten or fifteen others had the incense treatment
in the same way.  This was after the *sheikha* had called
on all the *mashayikh,* or demons, and had repeated the *Fatiha*
about five times, during which the drums played and all the
company chanted; at a given signal on the drums, each one
covered her face with a white veil.  The patient rose and
began swaying and contorting her body as she went slowly
around the table, followed by others.  When a performer
was too vigorous, an onlooker would take a little flour or
salt and sprinkle it over her head, following her around the
circle to prevent her falling.  In the midst of all the din,
some of the women gave the joy cry.  Two white hens and
a cock, which were to be sacrificed the next day, were brought
in and flew about the room.  The patient at last sank down
panting, and the *sheikha* took a large mouthful from a bottle
of rose water, and spattered it with force over each performer.

"The flour and other things are intended to make peace
between the patient and the *Asyad* (ruling demons).  'Do
not be angry with us, we will do all we can.'  At the beginning of these performances, the *sheikha,* with the incense in
her hand, and all the others standing around the table, repeated the *Fatiha;* [6] after which she alone recited: 'To

---

[6] *I. e.,* the first or opening chapter of the Koran.

those who belong to the house of God, may they have mercy on you by their favor, and we ask of you pardon, O *Asyad*. Have pity on us and on her in whom ye are, and forgive her with all forgiveness, because those who forgive died pious. Forgive, forgive, in the right of the Prophet (*hak-en-nebi*), upon him be prayers and peace.'

" The second round was in the name of others. After the *Fatiha*, ' To those who are of the house of God, the people of Jiddah, and Mecca, and the Arabs, by the right of the Prophet Mohammed, upon him be prayers and peace.'

### THE FATIHA

" ' To the mashayikh, Ahmed the Soudanese, all of them Sayyidi Amr, and Sayyedi Ahmed Zeidan.'

### THE FATIHA

" ' To the mashayikh of the convent, all of them, and Amir Tadrus and all those about him, and those who belong to the convent.' (Coptic.)

### THE FATIHA

" ' To the four angels, and the Wullayi, and Mamah, and Rumatu, and all the *mashayikh.*'

### THE FATIHA

" ' To those in the sea (or river), Lady Safina swimming in the river, and those of her household, and all those who belong to her.'

### THE FATIHA

" ' To Merri, the father of Abbassi, and sheikh-el-Arab, the Seyyid el Bedawi and Madbouli, and all the honored *mashayikh*. Come all, by the right of the Prophet, upon him be prayers and peace.'

" After the first round the *sheikha* put incense on the coals in the brazier, and with varied voices and gestures called on these personages to appear, the standing company joining in a low voice in the *Fatiha*. Then the incense was waved over the different articles on the table, then before the patient, the *sheikha* inclining the head of the woman toward the incense, afterwards her hands, feet, etc., and thus for all who wished it.

" We left at the end of the third round, but returned when they were in the middle of the tenth round. Some new women had taken the places of those who had become tired and who now sat chatting."

Miss Thompson, however, did not see the concluding ceremony, the climax of the Zar-ritual, namely, the sacrifice and the drinking of blood. She is not the only writer who omits the subject. Klunzinger [7] says nothing at all of a sacrifice, nor does Plowden. His account is one of the earliest we have:

" These Zars," he writes, " are spirits or devils of a somewhat humorous turn, who, taking possession of their victim, then cause him to perform the most curious antics, and sometimes become visible to him while they are so to no one else — somewhat after the fashion of the ' Erl-King,' I fancy. The favorite remedies are amulets and vigorous tom-toming, and screeching without cessation, till the possessed, doubtless distracted with the noise, rushes violently out of the house, pelted and beaten and driven to the nearest brook, where the Zar quits him and he becomes well. . . . As for defining the nature of a Zar more accurately, it is difficult . . . as it also is to state wherein the functions of a Zar differ from that of a *Ganeem* (*jinn*), save that the Zar is a more sportively malicious spirit and the Ganeem rather morose in his manners. The Zar is frequently heard,

[7] " Bilder aus Oberägypten," p. 389.

indeed, singing to himself in the woods, but woe betide the human eye that falls on him." [8]

The close connection between the Galla country and Oman since the Zanzibar Sultanate and the days of the Arab slave-traders make it probable that the Zar came to Muscat very early, if it was an imported superstition. Here the blood sacrifice is the main thing in exorcism.

" They have their houses of sorcery," writes Miss Fanny Lutton of the American Mission, " which have different names, and have different ceremonies in each one. The largest and most expensive one is called ' Bait-e-Zaar.' If one is afflicted with madness, or it may be some serious or incurable disease, she is taken to this house and the professionals are called; and the treatments sometimes last for days. The money extorted from the patient is exorbitant, and so, as a rule, it is only the rich who can afford to undergo this treatment. The poor are branded with a hot iron or suffer cupping (blood letting), which does not cost so very much. In these houses animals are slain and the sufferer is drenched with the blood and must drink the hot blood as it is taken from the animal. And then the devil dancing is performed by black slave women, and the patient is whirled around with them until she sinks exhausted."

In Egypt, the preparation for the sacrifice is closely related to one part of the ecstatic Zar dance. The sick person is dressed in white and ornamented with special charms, while the room is also prettily decorated. The *kursi* (chair) in the middle of the room is in fact an altar, which has been decorated with flowers, burning candles and various sweets, as a mark of honor for the spirits. These gifts and the burning incense are supposed to attract the spirit and cause him to appear; or drive away other demons.

[8] " Travels in Abyssinia and the Galla Country," quoted by Paul Kahle.

The animal sacrifice consists of sheep or fowls; sometimes a fowl is sacrificed in the beginning, and afterwards a sheep. Kahle is of the opinion that in former times only fowls were sacrificed, the sheep sacrifice being introduced later on, without, however, displacing the sacrifice of the fowl. According to Borelli, a black fowl is sacrificed in Abyssinia. In Luxor a brown or white cock is offered, and in Cairo one cock and two hens, which may be black or white. In Abyssinia the contact between the spirit and the sacrifice is performed by swinging the fowl several times around the head of the patient. Afterwards it is thrown on the floor, and if it does not die very soon, the sacrifice is considered to have been in vain. In Cairo, according to one report by Kahle, the animal is killed by the sheikha above the head of the Zar bride, who must open her mouth and drink the warm blood, the remainder running down her white garment. The theory is that it is not *she* who drinks, but the spirit in her. In Luxor one drop of the blood is placed on the forehead, the cheeks, the chin, the palms of the hands and on the soles of the feet. Probably the blood has to be drunk also. The claws and feathers of the fowl are laid aside carefully as a special gift to the spirit.

Of course the sacrifice must be an excellent animal. The possessed person is seated on its back and rides seven times around the *kursi.* If a sheikh leads the performance, he kills the beast immediately afterwards: if a sheikha is in charge, another person must do it instead, because it is unusual for women to kill sheep. The animal is slaughtered according to Moslem ritual, with its head toward Mecca, while the onlookers say the "Bismillah." Then the sick person is addressed as follows: "May God comfort you in this which has come upon you." If he is a man he stands near by and catches the warm blood in his mouth. In the case of a woman, the blood is poured into a bowl and given her to drink. With the remainder of the blood the hands and feet of the patient are stained. Almost the same ceremonies are observed at the sacrifice of both a fowl and a sheep, and so separate mention is unnecessary.

While the meat is being prepared, parts of the exorcism are repeated, the meal forming the closing act of the whole festival. The Zar bride, the sheikha, and her servants may eat only the inner parts (heart, stomach, etc.) of the animal and its head.

The charms which are given to the Zar bride during the performances must never be removed, or the spirit will return at once. These charms consist of silver ornaments and coins, worn on the breast beneath the dress, a ring with special inscriptions, or some other article. I have in my possession the following ornaments worn at the time of exorcism by the sheikh: First, a head-dress made of beads and cowrie shells with a fringe six inches wide, and a three-fold tassel. It is called *takiet kharz*. A belt of the same beadwork, green and white beads mounted on a red girdle with border of cowrie shells. In addition to these, two small amulets are worn of the same material; one square and containing Koran passages and the other circular of the same character with other potent material against demons.

The sheep or goat which is the sacrifice also has a special ornament on its head similar to those worn by brides in the villages. It consists of two palm twigs, two feet long, bound together in the shape of a T cross. Each twig is covered with colored paper and tinsel ornaments, and the whole is so adjusted that it can be tied to the head of the sacrifice.

Finally the woman who rides on the sacrificial sheep is armed with a cane forty-two inches in length. This is entirely covered with beadwork, brown, white, green, red, and has three chaplets of cowrie shells at equal distances from the top of the handle.

In Morocco, when a man or woman is possessed with the "devil" or jinn the people, including men and women, gather in a *zeriba* or mat hut where the proceedings are commenced by dances, chants, etc. Some chickens, or else a goat, are strangled and are afterwards boiled without salt. Some of the water that the animal has been boiled in is smeared all over the walls and floor by way of exorcism while the meat is eaten by those present, including the "possessed" one. ("Villes et Tribus du Maroc," Casablanca, vol. I, p. 64; Paris 1915.)

A fuller account of this sacrifice to demons as practiced in Arabia, "the Cradle of Islam," is given by Mrs. D. Dijkstra,[9] as follows:

"The great feast ordered by the zeeraan is called '*kabsh*,' meaning ram, and is so called because a sacrifice must be offered and this sacrifice is always a ram. The room for the *kabsh* is always a very large room. The meeting begins in the evening with a general dinner, but which is as a rule not an elaborate one. After the dinner the leader begins to chant, '*La illaha illa allah wa Mohammed rasul allah*,' all the others joining in chorus, and this exercise is kept up for about an hour, and all the while their bodies are swaying back and forth in rhythm to the chant. After this is ended the whole company get down on their knees and go through a crawling, grunting exercise which is kept up until they are exhausted. After a little rest the musicians begin their playing and do not stop until the next feature in the program, which is riding the ram by the party who is visited by the *zar*. Sometimes this is done at midnight if, as they say, the *zar* is not a very proud one, but if he considers himself very important this exercise takes place at dawn. The ram to be ridden is decorated with *mash-*

---

[9] *Neglected Arabia*, a quarterly published by the Arabian Mission, New York, January, 1918. Mrs. Dijkstra uses the word *zar* for the victim as well as for the ceremony.

*moum* (green twigs) and the rider is the one in whom the *zar* is. The rider goes around the circle three or four times. This is seldom accomplished except with great cruelty to the poor beast, which is pulled and prodded in a most unmerciful way, and it is a mercy that it is killed later, for it is usually injured in this exercise.

" After this first riding the company all take some rest until an hour or two after daybreak, when the second riding takes place, in the same way as the first. Immediately after this the ram is killed. This is done by the ' *abu* ' or ' *um*,' as the case may be, assisted by the *zar*, as the possessed one is called, and a third party. The head of the ram is held over a large tray or dish, for not a drop of blood must be spilled or wasted. When the beast is killed, a glass is filled with the blood and into it is put some saffron and some sugar and the *zar* drinks while the blood is warm. Three or four others of the company then strip the *zar* and give her the ' blood bath.' The *zar* is then dressed and put to sleep for an hour and after that is bathed to remove the blood and dressed in new clothes and new ornaments or decorations. In the meantime the sacrifice has been preparing. As with the blood so with the body; not a hair or bone or any of the entrails must be spilled or thrown away. The entrails and feet are boiled separately, but the skin, turned inside out and tied, is cooked with the rest of the body, including the head. When all is cooked, a portion is brought to each table (the table is a large mat spread on the floor), and all the rest of the food is placed around the central dish. A stick, which has been bathed in the blood of the animal, is placed before the *zar*. When all is in readiness, the leader asks the *zar*, ' Is everything here that you want? Are all the bones here of your sacrifice? Tell us now if there is anything amiss and don't say later that this or that was not done right and that, therefore, you will take revenge on us by bringing upon us some accident.' The *zar* is commanded to answer and if he does not he is beaten with the bloody stick until he does." . . .

In Cairo, the sacrificial ceremony was witnessed and described by Madame H. Rushdi Pasha.[10] She tells how after the preliminary music, dancing, and feasting, incense is burnt and the one possessed is properly fumigated. During the process of fumigating no prayers are offered. When this is over the dancing begins. The one possessed then takes hold of the ram which has now been brought in. She makes the tour of the room three times, acting the while like a drunken woman, amid the shrieks of the other women in the room. The ram is then dragged by the possessed to the door where it is butchered. The possessed reënters preceded by the *goudia* who carries a tray filled with jewels covered with the blood of the ram. In fact everybody gets covered with the blood of the ram, still warm. Blood is everywhere. They roll about on the animal until they are quite covered with it. The air becomes hot with incense and smoke. And when at last the women fall down on the ground, the *goudias* go around touching them on the ears and breathe on them whispering words in their ears, presumably from the Koran. After a while they regain their places as if nothing has happened.

Dr. Kahle also states that the *sheikha* or leader of the performance is called " Kudija " (goudia) but gives no explanation of the word; its derivation is obscure. *Zars* which are performed near sanctuaries and not in private houses, have neither a *kursi*, with candles, nor sheep offerings. But in most cases the *sheikha* comes to the house of the sick person the following morning to kill the animal there. The name *sheikha* (the feminine of *sheikh,* elder) is given her, be-

---

[10] " Harems et Musulmanes d'Egypte " (Paris), out of print, pp. 270–274.

cause she knows the method of casting out spirits. Her first task is to find out the right tune for a particular sufferer. If she knows the " Zar bride " from previous meetings, she at once begins the right one. The first time, one tune after another is tried (for Cairo spirits, Upper Egypt spirits, etc.), until the sick person becomes ecstatic, which proves that the right tune has been found and it is then continued. Each special tune requires special dressing, which, according to the sex of the spirit, may be that of men, women, boys or girls. The sick person herself acts as the incarnation of the spirit; sometimes, however, the *sheikha* speaks instead of the spirit.

The meetings for exorcising the *Zar* may be of short duration, or may continue for several nights. If the patient is rich, the feast is prolonged, and during the fourth night, called the " great night," the greatest feast is prepared. The *sheikha* and other visitors remain for the whole night with the sick person, and the following morning they have the solemn sacrifice, the supreme performance of the feast.[11]

Captain Tremearne in " the Ban of the Bori " and G. A. Herklot in his book on the customs of the Moslems of India, " Qanoon-e-Islam " (1832), relate similar practices prevailing in North Africa and India. In every land therefore, with variations due to local circumstances, the *Zar* must always be propitiated by three — incense, the *Zar*-dance with music and last, but not least, the sacrifice — all three of these are Pagan and repulsive to orthodox Islam and yet continue under its shadow. Between 1870–80 the practices spread to such an extent in Upper Egypt that the Government had to put a stop to them.[12] During the past four years the Cairo press has published many articles demanding that " these

[11] See *The Moslem World*, July, 1913. Article by Elizabet Franke, based on Kahle's investigations.
[12] Klunzinger, p. 388.

WOMEN AND CHILDREN VISITING A NEWLY MADE GRAVE
IN THE MOSLEM CEMETERY, CAIRO (See page 271)

infidel ceremonies " be abolished by law, but the custom dies hard.[13]    Not only is the superstition of the *Zar* degrading to morals and spiritual life judged even by Moslem standards but it is such an expensive bit of heathenism that families have been financially ruined through its demands.

"Sometimes a man will divorce his wife," says Mrs. Dijkstra, "because she has *zeeran,* or if he learns that the girl or woman he was going to marry has them he will break his marriage agreement.    And the reason in all these instances is a financial one.    People possessed by *zeeran* must give feasts at various times, and the women are prompted by their *zeeran* to demand from their husbands new clothing, new jewelry, and new house furnishings, and if these are not forthcoming the *zeeran* threaten that severe calamities will overtake them.    So unless the husband is prepared to assume such burdens he very promptly rids himself of the cause, and families refuse to entertain the very idea of *zeeran* because of the constant drain upon their time and strength and money."

The *Zar* spirits (*zeeran*) are divided into numerous tribes and classes.    In Cairo they have Abyssinian, Sudanese, Arab, and even Indian evil-spirits, for each of which a special ceremony is necessary at the time of exorcism.    They are male, female, or hermaphrodites.    They may belong to every class of society and different religions.    In Bahrein, East Arabia, " the outward sign of being possessed by a *Zar* is the wearing of a signet ring, with the name of the *Zar* and of the person himself engraven on a red stone, and also the *Shehadeh* or witness, ' La illaha illa allah, wa Mohammed rasoul allah,' there is no god but God and Mohammed is the prophet of God.    This signet ring must receive a bath

[13] Cf. for example the newspaper *Al Jareeda*, April 18, 1911, and the pamphlet " Mudarr ez Zar," " The Baneful Effect of the Zar," Cairo, 1903.

of blood before it becomes efficacious, and so a fowl must be killed and the stone soaked in the blood."

Among the fetich-worshipers of West Africa, where Islam has not yet entered, the same kind of demon-exorcism is practiced as in Arabia or in Cairo, the intellectual capital of Islam! Indeed, we need not ask what is the origin of the *Zar* for we have an almost exact description of it from the Rev. Robert H. Nassau as he witnessed pagan exorcism among a primitive people:

"Sick persons, and especially those that are afflicted with nervous disorders, are supposed to be possessed by one or other of these evil spirits. If the disease assumes a serious form, the patient is taken to a priest or a priestess, of either of these classes of spirits. Certain tests are applied, and it is soon ascertained to which class the disease belongs, and the patient is accordingly turned over to the proper priest. The ceremonies in the different cases are not materially different; they are alike, at least, in the employment of an almost endless round of absurd, unmeaning, and disgusting ceremonies which none but a heathenish and ignorant priesthood could invent, and none but a poor, ignorant, and superstitious people could ever tolerate. . . .

"In either case a temporary shanty is erected in the middle of the street for the occupancy of the patient, the priest, and such persons as are to take part in the ceremony of exorcism. The time employed in performing the ceremonies is seldom less than ten or fifteen days. During this period dancing, drumming, feasting, and drinking are kept up without intermission day and night, and all at the expense of the nearest relative of the invalid. The patient, if a female, is decked out in the most fantastic costume; her face, bosom, arms, and legs are streaked with red and white chalk, her head adorned with red feathers, and much of the time she promenades the open space in front of the shanty with a sword in her hand, which she brandishes in a very menacing way against the bystanders. At the same time she assumes as much of the maniac in her looks, actions, gestures, and walk as possible. . . . In speaking of the actions of these demoniacs, they are said to be done by the spirit, and not by the person who is possessed. If the person performs any unnatural or revolting act,— as the biting off of the head of a live chicken and sucking its blood,— it is said that the spirit, not the man, has done it." [14]

.    .    .    .    .    .    .    .    .    .

We have ended our studies on Animism in Islam. It has been rather a voyage along the coasts than a survey of the vast areas yet unexplored in a continent of superstition. Enough, however, has passed before our eyes to show that no real fundamental understanding of popular Islam is possible without taking account of Animism.

Regarding the effect of Animism and the fear of demons upon the mind of the Moslem we recall words written by De Groot in his " Religion of the Chinese," pp. 60–61; the fact that he says it in regard to China and that the same phenomena have passed before us as existing in Islam, makes his statement the more striking: " A religion in which the fear of devils performs so great a part that they are even worshiped and sacrificed to, certainly represents religion in a low stage. It is strange to see such a religion prevail among a nation so highly civilized as China is generally supposed to be; and does this not compel us to subject our high ideas of that civilization to some revision? No doubt, we ought to rid ourselves a little of the conception urged upon us by enthusiastic friends of China, that her religion stands high enough to want no foreign religion to supplant it. The truth is that its universalistic animism, with its concomitant

[14] " Fetichism in West Africa," New York, Charles Scribner's Sons, 1904, pp. 72–74.

demonistic doctrine renders the Chinese people unhappy; for most unhappy must be a people always living in a thousand — a hundred thousand — fears of invisible beings which surround the path of life with dangers on every hand, at every moment. If it is the will of God that man should have a religion in order to be happy, the Chinese religion is certainly no religion shaped by God." We likewise conclude that if it is the will of God that man shall have a religion in order to be happy and to have an assurance of deliverance from fear Animistic Islam is not that religion.

# BIBLIOGRAPHY

(In addition to correspondents and works referred to in the text.)

Abbott, G. F. Macedonian Folk-lore. (Cambridge Press), 1903.

Al Damiri. Zoölogy, article *Jinn*.

Baudin, P. Fetichism and Fetich Worshippers. 1885.

Bergen, Fanny D. Current Superstitions. Memoirs of American Folk-lore Society. Boston (Houghton), 1896.

Brinton, D. G. Religions of Primitive Peoples. 1897 or 1899. Putnam. American Lectures on the History of Religions.

Clouston, W. A. Popular Tales and Fiction — Their Migrations and Transformation. 2 vols. London (Blackwood), 1888.

Crawford, D. Thinking Black. New York (Revell), 1916.

Curtin, Jeremiah. Hero Tales of Ireland. London (Macmillan), 1894. Myths and Folk-tales of the Russians, Western Slavs and Magyars. Boston (Little, Brown & Co.), 1903.

Curtiss, Samuel Ives. Primitive Semitic Religions Today. 1902.

Cushing, Frank H. Zuni Folk-tales. New York (Putnam), 1901.

De Groot, J. J. M. Religion in China. pp. 342. New York (Putnam), 1912. A study of the animistic elements in the religions of China.

Dennett. Nigerian Studies.

Dennett, R. At the Back of the Black Man's Mind. 1906.

Dorman, Rushton M. The Origin of Primitive Superstitions. Philadelphia (Lippincott), 1881.

Doughty. Arabia Deserta. 2 vols. Cambridge, 1888.

Drake, Samuel G. Annals of Witchcraft in New England. (Woodward.)

Dresslar, Fletcher Bascom. Superstition and Education. University of California Publications. (The University Press), 1907.

Elmore, W. T. Dravidian Gods in Modern Hinduism: A Study of the Local and Village Deities of Southern India. Hamilton, New York (published by the author), 1915.

Encyclopedia Britannica, 11th edit. "Animism," Vol. II, pp. 53-9.

Encyclopedia of Religious Knowledge: Article on *Animism*.

El Shibli. Kitab al Mirjan fi Ahkam ul Jann.

Frazer, J. G. The Golden Bough: A Study in Magic and Religion. 3rd edit. in twelve vol. Macmillan, 1913-7, especially, The Scape Goat and The Taboo.

Garnett, L. M. J. Mysticism and Magic in Turkey. London, 1912.

Gordon: A Woman in the Sahara.

Herklots, G. A. Qanoon-e-Islam, or the Customs of the Moslems of India. London (Parbury Allen & Co.), 1832.

Hunt, Robert. Popular Romances of the West of England. London (Chatto & Windus), 1881.

Hutchinson, Horace G. Dreams and their Meaning. London (Longmans), 1901.

Jewish Encyclopedia: Articles on Angels, Demons, Kabala, Burials.

Junod, Henri A. "God's Ways in the Bantu Soul." Article in the *International Review of Missions*. III, pp. 96–106.

Kruyt, Albertus C. Het Animisme in den Indischen Archipel. (Leiden). A scientific account of animism.

Lane, E. W. Manners and Customs of the Modern Egyptians. 1860.

Meinhof, C. Africanische Rechtsgebräuche. pp. 162. Berlin, 1914.

Shems ul Ma'arif: Al Buni.

Simon, Gottfried. The Progress and Arrest of Islam in Sumatra.

Skeat, W. W. Malay Magic. London (Macmillan & Co.), 1899.

Smith, Robertson Religion of the Semites. New York, 1889.

Snouck Hurgronje. Het Mekkaansch Feest. Leiden, 1880.

Snouck Hurgronje. The Achenese. Translated by A. W. S. O'Sullivan (Luzac & Co.), 1906.

Tremearne. Hausa Superstitions and Customs. London, 1913.

Tremearne. The Ban of the Bori (Tripoli).

Wallis, W. D. Article in *American Journal of Theology*, April, 1915, on Missions from the Standpoint of an Anthropologist.

Wellhausen. Reste Arabischen Heidenthums. Berlin, 1897.

Wuttke, Adolf. Der deutsche Volksaberglaube der Gegenwart. Berlin (Wiegand & Grieben), 1869.

THE END

Printed in the United States
124946LV00001B/36/A

9 780766 177123